THE NARRATIVE OF ROBERT ADAMS,
A BARBARY CAPTIVE

First published in London in 1816, *The Narrative of Robert Adams* is an account of the adventures of Robert Adams, an African American seaman who survives shipwreck, slavery, and brutal efforts to convert him to Islam, before finally being ransomed to the British consul. In London, Adams is discovered by the Company of Merchants Trading to Africa, which publishes his story, including a fantastical account of a trip to Timbuctoo. Adams's story is accompanied by contemporary essays and notes that place his experience in the context of European exploration of Africa at the time, and weigh his credibility against other contemporary accounts. Professor Adams's Preface examines Adams's credibility in light of modern knowledge of Africa and discusses the significance of his story in relation to the early-nineteenth-century interest in Timbuctoo and to the literary genres of the slave narrative and the Barbary captivity narrative.

Charles Hansford Adams is Associate Professor of English at the University of Arkansas where he acts as Associate Dean for Academic Affairs and International Programs in the J. William Fulbright College of Arts & Sciences. He is the author of *The Guardian of the Law: Authority and Identity in James Fenimore Cooper* (1991). His essays have appeared in *The Kenyon Review*, *Southern Quarterly*, *American Studies*, *Western American Literature*, and numerous collections.

THE NARRATIVE OF ROBERT ADAMS,

A BARBARY CAPTIVE

A Critical Edition

Edited by

CHARLES HANSFORD ADAMS

University of Arkansas

CAMBRIDGE
UNIVERSITY PRESS

CAMBRIDGE UNIVERSITY PRESS

Cambridge, New York, Melbourne, Madrid, Cape Town, Singapore, São Paulo

Cambridge University Press

40 West 20th Street, New York, NY 10011-4211, USA

www.cambridge.org

Information on this title: www.cambridge.org/9780521842846

First published 2005

Printed in the United States of America

A catalog record for this publication is available from the British Library.

Library of Congress Cataloging in Publication Data

Adams, Robert, Sailor.
[Narrative of Robert Adams, a sailor who was wrecked on the western coast of Africa,
in the year 1810]
The narrative of Robert Adams, a barbary captive / edited, with notes and a preface,
by Charles Hansford Adams. – A critical ed.
p. cm.
Originally published as: A narrative of Robert Adams, a sailor who was wrecked on
the western coast of Africa, in the year 1810. London : J. Murray, 1816.
Includes bibliographical references and index.
ISBN-13: 978-0-521-84284-6 (hardback)
ISBN-10: 0-521-84284-0 (hardback)
ISBN-13: 978-0-521-60373-7 (pbk.)
ISBN-10: 0-521-60373-0 (pbk.)
1. Sahara – Description and travel.   2. Tombouctou (Mali) – Description and travel.
3. Slavery – Sahara.   4. Adams, Robert, Sailor – Travel – Africa.
I. Adams, Charles Hansford, 1954–   II. Title.
DT333.A33   2005
916.604'23 – dc22   2005002290

ISBN-13   978-0-521-84284-6 hardback
ISBN-10   0-521-84284-0 hardback

ISBN-13   978-0-521-60373-7 paperback
ISBN-10   0-521-60373-0 paperback

For My Parents, Again

CONTENTS

Preface   *page* ix
Bibliography   lvii
Acknowledgments   lxv

THE NARRATIVE OF ROBERT ADAMS

Contents   4

Introductory Details Respecting Adams   8

Advertisement to the Map   22

Chapter 1   26

Chapter 2   35

Chapter 3   49

Chapter 4   59

Notes and Illustrations   68

Concluding Remarks   106

Appendix No. I   125

Appendix No. II   136

CONTEMPORARY ESSAYS

"Interiour of Africa" (North American Review, *May 1817)*   147

"Article IX. The Narrative of Robert Adams." *A review essay
by Jared Sparks (*North American Review, *July 1817).*   162

Index   183

Figure 1. West Africa.

PREFACE

I

Through much of the month of November 1815, an illiterate African American sailor sat in an office in the City of London, talking with some of the most powerful men in Britain about Timbuctoo. Had they passed him in the crowded streets of Regency London, these men of affairs – merchants, statesmen, scientists, and military officers – would not even have glanced at the dark, impoverished, and sickly figure sitting before them. But he had a story to tell that they could not afford to ignore. He had, he claimed, crossed the deadly Sahara as a slave, spent six months in the fabled city on the Niger, and (most remarkably) returned to tell the tale. For those who listened to his narrative, this was important news indeed. No reliable witness – that is, no one from the West – had brought Europe information about Timbuctoo since Leo Africanus in the sixteenth century, and Leo was, after all, but a Christianized Moor of Granada. An account of Timbuctoo by an ignorant American "mulatto" might require some sifting, but his subject was worth the effort. For the City merchants in attendance, the word Timbuctoo triggered visions of a great emporium in the African interior, the wealth of which rested mainly on its trade in gold and slaves. Those who came from Westminster and Whitehall, fresh from conversations about Britain's role in the world five months after Waterloo, thought of both gold and national power. A lot might depend on what this black man had to say.

The sailor wanted to go home to New York, but he also needed the money that these men were giving him in return for his story. He was destitute, and they offered clothes, shelter, and cash as long as he answered their questions, with a promise of a bounty once they had finished. He needed their protection, too. Even eight months after the ratification of the Treaty of Ghent, renewed hostilities between Britain and the United States seemed possible. He had good reason to fear impressment if he were to risk a sea passage home without the guarantee of redemption that the Admiralty had offered. He could not bear another captivity – although a freeman at home, he had been a slave to several brutal masters in Africa, and, as he hinted to his London benefactors, he had already tasted of the brutal discipline of the Royal Navy.

His name was Robert Adams. Or, at least, that was the name that he gave to Mr. Simon Cock, Secretary to the Committee of the Company of Merchants Trading to Africa. Mr. Cock had found him living in the streets "in very ill plight, both from hunger and nakedness" (*Narrative* 9). More precisely, Mr. Cock had been led to him by a man lately arrived in London from Cadiz, who recognized the indigent sailor as the same one who had caused a stir just a few months earlier in that Spanish port by his fabulous tales of Timbuctoo. Mr. Cock knew that such a story, if credible, would be of great interest to the members of the Committee that employed him, and arranged for the American to be brought to the office of the Company of Merchants Trading to Africa. It was in the office of the African Company (as it was called) that this broken wanderer met the men of trade and empire interested in his tale. It was there, in Frederick's Place, off Old Jewry, that Simon Cock and his colleagues stitched the sailor's various answers to the gentlemen's questions into a consecutive narrative, assembled the supporting materials (introduction, map, notes, and appendices), and arranged for the house of John Murray to publish *The Narrative of Robert Adams*.

The sailor had used the name of Adams in Cadiz as well, but Mr. Cock would eventually discover that his name might actually be Benjamin Rose, the name that he had given to those who ransomed him from slavery in Africa, and under which he had shipped as a merchant seaman from New York five and a half years before he was found living in the streets of London. Or, he might be neither Rose nor Adams. He stuck with Adams throughout his time in London, but his name was of no particular interest to the Committee of the African Company, or to the "upwards of fifty" gentlemen who made their way to the African Company's office to see him, or even to the really important men to whose offices in Westminster and the West End Mr. Cock took the American for interviews (11). Sailors of this period often changed their names; and in any case, the capital was "crowded" with "distressed seamen," many of whom were black, and all of whom would be assumed by respectable people to have good reason to use more than one name (9; Bolster 19–20).

Still, the matter of his name bothered his sponsors. Mr. Cock included in his introduction to Adams's published narrative an extended discussion of the sailor's name by Joseph Dupuis, the British vice-consul at Mogador, in Morocco. Dupuis (whose numerous contributions to the finished *Narrative* make him Cock's co-editor) had ransomed an American calling himself Benjamin Rose from slavery among the desert Arabs in 1814, and had made notes of the man's tale of travel to Timbuctoo before sending him north to meet with the Emperor of Morocco. Two years later, Dupuis very publicly staked his rising reputation in the Foreign Office on the credibility of the publication by Mr. Cock and the African Company of this same American's tale, even if he now called himself Adams. Maybe, Dupuis ventured, he changed his name because he had been impressed by the Royal Navy; maybe he had been a prisoner of the Navy and was afraid of being apprehended; or maybe he did it because, as he had told Dupuis at Mogador, he had left America in order to escape a romantic entanglement which he was "unwilling to make good by marriage" (17). Maybe, or maybe not. The question of the sailor's name mattered to Cock and Dupuis as they prepared his narrative for publication because they knew that it stood for the central issue raised by *The Narrative of Robert Adams*, in 1816 and today – can we believe him, whoever he was?

Some who listened to him had their doubts. Most notably, Sir Joseph Banks and John (later Sir John) Barrow had their doubts. Banks was the President of the Royal Society, the founder of the Association for Promoting the Discovery of the Interior Parts of Africa (called the African Association), and one of the most famous men of science in Europe. Barrow, a Fellow of the Royal Society, had been Second Secretary to the Admiralty for more than a decade and enjoyed a reputation as one of the great scientific travelers of the age; his accounts of adventures in China and South Africa were on every educated man's bookshelf. Cock had to admit in his introduction that Adams "had the misfortune . . . to excite some doubts in their minds by his account of Tombuctoo, and by his mistakes on some subjects of natural history," though Cock felt at liberty to mention them as subscribers to the "*general* truth of his

Adams is discovered in the Tent with Isha.

Figure 2. Illustration for a retelling of *The Narrative of Robert Adams* in *Robinson Crusoe's Own Book* (1846).

Narrative" (13). Others, as we shall see, would not grant Adams even that. The bare outline of his story was too fantastic for some: shipwrecked along the Mauritanian coast, captured and enslaved by desert nomads, carried hundreds of miles across the Sahara into the interior of Africa, taken from his masters by black Africans who murdered the Moors and marched him to Timbuctoo, held there as human merchandise for six months, sold back into Moorish slavery and marched back across the Sahara, sold again and traded from one vicious master to another in southern Morocco (very publicly cuckolding one), ransomed by Dupuis at Mogador, taken to Meknes and interviewed by the Emperor himself, conveyed under imperial guard to Tangier, and placed aboard a ship to Cadiz, where he was put to work as a groom for more than a year by an English gentleman residing there, before finally making his way via Holyhead to London and the office of the African Company.

Fantastic though it was, most of those who listened to him in London had no trouble believing, with Banks and Barrow, the "*general* truth" of his story. That is, they believed that he had been shipwrecked and enslaved by the desert tribes, since such stories were familiar enough by this time; the reasons for their popularity will be addressed in Section V of this Preface. The question that vexed those who listened to Adams in 1815 and that continues to vex his readers right up until the present time concerns Timbuctoo.

Did he go there? Did this obscure African American accomplish on his own what several well-funded and widely publicized explorers before him had failed to do? Did he crack the mystery that had fascinated Europe for nearly five hundred years? Almost certainly, the answer to each question is no. "Almost" should be stressed, since Adams's story, as we have it, is so heavily mediated by the editorial presence of Simon Cock, Joseph Dupuis, and other unnamed members of the Committee of the African Company, that nothing is perfectly certain about the "very dark man" at the center of the *Narrative*. We know of him only what his English handlers chose to show. Still, by comparing what his amanuenses say he said, with what we know now about Timbuctoo and the Sahara, we may cautiously sort his tale into more and less credible portions. The "*general* truth" of his account of shipwreck and slavery among the desert peoples – that is, everything before and after the putative journey to Timbuctoo – is reasonably secure. Vice-Consul Dupuis, a man with a reputation to lose and no discernible reason to perpetrate or knowingly endorse a very public fraud, vouched personally for Adams's statements about life after ransom. He also assured the *Narrative*'s readers that he had conversed in Mogador with men who had either personally witnessed or reliably heard of the sailor's misadventures on the coast or in Moroccan settlements – Adams's shipmates, for example, or other enslaved sailors, or tribesmen and merchants fresh from the Saharan trade routes. Furthermore, some of his claims are corroborated by other captivity narratives from the period, and others are confirmed by more modern historical studies of the region. But even here, we should be careful. The narrative constructed in Cadiz by Samuel A. Storrow, a "gentleman of Boston" to whom Adams/Rose related his travels, differs in several particulars from the tale he told in London, including details warranted by Dupuis. The "Cadiz Narrative" (published under the title "Interiour of Africa" in the May 1817 issue of the *North American Review*) is included in this edition of the *Narrative*, along with an analysis by the *Review*'s editor, Jared Sparks, of its numerous contradictions of the London account. But if Adams's credibility is a bit wobbly regarding events along the coast and in the Sahara, it collapses where Timbuctoo is concerned. Why this is so will be the subject of the next section.

Although the particulars of the *Narrative*'s truth may be difficult to establish, and although Adams/Rose almost certainly invented his trip to Timbuctoo, the book retains enormous interest for modern readers. From the simplest historical perspective, the *Narrative* – both Adams's story as told by the African Company and the extensive notes appended to it – offers a rich source of information about North African society in the early nineteenth century. What Adams saw from a slave's viewpoint, and what Dupuis knew as a result of his extensive experience in the region, combine to provide a fascinating portrait of a complex world prior to its transformation by European colonialism. From a literary perspective, Adams's story is a good read, however mediated and however strictly true. His journey through Africa is a marvelous adventure tale, featuring shipwreck, slavery, exotic cities and strange people, a resourceful and determined hero, spiritual struggle, sexual transgression, and much more. The relationship of the *Narrative* to popular literary forms of the period – and especially to the Barbary captivity narrative – will be addressed in the final section of this essay.

But a different interest lies in placing the *Narrative* in contexts that help us both to understand its relationship to its time and to connect the *Narrative* and its time to our own day. One such context is the issue of slavery. The story involves slavery of several types: the North African enslavement of captured westerners like Adams, the desert trade in black slaves from Timbuctoo and elsewhere in sub-Saharan Africa, and the British slave trade in West Africa. Moslem slavery is Adams's interest, and that of his London editors. Christian slavery, though, informs the book at every turn and is the unwritten story behind the production of the *Narrative*; Section III of this Preface outlines the relationship of the African Company to the slave trade and explores the connection between the Company's decision to publish Adams's story and its role in the history of British slavery. Related to the matter of slavery is that of imperialism. The *Narrative*'s elaborate editorial material provides a snapshot of British attitudes toward Africa in the crucial years immediately following the abolition of the slave trade – an image that adumbrates the imminent expansion of British power on the continent. In this regard, the *Narrative* is a crucial document for understanding the development of European knowledge about Africa – a case study in the process by which knowledge was determined to be authoritative, and by which it was assimilated into the growing body of information deemed reliable according to standards that were frequently more social than strictly scientific (see Heffernan 203–5). Section IV considers the image of Timbuctoo in the western mind before 1815 and explores the purposes driving Dupuis and his colleagues to reconcile that image with Adams's unsettling story.

An aspect of the *Narrative* that is of particular and urgent interest today is the clash between the Christian and Moslem worlds. As a Barbary captivity narrative, Adams's tale shares with other examples of the genre an ugly picture of North African Islamic society. Depicted as hopelessly barbaric in their attitudes and manners, the Moslems who enslave Adams and sell him one to the other like a sack of dates are a uniformly cruel and capricious lot. The more devout the believer, the more vicious the master: Adams's only respite from suffering comes during his sojourn in a Timbuctoo he describes as being free of Moslem influence and indeed free of any significant religious activity at all. This view of Timbuctoo is, historically, the most implausible part of Adams's story, but considered in relation to the conventions of the captivity genre, it helps confirm the hero's essential role as a Christian martyr thrown into an Islamic lion's den. Section V surveys the orientalist assumptions (in Edward Said's sense) of the captivity genre and the particular popularity that it enjoyed in the United States in the period of Robert Adams's adventures. The anti-Islamic rhetoric of these stories, widely disseminated during a time of conflict between the young republic and the Barbary states, eerily anticipates similar vilifications of the Moslem world filling the popular media in the wake of the September 11 attacks.

In considering each of these spheres in which the *Narrative* moves – slavery, imperialism, the development of knowledge, and the clash of cultures – the strict truth of what Adams says is less important than what was believed about what he said. Adams's story is fascinating, but equally fascinating is the mediation of that story for purposes that resonate with some of the most vital topics of Adams's day, and of our own. Adams's narrative may not reveal very much reliable information about Timbuctoo *per se*, but the *Narrative* reveals a great deal about what Timbuctoo and North Africa meant to those who told his story and to those who read it.

II

Robert Adams, or whoever he was, disappeared from the historical record soon after telling his tale. Mr. Cock wrote in his introduction that Adams had gone back to America in December of 1815, leaving behind "a large balance of the bounty of the Lords of the Treasury, and the expected profits of his book." Adams said that he would be back, but, ocean crossings in the winter being what they were, he left with Cock "such particulars of his family" as might be needed to verify any claims on his money should he not return (*Narrative* 14). Unfortunately, Cock's minutes of the meetings of the Committee of the African Company do not reveal these "particulars," nor do the Company's accounts specifically show any money paid or held for Adams. Indeed, a search of various public records in Adams's stated hometown – Hudson, in Columbia County, New York – gives no sign that anyone of Adams/Rose's probable age and mixed race lived there in the years immediately before or after those described in the *Narrative*. If Cock did in fact make provision for Adams's financial future, the money went unclaimed. Where Adams went, and what he called himself, are unknown.

Jared Sparks did not feel a need to check Adams's assertions against the Columbia County records as he wrote his review of the first American edition of the *Narrative* in the *North American Review* in 1817. "We state with confidence," Sparks wrote, "on the authority of a gentleman who has resided at Hudson ever since its first settlement, that no . . . person of the character and pretensions of Adams has ever been heard of in that place." For Sparks, the doctrine of *falsus in uno, falsus in omnibus* applied; Adams's lie about Hudson just confirmed his mendacity in general. His methodical comparison of the stories Adams told in London and Cadiz remains one of the most devastating indictments of Adams's credibility. The general outline of the tale is the same in both versions, but the discrepancies between them are significant and inexplicable. If the Cadiz narrative is not itself a fake, and if Storrow recorded Adams's story faithfully, then either one or both versions are false in several details. Joseph Dupuis anticipates Sparks's skepticism in his awareness, expressed at several points in the "Notes and Illustrations," that the tale he heard in Mogador deviated in several respects from the London version. Occasionally Dupuis attempts to explain a discrepancy. More often, he notes it without comment.

Sparks may have been driven to dissect Adams's story by a cultural nationalism that distrusted everything British. He begins his assault with the double-edged remark that the sailor's relation "would not be worthy of serious attention, had it not excited so much interest, and gained universal belief in England." Adams might be an American, but his gullible sponsors were, Sparks observed gleefully, "some of the most distinguished men in England," and thus irresistible targets for a man whose entire career was devoted to establishing American cultural independence from Britain. The *North American Review* stood for a nascent national culture and offered an excellent platform on which to display the spectacle of an illiterate sailor hoodwinking some of Britain's brightest minds. Especially gratifying, from Sparks's perspective, would have been the fact that these "distinguished men" were obviously connected with the London *Quarterly Review*, a Tory publication mentioned with approbation in the *Narrative*.

Nationalism, and specifically Anglophobia, also may have motivated the attack on Adams's credibility that came from France in 1830; although, as in Sparks's case, the criticism was based on serious evidence. Edme-François Jomard, one of France's leading geographers and a distinguished member of the Société de Géographie de Paris, had an important advantage over both Sparks and the men who packaged Adams's story in 1816. In 1828, a Frenchman named Réné Caillié had gone to Timbuctoo with a trading caravan, disguised as a native Egyptian whose Arabic had been corrupted by a lifetime in France and Senegal. Secretly keeping his journal in a notebook made to look like a copy of the Koran, Caillié spent about a fortnight observing the city and its people, and brought back to France a richly detailed account. Jomard relied on Caillié's record to dispute nearly every piece of Adams's description of the city.

Jomard begins with geography, and he notes, in the spirit of Jared Sparks, that Adams could not keep his story straight. Adams claimed that the city is on a level plain, and yet a couple of times mentioned two mountains just to the south of the city, between which ran a river three-quarters of a mile wide and flowing to the southwest. Caillié had not seen any mountains near the city, nor had he seen a river matching Adams's description. In fact, there are no such mountains at Timbuctoo. Furthermore, the river, which Adams called the "La Mar Zarah" in London but "La Parsire" in Cadiz, and which he claimed to have followed upstream a couple of hundred miles to the northeast on his way back to Morocco, simply does not exist. The nearest large river is the Niger, which flows to the east past Cabara, the port serving Timbuctoo and located several miles to the south. Moreover, if Adams saw mountains and rivers that Caillié missed, he also saw a lot more people than the Frenchman saw. Adams's Timbuctoo was "as extensive, without being as populous, as Lisbon," while Caillié estimated the population at ten thousand to twelve thousand. Jomard wryly notes that between the two men's guesses there is a difference of perhaps a quarter-million people (244). More recent evidence about both cities suggests that Lisbon's population was around two hundred thousand in 1811 and that Caillié may have overestimated Timbuctoo's population in 1828. Whatever the precise figures, any comparison with Lisbon is difficult to defend.

One by one, Jomard ticks off Adams's mistakes. The royal palace is one example. Adams describes it as a walled compound half an acre in area, enclosing a two-story dwelling with "eight or ten" rooms on the ground floor. Caillié saw only a "small and extremely simple house" – the same one, apparently, described in the narrative of an Astrakhani merchant named Wargee, who visited Timbuctoo in 1821. Based on Wargee's testimony, one historian of Timbuctoo concludes that, in fact, "there was no 'royal palace' of any particular distinction at the time in Timbuctoo" (Saad 214). Jomard found Adams's zoology suspect as well. He claimed to have seen numerous elephants in the area, at least one of which (and a young one, at that) was more than twenty feet high and sported four tusks, two of them five feet long. Caillié saw none, and certainly none so fantastic. And so Jomard methodically compares Adams's observations of Timbuctoo – its language, customs, and architecture – with Caillié's eyewitness reports on the same subjects. He concludes that "ignorance" or "a want of memory" are not sufficient to explain the gross discrepancies between the two reports and declares himself "opposed to the authenticity of [Adams's] travels" (243). The modern reader, with the advantage of more and better information, is compelled to agree.

In short, the German explorer Heinrich Barth may have exaggerated only slightly when he wrote in 1857 that Adams's description of Timbuctoo "does not reveal a single trait which can be identified with its features" (310). Barth spent a month there in 1853, and although he was under virtual house arrest the entire time and had to observe the city mainly from the roof of his quarters, he saw enough to identify the most telling weakness of Adams's account: the assertion that the people of Timbuctoo do not "have any public religion, as they have no house of worship, no priest, and as far as Adams could discover, never meet to pray together" (*Narrative* 43). "It is," Barth scoffed, "unintelligible that a person could actually visit the town without becoming aware that it contained several mosques, and very large ones too, for such a place" (298).

Barth's judgment is hard to contest. The city had been a center of Moslem worship and learning for five hundred years before Adams told his tale, and the "large" mosques that Barth mentioned had been an integral part of the city's cultural and architectural fabric for nearly as long. Réné Caillié anticipated Barth's point in stating that "all the inhabitants of Timbuctoo are zealous Mohometans" whom he regularly observed attending the town's eight mosques, including two very large "houses of worship" on its northeastern and southwestern sides that were among the first things to strike the visitor's eye upon approaching the city (60, 71–6). Indeed, these two mosques, the Sankore and Jingereber, still dominate Timbuctoo's architectural profile and are, along with the Sidi Yahya mosque in the center of town, city landmarks. The Sankore, built in the early fifteenth century, housed the schools of numerous great imams whose teachings had made the name of Timbuctoo synonymous with wisdom throughout the Moslem world. Though the city's reputation for Islamic scholarship had declined by the early nineteenth century from its meridian just prior to the Moroccan invasion in 1591, Timbuctoo still produced great spiritual leaders. Until his death in 1811 – the very year that Robert Adams said he visited the city – Sidi al-Mukhtar al-Kunti led a spiritual *jihad* of mysticism and piety from the Timbuctoo region, attracting students from throughout western and central Sudan (Willis 548–9).

Indeed, according to the best scholarship on the city's history during this period, Sidi al-Mukhtar's influence was political as well as spiritual. Although the city was nominally ruled by a Pasha, as it had been (for the most part) since the Moroccan invasion, and its religious affairs were nominally overseen by a Qadi, the actual management of the city's secular and spiritual affairs was in the hands of a group of scholars of the Kunta clan. That group was led by Sidi al-Mukhtar al-Kunti. The Pasha was named Abu Bakr (d. 1230 A.H./1814–1815), and the

Qadi was most likely a cleric named Muhammed al-Aqib, but Sidi al-Mukhtar commanded actual power in Timbuctoo. According to Elias Saad, he dominated the city's *Jama'a*, the ruling group of Kunta scholars, for several years before his death in 1811 (213–15; see also Abitbol 261). Adams's irreligious King Woollo, whom he claimed to have met upon his arrival early in 1811, does not much resemble Pasha Abu Bakr, Qadi al-Aqib, or Sidi al-Mukhtar. Adams's Queen Fatima, with her "hair stuck full of bone ornaments," is also hard to find in the picture of the city's administration drawn by modern historians.

Assuming that Simon Cock faithfully recorded Adams's thoughts on the city's religious life, this point alone forces one of two conclusions: either Adams was the worst observer in the history of African exploration or he never set foot in Timbuctoo. One scholar, Brian Gardner, has bravely mounted an extended defense of Adams's credibility (27–34), but his arguments, while ingenious, do not much narrow the gap between Adams's Timbuctoo and the real thing. As Dupuis says, "Woollo" is obviously a name from sub-Saharan Africa, and indeed many items in Adams's description of Timbuctoo seem drawn from cultures found south or west of the city: for instance, the facial tattoos, the women's dress (or undress), the style of the communal dances, and the bodies greased with goat butter. Possibly Adams traveled to some place like the Soudenny he describes, outside the Moslem sphere, and attributed things he saw there to Timbuctoo. As we shall see in Section III of this Preface, though, one aspect of Adams's account of the city was confirmed by Caillié and others: compared to the legends of its splendor that had circulated for centuries, Timbuctoo was a distinctly unimpressive place. Adams may have inadvertently gotten this right either by describing (whether from hearsay or personal experience) some other modest trading town in West Africa and calling it Timbuctoo or by mingling things that he heard about the city with information from Bambara or further west. Whatever his sources and whatever his method, he managed to produce a story that was wrong in nearly every detail, but right in its repudiation of the myth of Timbuctoo.

Why did he do it? Money, attention, the plain fun of fooling people, especially important or self-important people – any or all of these may have motivated Robert Adams, or whoever he was. To their credit, Adams's London editors seemed aware that much about his Timbuctoo strained credulity. The motive of Simon Cock's "Introductory Details

Respecting Adams" is to assert his witness's credibility, and the "Concluding Remarks" is a long brief in Adams's defense, although the author admits that the only part of the story for which there is no corroborating evidence is the journey "from the Douar to which he was first conveyed from the coast, until his arrival at El Kabla" – that is, the journey to Timbuctoo. Cock makes much of the fact that Adams left behind most of the money offered him for his story, as though this demonstrates that a destitute and desperate man would not have told his story simply for the money, clothes, and shelter that he received before disappearing. Joseph Dupuis, a man with first-hand knowledge of Africa, is careful to distance himself from Adams's boldest inventions. The fantastical "courcoo" – a dog-like, tree-climbing creature, distinguished by a marsupial-like pouch on its back, and feeding on everything from coconuts to children – left Dupuis speechless; in his briefest note in the *Narrative*, he says only, "I have never before heard of this extraordinary animal, either from Adams [in Mogador] or any one else" (80). Like other statements by Dupuis regarding the sailor's name or the disagreements between his London and Mogador testimonies, this one reveals his unspoken awareness that the American could not, in fact, keep his story straight. Other lapses, such as Adams's inability to describe a coconut after assuring his audience that he saw them in Timbuctoo, are extenuated by reference to his social rank. Readers are admonished not to "attach much value to the botanical recollections of a common sailor," although the same readers are expected to attach a great deal of value to this sailor's other "recollections," botanical and otherwise (77).

The abiding anxiety of all those connected with the *Narrative* is suggested in a line from a letter written to Simon Cock by Sir Willoughby Gordon and introduced by Cock with a dramatic flourish among the "Introductory Details." Gordon, the Quartermaster of the Horse Guards at the time, had been among those listening to Adams in November of 1815. After announcing his faith in "the truth" of the story, Gordon concludes that "if he be proved an imposter, he will be second only to Psalmanazar" (13). The reference to England's most famous liar of the eighteenth century is telling. George Psalmanazar (1679?–1763) was the assumed name of a Frenchman who, between 1703 and 1708, deceived numerous luminaries of the English literary and scientific establishment with his claim to be a native of Formosa. He lectured and wrote extensively about the (fabricated) customs of his country and actually taught the (invented) Formosan language at Oxford for a few months in 1704. Sir Hans Sloane, a man whom Sir Joseph Banks resembled in his interests and range of accomplishments, was among Psalmanazar's sponsors before the hoax was discovered. Gordon's quoted reference is a hedge against embarrassment and represents an admission of its possibility. Even as he insists on Adams's veracity, Cock inserts a disclaimer: only the most accomplished of liars could gull such men as Sloan or Banks, or Simon Cock.

So why, despite their doubts, did Dupuis and Cock and the Committee of the African Company publish Adams's tale? Convinced, for good reasons, of the "*general* truth" of his story, and lacking sufficient knowledge of Timbuctoo to dismiss even the most outlandish statements on the subject, they published everything – and then spilled a great deal of ink in the notes, appendices, remarks, etc., striving to explain how it all might be true. But why did Mr. Simon Cock and the Committee of the Company of Merchants Trading to Africa spend so much time and energy on such a project? Why did a group of busy London traders care so much about a poor black sailor's tale of African adventure?

III

The most radically skeptical commentary on the *Narrative* to date is found in Ann Fabian's *Unvarnished Truths* (2000). Fabian suggests that "Robert Adams" may have been a fiction and that the same hoaxer may have created Simon Cock and the African Company as well – all, presumably, to sell books to an unsuspecting public hungry for exotic tales of Timbuctoo. Consider, she says, the dedication page, in which the *Narrative* is offered to the "African Committee" by "S. Cock": "Perhaps Cock's salutation was designed to alert readers to a ruse, suggesting that, like the long story that concludes Laurence Sterne's *Tristram Shandy* (1759–1767), Adams's tale was a 'cock and bull' story. It is also possible that Cock's 'African Committee' was a deliberate play on the African Association, the group of aristocrats and businessmen underwriting the European exploration of Africa" (30).

There is good reason to doubt some of Adams's story, but this goes too far. To believe that Adams never existed, we would have to believe that a number of very important men did not protest having their names attached to an elaborate joke about a matter that they took very seriously, the exploration of Africa. As for the "cock and bull" theory, there really was a Simon Cock and an African Committee. Fabian may be excused for suspecting that the African Company was a "ruse," since the Company and its Committee cast a dim light in historical studies of the period. But this lack of attention is surprising, since the African Company played for several decades a vital role in one of the most consequential social and economic phenomena of the late eighteenth and early nineteenth centuries – the slave trade.

The Company of Merchants Trading to Africa was created by Parliament in 1750, with the passage of "An Act for Extending and Improving the Trade to Africa" (Donnan 474). The legislation dissolved the Royal African Company, a joint-stock association founded in 1672, and replaced it with a Company of Merchants structured to avoid the dangers of monopoly while keeping the trade free of control by officers of the Crown. The Act of 1750 delivered to the Company all the African possessions of the Royal African Company and entrusted it with sole management of British trade "between the Port of Sallee in South Barbary, and the Cape of Good Hope," a coastline of about seven thousand miles. According to Eveline Martin, "the constitution of the company was extremely simple in design, consisting of two main parts, the general body of traders, all those who by paying forty shillings had become free of the company, and a committee of nine" that governed the Company (10). The Committee was composed of three merchants from each of the three cities principally involved in the African trade, with each committeeman elected by those merchants "free of the company" in his respective town: London, Bristol, or Liverpool. While Parliament controlled the Company's purse strings through an annual grant to support its London office and its African holdings, the Committee also reported to the Exchequer, the Admiralty, and, after 1782, the Secretary of State for War and Colonies – which explains why these offices are so well represented in the list of important men to whom Cock took Adams in November of 1815.

Control over British trade along a seven-thousand-mile coast sounds grand, but in reality the African Company inherited from the Royal African Company only nine rather humble African trading outposts, called forts or factories. All but one were situated on the Gold Coast, in what is now the nation of Ghana. Annamaboe, Accra, Succondee, Winnebah, Appolonia, Tantumquerry, Dixcove, Commenda, and the administrative center, Cape Coast Castle – each Company factory consisted of a fortified barrack, a storehouse, and, most importantly, a slave pen, called a barracoon (Craton 60). Each employed a contingent of up to a hundred soldiers, plus perhaps a couple of dozen assorted bookkeepers, craftsmen, surgeons, surveyors, scriveners, and, of course, the factors who traded with the peoples along the coast, principally the Ashanti.

While each factory did some trade in commodities like ivory, hides, beeswax, and gold, the real business of each factory before 1807 was to collect slaves and ship them to the West Indies. The Gold Coast factories run by the Royal African Company and the Company of Merchants Trading to Africa accounted for about 20% of the British slave trade to the New World between 1690 and 1800. While the "yield" from the Gold Coast was down to about 10% of the total by 1807, the African Company presided over the transportation of nearly four thousand slaves in the last six years of the (legal) trade (Craton 76–7). In short, Parliament created the African Company in 1750 to "improve" trade to Africa because it was better suited than the Royal African Company to "trade in Africans more efficiently, more nimbly, and more economically" in a time when the demand for slaves was increasing rapidly (Walvin, *Black Ivory* 35).

Everything changed for the Company and its Committee in 1807, when Parliament declared the slave trade illegal. Pressure to abolish the trade had been building since the 1780s, and significant action was taken as early as 1791, when Parliament created the Sierra Leone Company to compete with the African Company in trade along the coast without dealing in slaves. Other goals than trade, indeed, were increasingly championed by those interested in Africa. While it is difficult to tease commerce and empire out of the motives driving Sir Joseph Banks and others to create the African Association in 1788, that organization's very public goal to expand Europe's knowledge of African geography, ethnography, and natural history offered an embarrassing contrast to the African Company's bald pursuit of wealth through traffic in human bodies. In 1790, when the African Association had already underwritten expeditions of discovery by John Ledyard and Simon Lucas, the Committee of the African Company sponsored the publication of a treatise entitled *Slavery No Oppression: or, some new arguments and opinions against the idea of African liberty*. Pressure on the Company was added with the formation in 1807 of the African Institution, led by William Wilberforce and others who had been connected with the Sierra Leone Company. Their explicitly humanitarian purposes – dedicated to bringing civilization to Africa and fueled by an evangelical passion to save black souls – captured the popular imagination and further isolated politically the merchants of the African Committee.

After 1807, the African Company tried, as Martin says neatly, "to advance with the time, and, by accepting the new shibboleths of the early nineteenth century, to maintain their position in an age which had declared unlawful the pursuit of the object the Company had been created to promote" (145–6). Recognizing that their parliamentary grants were threatened by the new state of affairs, the Committee's Secretary, Mr. Simon Cock, assured the government in 1808 that trade in different commodities – rice, indigo, cotton, palm oil, or perhaps timber, in addition to the existing traffic in ivory and gold – would eventually replace the trade in humans, and asked for patience as they made the transition (Parliamentary Papers, VII 110–13). But the Company was perceived as a relic, and the Committee was suspected of being less than enthusiastic in abandoning the shameful practices that had generated so much wealth for its "freemen." A commission appointed by the Secretary for War and the Colonies to investigate the factories delivered a report to Parliament in 1810 that was sharply critical of the African Company; among other recommendations, the commissioners pointedly advocated removing a number of the sitting members of the Committee and replacing them with "other Gentlemen, whose long and public hostility to the Slave Trade had clearly proved their sincere desire to ameliorate the state of Africa" (Papers, VII 138). After this, the Company's end was just a matter of time. As the Company faced nearly annual assaults on its funding from Parliament and government, the factories deteriorated, the trade diminished, and the profits declined. The Committee and its faithful Secretary Cock put up a brave fight through the end of the Regency, until the passage in May 1821 of "An Act for abolishing the African Company and transferring to and vesting in His Majesty all the forts, possessions and property belonging to or held by them." With the fullness of empire on the horizon, the Gold Coast's bounty became Crown property.

Clearly, Simon Cock and the African Committee had a lot on their minds as they listened to Robert Adams and prepared his tale for publication in 1815–1816. Their precise concerns may be gleaned from the record of an inquiry by a Select Committee of the House of Commons into the operations of the African Company, undertaken just six weeks after Cock completed his introduction to the *Narrative* on 30 April 1816. Simon Cock was, indeed, the first witness called. For two days, 12 and 13 June 1816, the Secretary answered a volley of hard questions about matters of Company business: the salaries the Company paid its employees in Africa, the costs of supplying the factories, the prices paid for goods to be traded with the Africans, the qualifications of the Company's employees in Africa, and the means by which they were evaluated and promoted. The tone of Cock's exchange with the Select Committee was often tense – many of the members' questions were sharp and mistrustful, and Cock's replies were at times curt, evasive, or defensive. In these instances, the presumption of many of the committeemen was that the Company was wasting Parliament's money. The members demanded from Cock dozens of lists, tables, and letters detailing specific expenditures and administrative decisions over a period of several years, all of which he turned over and referred to frequently during his testimony (Parliamentary Papers, VII 5–24). He must have been gathering documents and preparing for this grilling even as he was pulling together the *Narrative* for publication. But the Select Committee was not solely concerned with accounting. Several times during these two days, members posed questions that exposed the often submerged theme informing every aspect of the inquiry: the Company's long and deep connection with the slave trade.

As they listened to Simon Cock talk about Africa and slavery, some among the Select Committee would have remembered earlier inquiries in which Mr. Cock had been a willing apologist for a very bad cause. His first appearance before a Commons committee had been in 1799, when he was an agent for the slave traders of Liverpool. At issue then was a proposal before Parliament to increase the amount of space allotted to each slave on vessels plying the Middle Passage. Cock's role was to provide a "Calculation upon the Returns," as he called it, demonstrating how much money the traders would lose if the proposal were enacted. The chart that he submitted to the House on this occasion is a perfect product of the bureaucracy of horror; in neat rows and columns filled with cargo sizes and ship dimensions, Cock demonstrated that the legislation being considered would cause an average reduction of one-third in the number of bodies the traders could pack in their holds. Add to this reduction in cargo that proportion of slaves who died of disease or despair on every voyage, and the loss to the merchants would be intolerable ("Minutes of Evidence" 4–6). A decade or so later, during the inquiry initiated by the Secretary for War and Colonies resulting in the report of 1810, he wrote ingratiating letters assuring Lord Castlereagh and others that the African Company would carry on its commerce with Africa "upon such principles as the legislature shall sanction, and in such manner as the Government may direct" (Martin 146). Such language would not have assured many in government that Mr. Cock or the African Committee were now born-again abolitionists.

So, as Simon Cock's 1816 appearance before the Select Committee wore on, the members focused less on the Company's business practices and more on its effect on the Africans themselves. Several questions illustrated the contrast in some members' minds between the Company and the other prominent bodies concerned with Africa, the African Association and the African Institution. "Have the [African] Committee," asked one, "ever taken measures to promote education upon the Coast of Africa?" Cock replied that they had recently sent their first schoolmaster – "a young mulatto, who had wounded his hand" – to one of the factories. This was the Company's first and only educational "measure" in the eight years since the abolition of the trade. Wondered another, "Have any measures been taken to promote religious instruction?" Cock pointed out that a black clergyman named Quaque had been residing at one of the factories "for fifty years; he was educated at Oxford, and about two years ago he sent for his tomb-stone." Cock admitted that the Committee had not yet been able to persuade anyone to take his place; although, as another witness later testified, Mr. Quaque was "superannuated" and "perfectly childish." By the time another committeeman asked Cock if "any measures for civilizing the natives [had] been adopted by the African Committee since the abolition of the Slave Trade," the Secretary could only refer the questioner to his earlier answers about the schoolteacher and the clergyman (Papers, VII 13–14, 23, 31). The Age of Improvement clearly had not yet arrived in the Company's office in Frederick's Place.

After Cock's testimony, the hearings went on for another two weeks, with the increasingly evident aim of some members being to confirm their suspicions that the Company was, if not actually engaging in the slave trade, at least aiding others who were. They were able to establish, through the testimony of a ship captain familiar with the Gold Coast, that the Company's officers had allowed fresh water to be sold and carried to passing slave vessels in Company canoes. Though this violated the Act of 1807, it was a minor matter, and no witness produced the smoking gun that some clearly sought in order to take action against the Company. The Select Committee of 1816 issued no report, but Simon Cock and others from the Company were summoned again to Westminster in May and June of 1817 to face yet another round of hostile questions. This second special committee drew on both years' testimonies to issue a report that began by perfunctorily recommending the continuation of the annual grant of £23,000 to the African Company, and then made a lengthy case for comprehensive reforms to its administration and stricter governmental control of its activities (Papers, VI 3–12). Wasteful, obtuse, and obsolete – the Committee of the African Company might have read its approaching demise on every page of the reports of 1817.

But in November of 1815, when Robert Adams was brought to his office, Cock had not yet faced the Select Committees and very likely believed that the situation could be saved. Such an old warrior in Westminster's battles would have understood that what the Company needed most in order to survive was credibility, and that the credibility it needed was of the sort possessed by its two rivals on the African stage, the African Association and the African Institution. Scientific credibility, on the one hand, and moral seriousness on the other – Robert Adams's extraordinary tale offered both. The quest for the first is reflected in nearly every line of what Jared Sparks mocked as "the greater part of the" published *Narrative*, "composed of introductory details, copious explanatory notes by various hands and on various subjects, elaborate concluding remarks in defense of the story and the notes, together with two learned and well written appendices, which have no connexion with any other part of the book" (163). Sparks was right that Adams's story is sometimes lost in the editorial scaffolding erected to support it, but he was wrong to assert a lack of "connexion" among the parts. These materials, which relentlessly test Adams's account against the touchstones of knowledge about Timbuctoo and West Africa provided by authorities from Leo Africanus to Mungo Park, are meant to work together to firmly place Robert Adams in this great scientific tradition. Or, more precisely, they are meant to place the African Company in the great tradition, since this ignorant son of a "mulatto" could not be properly ranked with a luminary such as Park. The achievement of the *Narrative*, from Cock's perspective, properly belonged to those informed and circumspect enough to know what to make of the sailor's story – that is, Simon Cock and the African Committee. The usefulness of the *Narrative*, to the Company, depended on Cock's ability to make its readers understand just whose achievement this poor man's story was.

In this sense, the *Narrative* may be read as a performance – a very public demonstration by the African Company that it was not, as so many thought, a wastrel with a scandalous past, but rather a player in the new game of African discovery and the march of human progress. This is probably why Cock began his introduction with a portrayal of his own foresight and perseverance in putting Adams's story on paper, as well as of the Committee's quick recognition that Cock was right to entice Adams to talk. We are to understand that without the Company's initiative, this important contribution to knowledge might have been lost. This is also why Cock quickly placed the Company's interest in Adams in the context of the "recent embarkation of Major Peddie and his companions." The Peddie expedition was a government initiative, undertaken by the Colonial Office to complete Mungo Park's fatal effort to discover the true course of the Niger in 1805. Cock's earnest, and unctuous, hope in searching for Adams in the London streets was that "the man might be rendered useful to the views of Government in the exploratory expedition" (*Narrative* 8). He should have said that he hoped that the African Company might be rendered useful, although he must have known that there was precious little to benefit Peddie in the tale that Adams told. Adams supposedly approached Timbuctoo from the Sahara, and said that he had not seen Niger while there; Peddie was to seek the Niger's headwaters from the Windward Coast, and then follow it to its termination, thought to be somewhere in the African interior.

But, having served its rhetorical purpose, Peddie's name quickly disappears. Mungo Park's presence in the *Narrative* is, on the other hand, ubiquitous. Indeed, the model for the structure of the *Narrative* was Park's popular and influential *Travels in the Interior Districts of Africa* (1799), describing his first mission to the Niger. Though Park's *Travels* is not quite so freighted with explanatory material as the Company's publication, it similarly features a map and an extended appendix examining the significance of Park's discoveries, both contributed by the famous geographer, Major James Rennell. Many features of the *Narrative* echo those of the *Travels*, while reference is made to Park's story and to Rennell's map and essay throughout the book. Notice is taken of every detail in which Adams's account is confirmed or made plausible by information from Park's. In those cases where Adams's tale contradicts Park's, Cock and his collaborators laboriously try to reconcile the two or delicately show that even the great Park might have been mistaken.

The deference shown to Park is based on his near legendary stature among both the scientific community and the general reading public of the time. His death on his second mission to the Niger in 1806, the details of which were still fresh in the minds of many after the publication in 1815 of his *Journal*, was broadly conceived as a glorious martyrdom dedicated, on the one hand, to the selfless pursuit of knowledge about the dark continent and, on the other, to British territorial expansion for the sake of the twin gods, civilization and commerce. But these abstract goals – knowledge, civilization, commerce – were given specific political meaning for the African Committee in 1816 by a consideration of the various sponsors of Park's expeditions and of his memory. His first patron was the African Association, which had sent him in 1795 as a "Geographical Missionary" to discover the "course, and, if possible, the rise and termination" of the River Niger (Hallett, *Records of the African Association* 158). His second was the government, specifically the Colonial Office, which in 1805 gave him a brevet commission of captain, put him in charge of a contingent of soldiers from Goree, and sent him off to Africa to "discover and ascertain whether any, and what commercial intercourse can be opened therein for the mutual benefit of the natives and of His Majesty's subjects" (Park, *Journal* liii). His third was the African Institution, to whose care the records of his second mission were entrusted, and which arranged for their publication in honor of Park's consistently stern condemnation of slavery (*Journal* xx–xxi). No wonder that Simon Cock and his friends gave Mungo Park a major part in their production of Robert Adams's *Narrative*.

Indeed, the political stagecraft of the *Narrative* becomes clear in light of the African Company's precarious position in 1816. The pressure from Westminster explains, for instance, the italics used at the end of the "Concluding Remarks" to highlight two points "which the present Narrative decidedly confirms; viz. *the mild and tractable natures of the Pagan Negroes of Soudan, and their friendly deportment toward strangers,* on the one hand, – and, on the other, *the extended and baneful range of that great original feature of African society – Slavery*" (124). The first point bodes well for commerce with the natives, and implicitly assures the world of the African Company's willingness to participate in this prosperous future "upon such principles as the legislature shall sanction, and in such manner as the Government may direct." This commitment is given an imperial twist by the unnamed member of the African Committee who penned the first appendix, in which he suggests that in order to control the trade in the Niger headwaters ahead of "some rival and more active European nation," Britain should immediately occupy the Gambia (134).

The second shouted point about the "baneful" extent of slavery seems strained, coming as it does from the sponsors of *Slavery No Oppression*. However, from a political perspective, the Company needed to shout such a point in 1816, and Robert Adams's tale of the horrors of slavery in the desert gave them an occasion to do so. Just how unconvincing the performance was may be gauged by the irony that one of those responsible for the Company's eventual demise in 1821 was none other than Vice-Consul Joseph Dupuis. In 1818, he was given a royal commission as consul at Kumasi and charged with promoting peace and good relations with the Ashanti. His reports from the Gold Coast, eventually published as a *Journal of a Residence in Ashantee* (1824), were highly critical of the African Company's management of its forts and factories and significantly contributed to the erosion of parliamentary support for the Company. He never commented again on Robert Adams after the publication of the *Narrative*, but we must wonder if the severity of his censure of the Company was motivated by an awareness that he had lent his good name to a very bad cause in 1816.

IV

If Robert Adams, or whoever he was, used the African Company for money and/or the pleasure of manipulating powerful men who would otherwise despise him, the Company used him to persuade the right people that these old slave traders had washed their hands and were fit to serve the pantheon of Britain's expanding interest in Africa: Trade, Civilization, Nation, and Knowledge. With regard to the last of these, the men of the African Committee would have known that publishing a book purporting to settle long-standing questions about Timbuctoo would attach the Company's name to one of the most fascinating subjects of the day, while giving it the leading position in a broadly European race to "discover" something certain about this storied city. Having decided to believe Adams, the main task facing Cock and Dupuis was to reconcile the sailor's tale with their meager knowledge of Timbuctoo, and thereby establish the *Narrative*'s relationship to the history of western interest in the place. If Adams's story could be established as an eyewitness account, the Company's book would achieve a goal that had eluded some of the best minds and deepest pockets in European science, despite a quarter-century of determined effort. Whether he actually went there or not, their effort, filling the many pages of the *Narrative*'s notes and appendices, is a revealing chapter in the history of Europe's attitude toward Africa.

With the exception of Park's second journey, all of the expeditions of this period that included Timbuctoo among their objectives were sponsored by Sir Joseph Banks's African Association. By the time Simon Cock found Adams/Rose in the London streets, the Association had sent seven explorers to Africa, recruited from nearly as many countries. An American, John Ledyard, was the first. Thomas Jefferson had, a few years earlier, encouraged this extraordinary man to try walking east from Europe to the Atlantic coast of America, a quixotic adventure that ended with his arrest in Siberia. Ledyard's African mission was even less successful; preparing in Cairo to cross the continent from the east, he suffered a "bilious complaint," which he treated with "too powerful a dose of the acid of vitriol," the painful effects of which he medicated with "the violent action of the strongest tartar emetic," the combined effects of which killed him (Hallett, *Records* 61). Next was Simon Lucas, an Englishman who set out a little after Ledyard in 1788, intending to make a northern approach across the Fezzan. He got only a hundred miles or so from Tripoli before tribal unrest in the desert forced him back. In 1790, the Association sent an Irishman, Major Daniel Houghton, to find Timbuctoo by way of the River Gambia. Late the following year, he disappeared, having been robbed of all his possessions and very likely murdered. Park tried the western approach again in 1795 and came the closest of all to succeeding, turning back only about three hundred miles up the Niger from Timbuctoo. A German was the next to go. Frederick Hornemann managed to cross the Sahara from Tripoli, but struck the Niger nearly a thousand miles downstream from Timbuctoo, in Nupe, where dysentery claimed him in 1800. Another Englishman named Nicholls was sent in 1804 to travel north from the Bight of Biafra, but he died of a fever in Calabar. Banks and his colleagues tried for the last time in 1808, when they sent a young Swiss, Johann Ludwig Burckhardt, to attempt Ledyard's Cairo route. Not surprisingly, considering the mortality rate among seekers of Timbuctoo, Burckhardt found occasion to spend several years exploring the Middle East before deciding that the time was right to challenge the Sahara. At last, in 1817, he made arrangements to join a caravan leaving Cairo for the Maghreb, but succumbed to dysentery before it departed (Hallett, Records 25–34; Bardner 10–19; Heffernan 206–8).

Why did they do it? Some, like Ledyard and Park, were restless men born at the right time for explorers. Others, like Burckhardt and Houghton, were at loose ends when Sir Joseph offered them a grand purpose, along with the chance for some glory and a little money. But why did the men of the Association spend so much time and cash to get them there? The simplest answer is that Timbuctoo had become, by the turn of the nineteenth century, one of a handful of places on which visionaries like Banks and John Barrow had fixed their dreams of Trade, Civilization, and National Glory, including the glory of scientific knowledge created by British initiative. Like Tibet or the North West Passage, other seemingly forbidden objects of passionate curiosity at the time, Timbuctoo had long promised great things for those who could get there and return alive. Like Tibet, especially, the power it exerted on the western imagination had its roots in gold.

In 1324, the great Mansa Musa, King of the Empire of Mali, set out on a *hadj* that would shape Europe's perception of the city for half a millennium. Mali was at the time the most powerful kingdom in the western Sudan, but few outside the trading routes had heard of it before Mansa Musa and his caravan marched into Cairo on his way to Mecca. The scale of the imperial train was spectacular enough: the King, mounted on horseback, was preceded by five hundred slaves and followed by thousands of attendants. But it was the gold that caused his name, and that of Timbuctoo, to spread quickly throughout the Mediterranean region. Each slave, it was reported, carried a staff of gold, and the royal caravan included nearly a hundred camel loads of gold, each weighing three hundred pounds. Mansa Musa showered gold on everyone he met, not just in Cairo, but all along his path to Mecca and back to Mali. So much gold was put into circulation in Egypt as a result of the King's generosity and extravagance that the market for the metal collapsed and remained depressed for nearly two decades after his *hadj*. Although Mansa Musa's caravan had probably set out from the Malian capital of Mande, it was popularly believed to have been assembled at Timbuctoo, and the city's reputation as a place of fabulous wealth was born (Bovill 86–87). A Catalan map made for Charles V in 1375 by Abraham Cresques, a Jewish cartographer of Majorca, featured a drawing of the Malian monarch in the center of the Sahara, holding a nugget of gold in his hand (see Bovill, Fig. 1).

The gold came mainly from around the headwaters of the Senegal or from the Hausa region, and for several centuries after Mansa Musa's *hadj* the supply seemed inexhaustible (Bovill 119–31). Or so the tale was told. Ibn Battuta, the illustrious Moroccan traveler, visited Mali for eight months in 1352–1353, and in his *Travels* described not just the abundant supply of gold in the court of the Mandingo king, but also the great trade in gold, copper, cloth, and other commodities (including slaves) between Mali and North Africa. Although Ibn Battuta actually had little to say about Timbuctoo, his account of Mali's commercial activity forged an impression of the empire as a great emporium, with Timbuctoo at its center. Speaking of the city of Takkeda, but applying the point to Mali generally, Ibn Battuta wrote that "the inhabitants . . . have no occupation except trade. They travel to Egypt every year, and import quantities of all the fine fabrics to be had there and of other Egyptian wares. They live in luxury and ease, and vie with one another in regard to the number of their slaves and serving women" (*Travels* 335). Over the next two hundred years, European traders along the African coast enthusiastically affirmed reports of the city's wealth and commercial power, though they merely repeated and elaborated stories they had heard. In 1488, the Portugese chronicler Ruy de Pina stated that the King of Portugal decided to build a fortress at the entrance to the Senegal River from a conviction that "the said river, penetrating far into the interior, flowed from the city of Tambuctu . . . where are the richest trades and markets of gold in the world, from which all Berberia [Barbary] from east to west up to Jerusalem is supplied and provided" (Blake 85). Popular narratives by the Venetian explorer Alvise Cadamosto (1507) and the Portugese João de Barros (1552) celebrated the fabulous trade in gold moving both north and west from Timbuctoo, though at least two missions sent by the Portugese crown in the late fifteenth century to locate the city proved fruitless (Crone 21, 140; Gardner 198). Timbuctoo's very impenetrability only magnified the general belief that there must be something very special behind its veil.

Excepting Mungo Park's two volumes of travels, the account against which the editors of Robert Adams's *Narrative* most often measured his credibility was that of Leo Africanus, the Moor of Granada who visited Timbuctoo around 1510 on a diplomatic mission for the Sharif of Fez. At that time, he was known as al-Fasi, the man of Fez, but in 1518 he was captured by Christian corsairs, who, recognizing the value of such a learned and well-traveled slave, carried him to Rome and presented him to Pope Leo X. Leo arranged for al-Fasi's baptism and christened him with his own names, Giovanni Leone, though he soon became known as Leo Africanus. At the time of his capture, he was carrying a draft in Arabic of a narrative of his African travels, which he completed in Italian; it was eventually published in Italian in 1550 and translated into English in 1600 by John Pory, one of Richard Hakluyt's circle. Leo's rendering of Timbuctoo was everything his European audience expected to hear. The city was truly opulent: "the inhabitants, & especially strangers there residing, are exceeding rich," while "the rich king of Tombuto hath many plates and scepters of gold, some whereof weigh 1300 pounds: and he keeps a magnificent and well furnished court." There was plenty of "sweete water" from the city's many wells, while the Niger provided abundant irrigation with which to sustain both livestock and agriculture. Trade flourished: "here there are many shops of artificers, and merchants, and especially of such as weave linnen and cotton cloth. And hither do the Barbarie-merchants bring cloth of Europe.... And hither are brought divers manuscripts or written books out of Barbarie, which are sold for more money than any other merchandize." Leo was, indeed, especially impressed with the city's learning and celebrated its "great store of doctors, judges, priests, and other learned men, that are bountifully maintained at the king's cost and charges." Perhaps best of all, "the inhabitants are people of a gentle and chereful disposition, and spend a great part of the night in singing and dancing through all the streets of the citie" (*History* 824–5), so they would not oppose anyone hoping for a share of Timbuctoo's riches.

For the next two hundred years, fragmentary reports drifted back to Europe from the northern and western edges of the African continent describing enormous wealth arriving in caravans from Timbuctoo. Mostly, it was the stuff of fantasy. One fevered English merchant assured his buyer in London of the arrival in Marrakesh of a "great store of pepper, unicorns' horns...eunuchs, dwarfs, and women and men slaves, besides fifteen virgins" and thirty camels laden with gold (Gardner 8). By the end of the eighteenth century, even those skeptical of unicorns were sure that Timbuctoo, wherever it might be found, was a grand mercantile metropolis, a center of learning and luxury, the heart of a vast inland network of trade. For the less skeptical sort, Timbuctoo was the "city of the golden roofs," the African El Dorado, a city where the beds of the rivers glistened with precious metal. One of the founders of the African Association, Sir John Sinclair, was so moved by such stories that he fairly squirmed with expectation: "We have heard of a city called Tombuctoo.... Gold is so plentiful there as to adorn even the slaves.... If we could get our manufactures into that country, we should soon have gold enough" (Hallett, *Records* 108).

The most recent corroboration of the myth available to the men of the African Committee as they listened to Robert Adams was James Grey Jackson's redaction of reports from "the Guides of the Caravans, Itinerant Merchants of Soudan, and other creditable sources of Intelligence" regarding Timbuctoo, appended to his *Account of the Empire of Marocco* (1809). Jackson excitedly confirmed that Timbuctoo was "the great emporium of central Africa" and offered an expanded version of the familiar list of goods coming north, the very specificity of which must have been compelling to London merchants. "The produce of the Soudan," according to Jackson's sources, "consists principally in gold dust, twisted gold rings of Wangara, gold rings made at Jinnie, bars of gold, elephants' teeth, gum of Soudan,...a great number of slaves, purchased at Timbuctoo," as well as ostrich feathers and ambergris "collected on the confines of the desert." In a paragraph that may have stung Simon Cock and other losers in the recently concluded battle over the slave trade, Jackson added that the slaves from Timbuctoo "are treated very differently from the unhappy victims who used to be transported from the coast of Guinea, and our settlements on the Gambia, to the West India islands" (Jackson, *An Account of the Empire of Marocco* 282, 290–3).

Robert Adams's testimony was startling and worthy of attention because he claimed to have seen the place, and what he saw challenged much of what had been said about it. We now know that much of his information was unexpected because it was erroneous, but in 1815 no news could be disallowed simply because it was surprising. His natural history and geography of the place required some explanation, and his failure to find any significant religious activity gave his London audience pause, but their particular attention was drawn by Adams's revelation that Timbuctoo was far from the El Dorado of dreams. There was gold in the city, surely, since Adams mentioned that the natives wore gold earrings and gave gold dust in trade for other goods, but where were the great markets, or the Moors who supposedly filled them with goods from the Maghreb, or the shops that a great emporium ought to have? No golden roofs and no gold lying on the ground: "he never saw the Negroes find any gold," though he understood that some was to be found somewhere "southward of Tombuctoo" (46). How could Jackson's information, gathered just a few years before Adams's supposed visit, be so completely wrong about the city's wealth? What had happened to the wealth of Mansa Musa, or the city that Leo and Ibn Battuta had described?

The very unexpectedness of Adams's report in this regard may have contributed to the African Company's determination to publish the *Narrative*. Given the state of knowledge of the African interior, any novel information was potentially a scientific and commercial breakthrough, so that the very singularity of Adams's account served well the merchants' purpose to position themselves as legitimate and leading members of the community of African interests in London. Of course, the deviation of Adams's account from material like Jackson's required Cock and his colleagues to toil mightily indeed to establish that Adams was not, after all, the outlier he seemed. The "Concluding Remarks" of the *Narrative* is, when viewed in the context of the history of African exploration, a fascinating balancing act. While conceding the danger of relying on the word of such an "unscientific individual," the author (an unnamed member of the Committee of the Company) wrestles to position this poor sailor's testimony as a veritable revolution in knowledge about Africa. Even as Adams's more improbable disclosures, such as the courcoo, are dismissed as products of his ignorance, the "*general truth*" of his tale before and after the Timbuctoo episode is deemed "sufficient . . . to prepare us for a disappointment of the many of the extravagant expectations which have been indulged respecting this boasted city." Five hundred years of received wisdom regarding Timbuctoo are discarded on the evidence of a man whose very name is uncertain: "And here, we may remark, that the relative rank of Tombuctoo amongst the cities of central Africa, and its present importance with reference to European objects, appear to us, to be considerably over-rated" (118).

Even Mungo Park's contributions could be amended by what Adams had to say, though it was a "species of sacrilege" to directly contradict the martyr (114). Leo Africanus, too, might be corrected by the Company's unwitting explorer; the final paragraphs of the "Concluding Remarks" are a reinterpretation of his account of the city based on Adams's information. Simon Cock and his colleagues surely understood that if Adams had sat in the City retelling tales of golden roofs and bustling markets, men like Banks and Barrow would not have been nearly so intrigued. Unsettling as such new information was, its publication with the imprimatur of such men represented, at least potentially, a triumph for British science and an embarrassment to other European powers interested in Timbuctoo, especially France. There were more immediate and practical considerations as well. The quest for Timbuctoo and its riches had already cost the lives of several good men, a good deal of money, and some loss of face for the African Association and the British scientific establishment generally. Was the prize worth the sacrifice? If the African Company could provide the answer, perhaps everyone concerned – from Whitehall to Westminster to the African Association's rooms in Pall Mall – would grant the old slave traders from the City the authority in African affairs that they once had, and needed desperately to regain.

Indeed, given the Company's circumstances in 1816, it would be reasonable to surmise that its historical connection with slavery influenced its leaders' willingness to challenge the myth of Timbuctoo through the publication of the *Narrative*. Prior to the abolition of the trade, the type of men seated on the Company's Committee would have been interested in Timbuctoo primarily as a fresh source of bodies for sale to the Americas. The ancient reports of the arrival in markets across the Maghreb of "great numbers of slaves, purchased at Timbuctoo" (Jackson 293; see also Segal 55–65 and Ennaji 1–10) might have promised relief for the Committeemen facing the challenges to the slave trade along the Gold Coast during its final two or three decades: increasing demand, dwindling supply, rising prices commanded by the coffle-masters, and escalating competition from other European traders (Craton 75). But after 1807, it was in the Company's interest to demonstrate that its concern with the African interior rested on an earnest desire for legitimate trade. Adams's confirmation that the authorities in Timbuctoo were still mounting slave raids on neighboring Bambara (45) worked to the Company's benefit in this regard, since the editors could surround such news with italicized condemnations of slavery complemented by asseverations of the Company's interest in other types of trade with the African interior. Gold was a worthy object, even if the supply might not be as plentiful as had been supposed; and the ivory, gums, ambergris, feathers, and other such commodities would find a European market. In this regard, the Company's motive in publishing Adams's narrative and its various appendages was only partly to determine his accuracy regarding the true nature of Timbuctoo's vaunted trade, though of course that mattered. A broader purpose would have been to make its voice heard in the national determination of what material good could be made of Africa after the slave trade.

Other accounts of Timbuctoo appeared in England in the wake of Adams's, most notably that of the merchant Abd Salam Shabeeny, whose tale of a visit to the city some thirty years earlier appeared in James Grey Jackson's *An Account of Timbuctoo and Housa* (1820). Shabeeny's tale bears a curious resemblance to Adams's in some aspects, and is implausible for many of the same reasons; he claims, for instance, that the people of Timbuctoo are completely without religion and that the city is bordered by a great forest in which live a large number of elephants. These and similar fables were finally silenced when twelve years after the publication of Adams's *Narrative* René Caillié walked into Timbuctoo with a caravan from Senegal. In his *Journal d'un Voyage à Temboctoo* (1829; published as *Travels Through Africa to Timbuctoo* in 1830), he described his entry into the city that he had spent all his life dreaming about and several years preparing to visit. "The sight before me," he recalled, "did not answer my expectations. I had formed a totally different idea of the grandeur and wealth of Timbuctoo. The city presented, at first view, nothing but a mass of ill-looking houses, built of earth. Nothing was to be seen in all directions but immense plains of quicksand of a yellowish white colour. The sky was pale red as far as the horizon: all nature wore a dreary aspect, and the most profound silence prevailed." The next few days confirmed his initial impression. The city was "neither so large nor so populous" as he had expected, and "its commerce . . . not so considerable as fame [had] reported." Many goods were exchanged in a market there, including slaves and ivory, but the trade was mainly in subsistence goods: dried fish and earthen pots from the nearby Niger, grains and nuts from Djenné, salt from Toudenny. Those Moors who traded for gold to carry across the Sahara did so further upriver, "at Sansanding and Yamina, on account of the vicinity of the gold mines of Bouré, whence they obtain considerable supplies of this precious metal." As Edme-François Jomard documented in his postscript to Caillié's *Travels*, the Frenchman contradicted Adams's account in many particulars regarding life in the city, but his reflections on the general "inactivity, I may even say, indolence" of Timbuctoo confirmed the disappointment for which Adams's story, however obtained, had prepared the world (*Travels*, vol. 2, 49–69).

Of course, Timbuctoo had never been the Timbuctoo of dreams. Doubtless, for several centuries – roughly, from the twelfth through the sixteenth – it was a relatively rich and sophisticated place: a major entrepôt for the trading centers up and down the Niger, and an intellectual center to which students traveled from throughout the Islamic world. And it remained relatively important at the beginning of the nineteenth century, despite the assumption, shared by many who have written about the city, that its fortunes suffered a precipitous collapse after the Moroccan invasion of 1591 (see Willis). But it was only relatively rich and relatively important. More careful attention to the words of those principally responsible for creating the myth of Timbuctoo's magnificence should have given Europeans pause, long before Caillié confirmed the truth first broached in the *Narrative*. Right alongside Leo Africanus's description of the king's 1300-pound gold plates was his comment that "all the houses" of the city are "built of chalke, and covered with thatch" (824). Leo also mentioned that outside the city there "are no gardens nor orchards at all," a harbinger of Caillié's "immense plains of quicksand." Ibn Battuta wrote of the great trade of Mali, but of Timbuctoo he actually says very little, and certainly nothing about its opulence (333). From willful misreadings, inspired by desire, Europeans fashioned their African paradise.

The same year in which Caillié's *Journal* was published in France, a young English poet summarized the new understanding of Timbuctoo. Alfred Tennyson launched his poetic career by winning the Chancellor's Gold Medal at Cambridge for his poem "Timbuctoo," a 248-line blank-verse elegy for the African El Dorado. Tennyson probably had not read Caillié's book, but word of the Frenchman's adventure and his disappointment was circulating through intellectual centers like Cambridge. British interest in the subject had been stirred with reports (correct, as things turned out) that a Scot named Gordon Laing had earned the honor of being the first European to enter the city in 1826, only to be murdered a few miles along his route back north across the Sahara (see Gardner 43–108). And, of course, Adams's story was still part of any conversation about Timbuctoo. Disillusionment was thus very much in the cultural air when Tennyson wrote his memorial for a five-hundred-year-old dream, spoken by an angel sent to wake the poet from his reverie.

> Child of Man,
> Seest thou yon river, whose translucent wave,
> Forth issuing from the darkness, windeth through
> The argent streets of the city, imaging
> The soft inversion of her tremulous Domes,
> Her gardens frequent with the stately Palm,
> Her pagods hung with the music of sweet bells,
> Her obelisks of rangèd Chrysolite,
> Minarets and towers? Lo! how he passeth by,
> And gulphs himself in sands, as not enduring
> To carry through the world those waves, which bore
> The reflex of my City in their depths.
> Oh City! oh latest Throne! where I was raised
> To be a mystery of loveliness
> Unto all eyes, the time is well-nigh come
> When I must render up this glorious home
> To keen *Discovery*; soon yon brilliant towers

Shall darken with the waving of her wand;
Darken, and shrink and shiver into huts,
Black specks amid a waste of dreary sand,
Low-built, mud-walled, Barbarian settlements.
How changed from this fair City!
(Ricks, vol. 2, 224–45)

It is telling, in light of the history of Europe's relationship with Africa after 1829, that Tennyson's poem offers as knowledge of Timbuctoo only a choice between "argent streets" and the "black specks" of "Barbarian settlements." When the beautiful illusion finally dissolved, Europeans replaced one fantasy about Timbuctoo with another – one better suited to an age of dominion.

V

Tennyson's "black specks" evoke, of course, not merely Timbuctoo's shriveled towers, but their black inhabitants as well. Race was always central to the myth of Timbuctoo; part of its allure was the apparent conundrum of a black city boasting fabulous wealth and deep learning. The exotic image of Mansa Musa holding his gold nugget on Cresques's 1375 map was tantalizing to some precisely because of the unspoken understanding that such an unsophisticated creature might be easily separated from his riches, if only he could be found. Race is also central to *The Narrative of Robert Adams*, a book in which the riddle of the black metropolis is supposedly solved by a son of slaves. The political context of the African Company's decision to publish Adams's account was largely shaped by its long and dismal relationship with black Africans, and nearly every page of the published volume reveals that the racial attitudes informing the slave trade still shaped the Company's conception of Africa.

For instance, Dupuis's Appendix II, which he provided at Cock's urging, presents a fine specimen of early-nineteenth-century ethnography. Greater Morocco is sliced into neat racial sections, and each group discernible to the western eye – Arab, Berber, and Moor (with a passing glance at the Jews) – is classified and subclassified according to physical appearance, customs, and moral character. Dupuis paints with a broad brush; like James Fenimore Cooper's Indians, these North Africans divide into those who are "brave" or "honest" and those who are "brutal" or "cowardly." Everywhere in the text, Africans, whether above or below the Sahara, are deemed good or bad depending on their tractability for European purposes. Complex groups such as the Bambara and the Fulani – whose complexity could be surmised even at this early date from a careful reading of Park's two narratives – are reduced to a phrase pinned to a moral map of the continent.

Oddly, though, the matter of Adams's race is deliberately muted by his editors. In the "Introductory Remarks," Dupuis reports Adams's comment in Mogador that his mother was a "mulatto," a statement confirmed for Dupuis by a glance at "his features and complexion" (17). Later, Dupuis mentions that Adams's "complexion" was similar to that of "many Moors, especially those from Fez" (89). The most complete physical description of Adams is that he was "a very dark man, with short curly black hair" (47). But these comments exhaust the references to his race. In those passages where his more implausible assertions or omissions are written off as the mistakes an ignorant sailor might make, his race is never offered as an extenuating consideration. His credibility was understood to be a function of his class and his education, but only implicitly of his race.

Indeed, Adams's racial identity seems oddly blurred throughout the *Narrative*. As Paul Baepler has written, Adams is a racial "chameleon" throughout the tale, changing color depending on the racial identity of those around him (*White Slaves* 25). Compared with the Moors who capture him and his shipmates, he is one of the whites. When (in one of the terrible ironies of his story) the Moors take this free black man hunting for slaves, he is captured by blacks who imprison him along with all the other Moors. Cock's telling of the story indicates that while in Timbuctoo, Adams and a Portugese boy are distinguished as white compared to both Moors and blacks, but when Dupuis first sees him after the ransom, he appears to be Arab, Negro, and Berber all at once: his "appearance, features, and dress...perfectly resembled those of an Arab, or rather of a Shilluh," though "his pronunciation of Arabic resembled that of a Negro" (15).

The reason for this veiling of Adams's blackness may be guessed, considering the political and scientific weight that the *Narrative* had to bear for the African Company. Adams's class and education were weak enough foundations on which to rest the rehabilitation of the Company's image and the revision of the myth of Timbuctoo; but his race, if too plainly stated, might have seriously compromised his credibility. Just how seriously may be gauged by a parody of Adams's narrative published in London's *New Monthly Magazine and Literary Journal* in 1826. "Specimens of a Timbuctoo Anthology" recounts the adventures of a fictional American "mulatto," Captain Jonathan Washington Muggs, "the son of a Timbuctoo slave by an American residing on the banks of the Turtle River in Georgia." Muggs is wrecked on the coast of Africa and taken prisoner by "the savage Mandingoes," who eventually help him on his way to find Timbuctoo. Like Adams, Muggs spends "several months" there, and eventually brings back to England a story disbelieved by many "merely because it contains facts that may startle the narrow intellects of Europe." The most startling news is that "this celebrated and long-sought city" is a forlorn assembly of mud huts presided over by "His wooly majesty," a king with a crocodile jaw for a scepter. Timbuctoo's degradation is presented ironically: Muggs reports that the city's "aspect" is "decidedly superior to that of the finest Kraal of Hottentots in all Caffraria," since the "mud of which the hovels are constructed is of a finer texture," while "the architecture approache[s] in several instances the ingenuity displayed in the nidification of birds" (22, 25).

The imputation is that the "mulatto" Muggs, like Adams, is unqualified to judge what he sees in Timbuctoo, and that whatever valuable information he possesses must be culled by those of broader knowledge. The anonymous satirist invokes ugly stereotypes to make his point. Captain Muggs provides translations of "specimens" of Timbuctoo's poetry, ostensibly illustrating the "refined and delicate sentiments" characteristic of the city's culture. One love poem, "To Tambooshie," features this quatrain: "O wert thou mine, Tambooshie! I would make/Suet and soot pomatum for thy head/Then powder it with bucku dust, and take/Cowdung cosmetics o'er thy face to spread." Black civilization and its hapless black chronicler are both mocked, and the sacrifice of valuable European lives to reach Timbuctoo is denounced by the "editor" of Muggs's report as a "hopeless and desperate" effort that he means to "discourage" (26, 22).

Considered in light of such racist skepticism, Simon Cock's decision to surround the actual narrative with the testimonies of important white men is identical to a strategy familiar to readers of American slave narratives. In both cases, a black man's statement required white certification so that readers could have faith in the narrative's authenticity. Frederick Douglass's *Narrative* (1845), the most famous slave narrative, is prefaced with essays by William Lloyd Garrison and Wendell Phillips, prominent abolitionists whose task was to assure Douglass's readers that he was not a fraud – that he really was a runaway slave and that he really could read and write well enough to produce such a remarkable book. Such pledges did not persuade everyone, of course. Douglass's credibility continued to be assailed by apologists for slavery after his story was published, just as Adams's was attacked by those who, like Sparks, were predisposed to attack anything bearing the imprimatur of the British scientific establishment or of the Tory *Quarterly Review*. Hostility to the latter may partly explain the *New Monthly Magazine*'s parody.

Of course, Adams's story is not quite a slave narrative in the sense of Douglass's. He was not born to slavery, having put himself in harm's way aboard the *Charles*, and the slavery that he endured in North Africa was of a type that, while often brutal, was rarely lifelong. (The works by Segal and Ennaji listed in the Bibliography provide excellent discussions, from very different viewpoints, of Islamic slavery of this period.) The rituals of ransom that Dupuis describes are repeated in the tales of James Riley, Archibald Robbins, Judah Paddock, and others shipwrecked along the coast and sold slowly northward until redeemed. Adams's *Narrative* is more closely related to the dozens of so-called Barbary captivity narratives published on both sides of the Atlantic between the late sixteenth and early twentieth centuries. For the most part, the genre consists of accounts of captivity and/or slavery written by British and American seamen seized by corsairs operating from the principalities of the North African coast: Tripoli and Algiers especially, but also Tangier and Tunis. Held in prisons, put to work, or sold into slavery by the Bey, these westerners often spent years in captivity, waiting for ransom or a chance to escape. Obviously, the narratives of Barbary captivity were written by (or written for, as in Adams's case) those who managed to return home, so the relatively modest number of full-length published accounts cloaks the staggering total number of those held captive. Linda Colley, in her study of British captives worldwide, counts about fifteen full and reasonably credible autobiographical tales of Barbary captivity published in Britain during the seventeenth and eighteenth centuries. Dozens of printed accounts appeared in newspapers, magazines, books, and pamphlets during the same period, but many of those belong more to folklore than to history, since they are told at second or third hand by anonymous redactors, often drawing on stock stories of atrocities committed in Barbary prisons. By contrast, Colley estimates that 20,000 British and Irish captives were held in North Africa from the beginning of the seventeenth century through the middle of the eighteenth – a more responsible estimate than that of the historian al-Zayani (1734–1809), who wrote that the Moroccan emperor alone held "more than 25,000 captives from among the infidels" at one time in the early seventeenth century (Colley 88, 56; Vitkus 5). The number of Americans detained or enslaved was smaller, though those who escaped or were ransomed produced a remarkable number of captivity narratives. About seven hundred Americans were held captive in the Barbary states between 1785 and 1815, producing more than one hundred editions of about forty full-length narratives from 1798 to 1817 (Allison 107; Baepler, *White Slaves* 24).

Whether American or British, and whether autobiographical or mediated by an editor such as Simon Cock, the form of the Barbary captivity narrative was designed to accomplish very specific rhetorical goals. Each captivity drama enacts an orientalist drama: a contest between Christian civilization and Moslem barbarity. At its heart, the Barbary captivity narrative is a morality play, cut from the pattern of Christ's captivity and torment. Innocent Christian victims – sailors, soldiers, passengers on ships going about their business – are unlawfully seized by Moslem pirates or coastal scavengers and subjected to the cruelest treatment imaginable. The sufferings of the martyr are carefully detailed: their skin peels off in sheets under the African sun, their mouths swell shut from drought, their bones are broken by vicious masters, and their stomachs shrink as they wait for their next ghastly meal, such as Adams's repast of donkey flesh and camel urine. Through it all, the victim maintains his moral integrity, doing what is necessary to survive and ultimately escape, while resisting the constant temptation to descend to his captors' depravity or accept their false religion. Like its close literary cousin, the Indian captivity narrative, the Barbary narrative tells the story of a Christian stolen by savage infidels, imprisoned and/or carried into a literal and spiritual desert, subjected to horrific torments, tempted to apostatize, and finally redeemed because of a superior faith and a commitment to the values of a superior civilization.

Adams's editors were surely aware of the cultural power of the Barbary captivity tales; to what extent they shaped his story to conform to its readers' expectations of the genre cannot be known, though there is evidence throughout that they were conscious that certain events possessed a particular dramatic and emotional energy by virtue of their resonance with the genre's conventions. Adams is specifically a Christian hero at Wed-Noon, where he resists the demands of his master to convert to Islam, despite being a special "object of the derision and persecution of the Moors" because of his strength of character. Like Milton's Jesus, assailed by Lucifer in the desert, Adams's desert tormenters were "constantly upbraiding and reviling him, and telling him that his soul would be lost unless he became a Mohammedan," and still he refused to yield. Adams's spiritual fortitude is contrasted with the infirmity of the sailors Williams and Davison, who renounce their faith for better treatment only to regret bitterly their weakness when help arrives from Mogador. Other foils illuminating Adams's constancy appear elsewhere in the *Narrative*. Shortly after being captured on the coast, Adams encounters a "French renegade," whose cowardly denial that he had "turned Mohammedan" despite eating and sleeping with the Moors only marks him a figure of particular shame (*Narrative* 29). Later, another Frenchman appears, a "man who had turned Mohammedan, and was named *Absalom*." His adopted name underscores clearly enough his betrayal of the King, while the description of his work manufacturing gunpowder for the Moors suggests a man living in the fires of hell (60). Doubtless Adams's English editors were pleased to find, or cast, Frenchmen in the role of apostate (see Heffernan 210–14). Again, we cannot be certain whether they simply recorded what Adams told them, shaded his account to foreground such details, or shamelessly fabricated "French renegades" (with or without biblically symbolic names) to satisfy their audience's prejudices. Whatever the case, the sudden emergence of Robert Adams in Chapter Four of the *Narrative* as a man of God confirmed well-established expectations for Barbary narratives, and thereby contributed to the aura of credibility that Cock strove to throw around his unlikely hero.

Coupled with the celebration of Christian perseverance in the Barbary narrative was an often explicit condemnation of the inherent evils of North African Islamic society – despotism, violence, despair, and bondage. A large part of the appeal of the captivity story, on both sides of the Atlantic, was its rendering of the Moslem world as the Other, "a reverse and minatory image," in Colley's phrase, of the glories of western civilization (101; see also Matar 562–72). Returning captives routinely represented their experience in the desert as a struggle between the forces of "rationality, progress,... and self-control" against those of barbarism, atavism, and base instinct (Baepler, *White Slaves* 33). Adams's sufferings as a slave are paradigmatic of the genre's orientalism. After nearly a year of hard work and meager rations at the hands of the Bel-Cossims, father and son, Adams defies his masters in a scene that dramatizes the broader clash of cultures described by the *Narrative*. When Adams refuses to plow his master's field on the "Moorish sabbath," by custom a day of rest even for slaves, young Hameda Bel-Cossim strikes him on the forehead with a cutlass, and Adams repays the blow by knocking Hameda down. The American is promptly put in irons and told that he will remain confined until he kisses Hameda's feet and hands in apology. This Adams refuses to do, saying that is "contrary to his religion" to kiss anyone's feet, and that he had never been required to do so "in his own country" (61–2).

Adams is conspicuously a Christian hero in this episode, but he is more broadly posed as a champion of civilization against barbarism. In his argument with Bel-Cossim about the justice of working on the sabbath, he represents law, reason, and history. His master, he says, is violating the custom of his own religion and capriciously denying Adams his rights. Hameda's response is enraged violence. In his refusal to submit to the inhumanity and degradation of his master's demands, Adams stands for individual dignity. Bel-Cossim's only principle is greed, and his professed religion is a sham. Again, the mediation of Adams's story makes it impossible to know whether the moral drama at Wed-Noon happened this way, although Dupuis heard from several informants of Adams's harsh treatment from the Bel-Cossims (see Note 52). Edward Said would say that its veracity is beside the point: considered as a story element, it gives its western audience what they expect to find when West meets East. Significantly, when the *Narrative* was retold by Charles Ellms in an anthology of adventure stories published in 1846, Adams's punch to Bel-Cossim is one of the two incidents chosen for graphic illustration. The other scene drawn, that of (a very white-looking) Adams fleeing from the tent of his master's wife after her adultery is discovered, perhaps

Hameda Bel Cossim is knocked down by Adams.

Figure 3. From *Robinson Crusoe's Own Book* (1846).

alludes to the orientalist trope of the effeminate easterner by drawing the reader's attention to Adams's masculine triumph.

In *The Crescent Obscured*, Robert Allison explores the significance to early American culture of this disparaging portrait of the Moslem world in the Barbary narratives and argues persuasively that the image of North Africa exerted a powerful, albeit negative, influence on discussions of the young republic's future. The political despotism, religious fanaticism, and institutionalized cruelty of the Barbary states were displayed as examples of what the new nation must avoid as it defined itself in the first half century after the Revolution. The Barbary states were much on Americans' minds in this period, of course; American shipping had lost the protection of the Royal Navy and British treaties with the North African city-states, and corsairs preying on American vessels quickly added hundreds of Yankees to the European prisoners held in Tripoli, Algiers, Tunis, and Tangier. North Africa posed the first significant test to American foreign policy, forcing presidents from George Washington through James Madison to employ different combinations of diplomacy and military force to contain the threat to national sovereignty and commercial activity. The nation's first war was an inconclusive contest with Tripoli between 1801 and 1803, and the rapid development of the United States Navy under Adams and Jefferson was largely in response to the corsair threat in the Mediterranean and eastern Atlantic. Though abductions of American seamen dropped off sharply after Stephen Decatur's heavily armed diplomatic mission to the Barbary coast in 1815, the so-called corsair states were, along with Great Britain, the most persistent foreign threat to American security during the nation's formative decades, and they shared with the British the distinction of being the most consistent objects of American vilification.

The flood of captivity narratives printed and reprinted between the mid-1790s and the late 1810s drew and redrew the image of the Moslem as the quintessential antirepublican, determined to crush the spirit of liberty and democracy carried in the hearts of those Americans unfortunate enough to fall into his clutches. As occurred in England in the seventeenth and eighteenth centuries, the American captivity narratives of the early republic were accompanied by a host of material in other media – newspapers, songs, plays, and verse – condemning "the Turk" or "the Moor" as the natural antagonist of (in Crèvecoeur's famous formulation) the "new man" on the historical stage, the American. Not for the last time, Americans fashioned their national identity and mission in the world in explicit contrast to a popular conception of the Moslem world based on sensational accounts of cruelties perpetrated by a minority of its inhabitants.

The *Narrative* was reprinted in 1817 by the Boston house of Wells and Lily in part to satisfy American interest in the Timbuctoo question, but mainly to capitalize on the market for tales of Americans abused by Moslem masters. Adams's "involuntary exultation at the sight of the American flag" after his ransom (17) resonated with the mood of Monroe's America, in which the Barbary and British threats were receding and a period of national expansion was looming. But the freed slave's "exultation" would have touched British emotions as well; the moment of return from Barbary captivity was, in both national traditions, often dwelt upon as a sign both of the redemptive power of true civilization and religion and of the impotence of barbarism to extinguish

1

the finest sentiments of the human heart (Ben Rejeb 349). By the Regency, though, the anti-Islamic fever in Britain was milder and more subtle than the American strain. American attitudes were shaped by the Barbary states' aggression against American shipping in the era just after Independence, just as the more virulent British hatred of Moslems characteristic of the seventeenth and early eighteenth centuries had been sparked by the corsairs' kidnapping of tens of thousands of British seamen. Through the late eighteenth century, Britain's relationship with the Islamic world became principally commercial, as trade grew with the Ottomans and their North African dependencies. By the turn of the nineteenth century, Moslems were viewed by Britons less as natural antagonists of the civilized world than as, in Linda Colley's phrase, "vital auxiliaries in the business of the British empire" (103). The expansion of British commerce might necessitate imperial conquest (as it had and would again), but in 1816 the main goal of commercial men like those of the African Company was to understand the Moslem world in order to more effectively seize the economic opportunity that it represented.

Thus, while the *Narrative* appealed to an abiding English interest in the Barbary captivity story, Adams's suffering at the hands of the Moslems is subordinated to the avowedly commercial and scientific interests driving the composition of the notes and appendices. The *Narrative* stands slightly apart from most Barbary tales in another important respect as well. On both sides of the Atlantic, the captivity narratives typically engaged the interest of a very specific readership, those in the antislavery movement. All of the captivity narratives that are also slave narratives told a story that those working for the abolition of slavery could use to illustrate the essential cruelty of the institution: a free man, caught by mere chance in the brutalizing engine of slavery. The abolitionists insisted that slavery was slavery and demanded that the moral outrage directed at Moslem slaveholders be turned on Christian slaveholders as well. If, they asked, free (and, in every case except Adams's, white) men and women could tell dreadful tales of enslavement by dark-skinned people in far-off lands, and those dark-skinned people could be justly condemned by their free white readers, how could those same free white readers justify keeping the dark-skinned people of their own nation in bondage? Sometimes the writer of a captivity narrative had an epiphany regarding slavery as a result of his experiences, as did Captain James Riley after surviving shipwreck and slavery in the Sahara. Having endured "cruelty and religious intolerance and bigotry" in Africa, he could not tolerate the enslavement of Africans "who have been snatched & torn from their native country . . . by professors too of moral & political freedom & christian benevolence. . . . The hypocritical advocate of slavery shall be detested by all mankind" (King 314). Abraham Lincoln, for one, was deeply impressed by Riley's story and took to heart the author's lesson (McMurtry 137). More often, the captive himself remained silent on the slavery issue at home, leaving others to draw an abolitionist moral from his story. In *White Slavery in the Barbary States* (1853), for example, Senator Charles Sumner of the Free Soil Party looked back at the narratives so popular around the turn of the century and read a message for his generation: "The interest awakened for the slave in Algiers embraced also the slave at home. Sometimes they were said to be alike in their condition; sometimes, indeed, it was openly declared that the horrors of our American slavery surpassed that of Algiers" (83). The patriotism originally stirred by the Barbary narratives becomes, in Sumner's hands, a mirror held up to expose the illogic of those who claimed to cherish American values while defending a system built on the same vicious principles motivating the Beys of North Africa.

But as a "very dark man," Robert Adams was different from other tellers of captivity tales in a way that complicated any effort to deploy his story in the fight against slavery. There is, in fact, no evidence that his tale was ever mentioned by the abolitionists in either Britain or America. The problem was not merely that the logic of the abolitionists' "there but for the grace of God" argument worked only when the Barbary captive was white. A more serious danger was that a black captive's tale might actually be used by slavery's apologists as confirmation of nineteenth-century pseudoscientific theories of the inherent inferiority of the black race. A relatively temperate form of such theories held that since Africans enslaved each other, blacks must by nature be made for slavery. A more radical iteration, though, argued that blacks were a different species from whites, sufficiently distinct that white enslavement of blacks was thought to be morally equivalent to human ownership of animals. Pseudoscientists produced dismal tracts marshaling physiological, theological, and historical "evidence" in support of their conviction that slavery was not the product of unequal power or historical accident, but rather built into God's (or at least Nature's) well-ordered plan. As numerous writers have noted, this pseudoscientific racism had deep roots in western culture and would persist well beyond the full abolition of slavery in either Britain or America – indeed, it still persists, though in less obvious forms. But the period between the first serious restrictions on the slave trade in the first decade of the nineteenth century (the ban on importation of slaves to the United States in 1803, and the British prohibition of the trade in 1807) and the final abolition of slavery (1838 in Britain, 1863 in America) saw a rapid development of ethnological theories designed to defend the institution. After abolition, these same theories would be elaborated to justify the imperial subjugation of nonwhite races throughout the world, but the focus in 1816 and for several decades afterward was the black African. "The Negroes are made on purpose to serve the whites, just as the black ants are made on purpose to serve the red," declared one English essayist (Fryer 173). "The social, moral, and political, as well as the physical history of the negro race bears strong testimony against them; it furnishes the most undeniable proof of their mental inferiority," echoed an American apologist for "Southern institutions" on the eve of the Civil War (Sawyer 192). Modern readers may cringe at such language, but it was hardly confined to obscure crackpots on either side of the Atlantic. Thomas Carlyle described the "Nigger" as "evidently a poor blockhead with good dispositions.... The Almighty Maker has appointed him to be a servant" (321); Thomas Jefferson, in *Notes on the State of Virginia* (1785), anticipated the ethnology of the next century by carefully outlining the observations leading to his conclusion that "the blacks ... are inferior to the whites in the endowments both of body and mind" (150–1; see also Walvin, *England, Slaves and Freedom* 69–94; Baepler, *White Slaves* 25–31; and Jenkins 242–84).

Considered in this context, the publication of the sole Barbary captivity narrative relating a black man's story by a Company of Merchants that had been forcibly retired from the slavery business inevitably raises another question about that company's motives. Did the men of the African Company, in sponsoring the publication of the *Narrative*, quietly intend Adams's slavery to suggest that the liberalism of the age with regard to race was unnatural? Even as they brought before the world a text meant to confirm their commitment to the new century's definition of legitimate African commerce and to establish their credentials as earnest contributors to the noble work of discovering and civilizing Africa, were they also invoking a popular set of assumptions about blackness that created a rhetorical undertow in the *Narrative*, pulling against the tide of freedom and equality for blacks? Whether such a smuggled message was intended or not, the editors' determination to offer the book as a contribution to science invites its readers to consider it in relation to the ethnological science of the day, and find wrapped in the pious rhetoric of "baneful" slavery and "joyous" redemption an image of the black man as, in the words of a Louisianan, *"the submissive knee-bender . . .* which the Almighty declared he should be" (Breeden 173).

In serving any of its various and contradictory cultural purposes in western culture – orientalism, jingoism, anti-Islamism, abolitionism, racism, or Christian spiritualism – the Barbary captivity narrative was an intensely affective genre. The stories of innocent suffering, brutal villains, and narrow escapes appealed to their readers' passions: their love for Self, variously defined, and their hatred of the Other, variously defined. Paul Baepler has noticed the ways in which the genre's sensationalism aligns it with other popular literary forms of the day, especially the sentimental novel, the gothic novel, and the adventure tale (*White Slaves* 11–12). The link with fiction is significant, since several scholars have observed that, in their pursuit of an affecting tale, neither the writers of Barbary narratives nor their amanuenses hesitated to invent situations or borrow them from other works. Like the eighteenth-century adventure tale, the Barbary narratives often blurred the line between fact and fiction in the pursuit of a powerful story; their authors or their editors regularly exaggerated the truth, repeated stock tales from earlier narratives, or simply made things up in order to meet their obligation to entertain and move the reader.

The Narrative of Robert Adams is distinctive in this regard, as in many others. Its particular complexity and interest lie in its deep and pervasive tension between the imaginative and the historical. Part fable, part treatise, part travel narrative, part polemic, the literary and discursive elements are generally identifiable yet thoroughly entwined to produce a text that resists easy classification. Students of both literature and history will find much to reward their attention, since each aspect of the book provides an interpretive context for the other, and both are required for a full appreciation of the text's place in the culture that produced it. At the center of the *Narrative* is a compelling encounter between a man whose only social power lay in the story he had to tell and the men who made his story their own for the sake of power of various kinds: personal, economic, scientific, and imperial. The "very dark man" telling a tale both true and untrue found eager listeners because he told them something they wanted to hear and gave them something they could use.

This edition of *The Narrative of Robert Adams* follows the text published in London by John Murray in 1816, and includes a copy of the map tracing Adams's supposed course that was bound with the first edition. Original spellings in the text have been preserved, although obvious typographical or printing errors have been silently corrected. My explanatory notes are found in brackets.

Charles Hansford Adams

BIBLIOGRAPHY

EDITIONS OF *THE NARRATIVE OF ROBERT ADAMS*

The Narrative of Robert Adams, a sailor, who was wrecked on the western coast of Africa, in the year 1810, was detained three years in slavery by the Arabs of the Great Desert, and resided several months in the city of Tombuctoo. With a map, notes, and an appendix. London: John Murray, 1816.

The Narrative of Robert Adams, an American sailor, who was wrecked on the western coast of Africa, in the year 1810, was detained three years in slavery by the Arabs of the Great Desert, and resided several months in the city of Tombuctoo. With a map, notes, and an appendix. Boston: Wells and Lilly, 1817.

Nouveau voyage dans l'interieur de l'Afrique, fait en 1810, 1811, 1812, 1813, et 1814; ou, Relation de Robert Adams, Americain des États-Unis. Paris: L. G. Michaud, 1817.

Resa i det inre af Afrika och till Tombuctu. Stockholm: A. Gadelius, 1817.

Jongste in echte berigten betrekkelijk Tombuctoo, in eenige andere nog onbezochte deelen der binnenlander van Afrika. Trans. Herman Van Lil. Amsterdam: J. C. Sepp en Zoon, 1818.

"The Narrative of Robert Adams, An American Sailor, who was wrecked on the western coast of Africa, in the year 1810, and was detained three years in slavery by the Arabs of the Great Desert. He was the first White Man who ever visited the great city of Tombuctoo, where he resided several months." In *Robinson Crusoe's Own Book; or, the voice of adventure, from the civilized man cut off from his fellows, by force, accident, or inclination, and from the wanderer in strange seas and lands,* by Charles Ellms. Boston: Joshua V. Pierce, 1846. [A retelling, through a combination of direct quotation and close paraphrase, of the narrative as originally published.]

PRIMARY WORKS CITED

"Article IX. [Review of] *The Narrative of Robert Adams, a sailor.* . . . pp. 200. Boston, Wells and Lilly, 1817." *North American Review* 5 (1817): 204–24.

Barrow, Sir John. *An Account of Travels into the Interior of Southern Africa, in the Years 1797 and 1798; Including Cursory Observations on the Geology and Geography of the Southern Part of that Continent; The Natural History of such Objects as Occurred in the Animal, Vegetable, and Mineral Kingdoms; and Sketches of the Moral and Physical Characters of the various Tribes of Inhabitants surrounding the Settlement of the Cape of Good Hope. To which is annexed, a Description of the present State, Population, and Produce of that extensive Colony; with a Map constructed entirely from actual Observations made in the Course of his Travels.* London: T. Cadell, jun., and W. Davies, 1801.

Barth, Heinrich. *Travels and Discoveries in North and Central Africa, being a journal of an Expedition undertaken under the auspices of H.B.M.'s Government in the years 1849–1855. 1857.* Reprint, 3 vols., London: Frank Cass & Co. Ltd., 1965.

Blake, John William, ed. and trans. *Europeans in West Africa.* 2 vols. London: Hakluyt Society, 1942.

British Parliamentary Papers: Colonies. Africa, Volume 1: Reports from Select Committees on Petitions of the Court of Directors of the Sierra Leone Company, and the Company of Merchants Trading to Africa, and on the State of the Settlements and Forts on the Coast of Africa. Shannon: Irish University Press, 1968.

Bruce, James. *Travels to Discover the Source of the Nile, in the Years 1768, 1769, 1770, 1771, 1772, and 1773.* Edinburgh: Printed by J. Ruthven, for G.G.J. and J. Robinson, London, 1790.

Caillié, Réné. *Travels Through Central Africa to Timbuctoo and Across the Great Desert to Morocco, Performed in the Years 1824–1828.* London: Colburn and Bentley, 1830.

Crone, G. R., ed. *The Voyages of Cadamosto and Other Documents on Western Africa in the Second Half of the Fifteenth Century.* London: The Hakluyt Society, 1937.

Despatches from United States Consuls in London, 1790–1906. National Archives and Records Administration Microcopy No. T-168, Roll 10 (August 3, 1812–November 28, 1816).

Douglass, Frederick. *Narrative of the Life of Frederick Douglass, an American Slave, Written by Himself.* Boston: The Anti-Slavery Office, 1845.

Dupuis, Joseph. *Journal of a Residence in Ashantee.* London: H. Colburn, 1824. Reprint, London: Frank Cass & Co. Ltd., 1966.

Gray, William, Major. *Travels in West Africa: in the Years 1818, 19, 20, and 21, from the River Gambia through Woolli, Bondoo, Galam, Kasson, Kaarta, and Foolidoo, to the River Niger.* London: John Murray, 1825.

Hallett, Robin, ed. *Records of the African Association, 1788–1831.* London: Thomas Nelson and Sons Ltd., 1964.

Hornemann, Friedrich. *The Journal of Frederick Hornemann's Travels, from Cairo to Mourzouk, the Capital of the Kingdom of Fezzan, in Africa, in the Years 1797–8.* London: Printed by W. Bulmer and Co., Cleveland-Row, St. James's, for G.&W. Nicol, Booksellers to His Majesty, Pall-Mall, 1802.

"Interiour of Africa." *North American Review* 5 (1817):11–26.

Ibn Battuta, Abu Abdullah Muhammed. *Travels in Asia and Africa, 1325–1354.* Trans. H. A. R. Gibb. London: Routledge and Kegan Paul, Ltd., 1929.

Jackson, James Grey. *An Account of the Empire of Marocco, and the District of Suse: compiled from miscellaneous observations made during a long residence in, and various journeys through these countries; to which is added, an accurate and interesting account of Timbuctoo, the great emporium of central Africa.* London: G. and W. Nicol, 1809.

———. *An Account of Timbuctoo and Housa, Territories in the Interior of Africa.* London: Longman, Hurst, Rees, Orme and Brown, 1820.

Jomard, Edme-François. "Geographical Remarks and Inquiries concerning the travels of M. Caillié, in central Africa." In R. Caillié, *Travels Through Central Africa* (1830), 225–501.

Labat, Jean Baptiste. *Nouvelle Relation de l'Afrique Occidentale, Contenant une Description Exacte du Senegal et des Païs Situés Entre le Cap-Blanc et la Riviere de Serrelione, Jusqu'à Plus de 300 Lieüs en Avant Dans les Terres. L'Histoire Naturelle de ces Païs, les differentes Nations qui y sont répandües, leurs Religions et les Moeurs. Avec l'Etat ancien et present des Compagnies qui y font le Commerce. Ouvrage enrichi de quantité de Cartes, de Plans, et de Figures en Taille-Douce.* Paris: Chez G. Cavelier, 1728.

Le Vaillant, François. *Voyage de Monsieur Le Vaillant dans L'Intérieur de l'Afrique par le Cap de Bonne-Espérance, dans les Années 1780, 81, 82, 83, 84, & 85.* Paris: Chez LeRoy, 1790.

Leo Africanus. *Historiale Description de l'Afrique, Tierce Partie du Monde, Contenant ses Royaumes, Iles, Coutumes; Escrite de Nôtre Temps par Iean Leon, Premierement en Langue Arabesque, Puis en Toscane, et à Present Mise en François. Plus, Cinq Navigations au Païs des Noirs, avec les Discours sur Celles.* Trans. Jean Temporal. 3 vols. Lyon: par Jean Temporal, 1556.

Leo Africanus. *The History and Description of Africa, and of the notable things therein contained, written by Al-Hassan Ibn-Mohammed Al-Wezaz Al-Fasi, a Moor, baptised as Giovanni Leone, but better known as Leo Africanus.* Tr. John Pory, 1600. Reissued, ed. Robert Brown, 3 vols., London: Hakluyt Society, 1896.

Mármol Carvajal, Luis del. *Descripción General de Áffrica, con Todos los Successos de Guerras que a Aiudo entre los Infieles, y el Pueblo Christiano, y entre Ellos Mesmos desde que Mahoma Inueto su Secta, hasta el Año del Señor Mil y Quinientos y Setenta y Uno.* Granada: Rene Rabut, 1573–99.

"Minutes of evidence [of Mr. Rigby, Mr. Gyles, and Mr. Cock] respecting the shipping and carrying of slaves." London: n.p., 1799.

Minutes of the Committee of the Company of Merchants Trading to Africa, 1814–1816. British Public Records Office, T 70/150.

Paddock, Judah. *A Narrative of the Shipwreck of the Ship Oswego, on the Coast of South Barbary, and of the Sufferings of the Master and the Crew while in Bondage among the Arabs: Interspersed with Numerous Remarks upon the Country and its Inhabitants, and Concerning the Peculiar Perils of that Coast.* New York: Collins & Co., 1818.

Park, Mungo. *A Journal of a Mission to the Interior of Africa in the Year 1805.* London: John Murray, 1815.

———. *Travels in the Interior Districts of Africa.* London: William Bulmer and Co., 1799. Reprint New York: Arno Press and the New York Times, 1971.

Pennant, Thomas. *History of Quadrupeds.* London: B. White, 1781.

Ramusio, Giovanni Battista. *Primo Volume delle Navigationi et Viaggi nel qual si Contiene la Descrittione dell'Africa: et del paese del Prete Ianni, con varii Viaggi, dal Mar Rosso à Calicut, et insin all'isole Molucce, dove nascono le spetierie, et la Navigationi attorno il Mondo; li Nomi de gli Auttori, et le Navigationi, et i Viaggi piu Particolarmente si Mostrano nel Foglio Seguente.* Venetia: Appresso gli Heredi Lucantonio Giunti, 1550.

Riley, James. *An Authentic Narrative of the Loss of the American Brig Commerce, Wrecked on the Western Coast of Africa, in the Month of August, 1815. With an Account of the Sufferings of Her Surviving Officers and Crew, Who Were Enslaved by the Wandering Arabs on the Great African Desart, or Zahahrah; and Observations Historical, Geographical, &c., Made During the Travels of the Author, While a Slave to the Arabs, and in the Empire of Morocco.* New York: James Riley, 1817.

Robbins, Archibald. *A Journal: Comprising an Account of the Loss of the Brig Commerce, of Hartford (Conn.), James Riley, Master, Upon the Western Coast of Africa, August 28, 1815; Also of the Slavery and Sufferings of the Author and the Rest of the Crew, Upon the Desert of the Zahara, in the Years 1815, 1816, 1817; with Accounts of the Manners, Customs, and Habits of the Wandering Arabs; also, a Brief Historical and Geographical View of the Continent of Africa.* 1817. Reprint. Hartford: S. Andrus, 1851.

St. John de Crèvecoeur, J. Hector. *Letters from an American Farmer, Describing Certain Provincial Situations, Manners, and Customs, and Conveying Some Idea of the Late and Present Interior Circumstances of the British Colonies in North America.* London: T. Davis, 1782.

Sawyer, George S. *Southern Institutes; or, an inquiry into the origin and early prevalence of slavery and the slave trade: With an analysis of the laws, history, and government of the institution in the principal nations, ancient and modern, from the earliest ages down to the present time. With notes and comments in defense of the Southern institutions.* Philadelphia: J.B. Lippincott and Co., 1858.

Slavery No Oppression: or, some new arguments and opinions against the idea of African liberty, dedicated to the Committee of the Company of Merchants that Trade to Africa. London: Lowndes and Christie, 1790?

"Specimens of a Timbuctoo Anthology." *New Monthly Magazine and Literary Journal* 8 (1826): 22–28.

SECONDARY WORKS CONSULTED

Abitbol, Michel. *Tombouctou et les Arma: De la Conquête marocaine du Soudan nigérien en 1591 à l'hégémonie de l'Empire Peulh du Macina en 1833.* Paris: G.-P. Maisonneuve et Larose, 1979.

Africana: The Encyclopedia of the African and African American Experience. Ed. Henry Louis Gates and Kwamme Anthony Appiah. New York: Basic Civitas Books, 1999.

Allison, Robert. *The Crescent Obscured: The United States and the Muslim World, 1776–1815.* New York: Oxford University Press, 1995.

Ajayi, J. F. A., and Michael Crowder, eds. *History of West Africa.* 2 vols. 2nd ed. New York: Longman Group Ltd., 1976.

Baepler, Paul. *White Slaves, African Masters: An Anthology of American Barbary Captivity Narratives.* Chicago: University of Chicago Press, 1999.

———. "The Barbary Captivity Narrative in Early America." *Early American Literature* 30 (1995): 95–120.

Ben Rejeb, Lofti. "Barbary's 'Character' in European Letters, 1514–1830." *Dialectical Anthropology* 6 (1982): 345–55.

Boahen, A. Adu. *Britain, the Sahara, and the Western Sudan, 1788–1861*. Oxford: Clarendon Press, 1964.

Bolster, W. Jeffrey. *Black Jacks: African American Seamen in the Age of Sail*. Cambridge: Harvard University Press, 1997.

Bovill, E. W. *The Golden Trade of the Moors*. 2nd ed. London: Oxford University Press, 1968.

Breeden, James O., ed. *Advice Among Masters: The Ideal in Slave Management in the Old South*. Westport, CT: Greenwood Press, 1980.

Briggs, Lloyd Cabot. *Tribes of the Sahara*. Cambridge: Harvard University Press, 1960.

Bulliet, Richard W. *The Camel and the Wheel*. 1975. Reprint, New York: Columbia University Press, 1990.

Carlyle, Thomas. *Shooting Niagara; and After?* London: Chapman and Hall, 1867.

Clissold, Stephen. *The Barbary Slaves*. New York: Barnes & Noble Books, 1977.

Colley, Linda. *Captives*. New York: Pantheon Books, 2002.

Craton, Michael. *Sinews of Empire: A Short History of British Slavery*. Garden City, NY: Anchor Books, 1974.

Curtin, Philip D. *The Image of Africa: British Ideas and Action, 1780–1850*. Madison: University of Wisconsin Press, 1964.

Davies, K. G. *The Royal African Company*. London: Longmans, Green and Co., 1957.

De Villiers, Marq, and Sheila Hirtle. *Sahara: The Extraordinary History of the World's Largest Desert*. New York: Walker & Co., 2002.

Donnan, Elizabeth, ed. *Documents Illustrative of the History of the Slave Trade to America*. Vol. 2: *The Eighteenth Century*. Washington, DC: Carnegie Institution, 1931.

Encyclopedia of Africa South of the Sahara. Ed. John Middleton. New York: Charles Scribner's Sons, 1997.

Encyclopedia of Islam: A Dictionary of the Geography, Ethnology, and Biography of the Muhammedan Peoples. 4 vols. London: Luzac & Co., 1913.

Ennaji, Mohammed. *Serving the Master: Slavery and Society in Nineteenth-Century Morocco*. Trans. Seth Graebner. New York: St. Martin's Press, 1999.

Fabian, Ann. *The Unvarnished Truth: Personal Narratives in Nineteenth-Century America*. Berkeley: University of California Press, 2000.

Ferro, João Pedro. *A População Portuguesa no Final do Antigo Regime (1750–1815)*. Lisbon: Editorial Presença, 1995.

Fleming, Fergus. *Barrow's Boys*. New York: Atlantic Monthly Press, 2000.

Fryer, Peter. *Staying Power: The History of Black People in Britain*. London: Pluto Press, 1984.

Gascoigne, John. *Joseph Banks and the English Enlightenment: Useful Knowledge and Polite Culture*. Cambridge: Cambridge University Press, 1994.

Gash, Norman. *Lord Liverpool: The Life and Political Career of Robert Banks Jenkinson, Second Earl of Liverpool, 1770–1828.* Cambridge: Harvard University Press, 1984.

Gardner, Brian. *The Quest for Timbuctoo.* New York: Harcourt, Brace & World, 1968.

Hallett, Robin. *Africa to 1875: A Modern History.* Ann Arbor: University of Michigan Press, 1970.

Hall, Luella J. *The United States and Morocco, 1776–1956.* Metuchen, NJ: Scarecrow Press, 1971.

Heath, Jeffrey. *Dictionnaire Songhay-Anglais-Français.* 3 vols. Paris: L'Harmattan, 1998.

Heffernan, Michael. " 'A dream as frail as those of ancient Time': The Incredible Geographies of Timbuctoo." *Environment and Planning D: Society and Space* 19 (2001): 203–25.

Hickey, Donald R. *The War of 1812: A Forgotten Conflict.* Urbana: University of Illinois Press, 1989.

Imperato, Pascal James. *Historical Dictionary of Mali.* 2nd ed. Metuchen, NJ: Scarecrow Press, 1986.

Jenkins, William Sumner. *Pro-Slavery Thought in the Old South.* Chapel Hill: University of North Carolina Press, 1935.

Jefferson, Thomas. *Notes on the State of Virginia.* Ed. Frank Shuffleton. New York: Penguin Books, 1999.

King, Dean. *Skeletons on the Zahara: A True Tale of Survival.* New York: Little, Brown and Company, 2004.

Lipschutz, Mark P., and R. Kent Rasmussen. *Dictionary of African Historical Biography.* Berkeley: University of California Press, 1986.

Martin, Eveline C. *The British West African Settlements, 1750–1821.* 1927. Reprint, New York: Negro Universities Press, 1970.

Matar, Nabil. "English Accounts of Captivity in North Africa and the Middle East: 1577–1625." *Renaissance Quarterly* 54 (2001): 553–72.

Maugham, Robin. *The Slaves of Timbuktu.* New York: Harper & Brothers, 1961.

McCarthy, Mary. *Social Change and the Growth of British Power in the Gold Coast: The Fante States, 1807–1874.* Lanham, MD: University Press of America, 1983.

McMurtry, R. Gerald. "The Influence of Riley's *Narrative* upon Abraham Lincoln." *Indiana Magazine of History* 30 (1934): 133–8.

Miner, Horace. *The Primitive City of Timbuctoo.* Garden City, NY: Doubleday, 1965.

Mountfield, David. *A History of African Exploration.* London: Domus Books, 1976.

Nouvelle Biographie Générale, Depuis les Temps Plus Reculés Jusqu'a nos Jours. 46 vols. Paris: Firmin Didot, Fréres, 1855–70.

Oxford Dictionary of National Biography. 60 vols. Oxford: Oxford University Press, 2004.

Park, Mungo. *Travels in the Interior Districts of Africa.* Ed. Kate Ferguson Marsters. Durham, NC: Duke University Press, 2000.

Pazzanita, Anthony, and Tony Hodges, eds. *Historical Dictionary of Western Sahara.* Metuchen, NJ: Scarecrow Press, 1994.

Ricks, Christopher, ed. *The Poems of Tennyson*. 3 vols. Berkeley: University of California Press, 1987.

Saad, Elias N. *Social History of Timbuktu: The Role of Muslim Scholars and Notables, 1400–1900*. Cambridge: Cambridge University Press, 1983.

Said, Edward W. *Orientalism*. New York: Random House, 1978.

Segal, Ronald. *Islam's Black Slaves: The Other Black Diaspora*. New York: Farrar, Straus and Giroux, 2001.

Spencer, William. *Historical Dictionary of Morocco*. Metuchen, NJ: Scarecrow Press, 1980.

Sumner, Charles. *White Slavery in the Barbary States*. Boston: John P. Jewett, 1853.

Vitkus, Daniel J., ed. *Piracy, Slavery, and Redemption: Barbary Captivity Narratives from Early Modern England*. New York: Columbia University Press, 2001.

Walvin, James. *Black Ivory: A History of British Slavery*. London: Fontana Press, 1993.

———. *England, Slaves and Freedom, 1776–1838*. Jackson: University Press of Mississippi, 1986.

Willis, John Ralph. "The Western Sudan from the Moroccan Invasion (1591) to the death of Al-Mukhtar Al-Kunti (1811)." In *History of West Africa*, ed. J. F. A. Ajayi and Michael Crowder. 2nd ed., vol. 1. New York: Longman, 1976.

ACKNOWLEDGMENTS

Many people helped me bring Robert Adams and the African Company back to life.

James O. Horton, Benjamin Banneker Professor of American Civilization and History at George Washington University, and his wife Lois Horton, Professor of Sociology and Cultural Studies at George Mason University, first encouraged me to undertake this project and lent their enthusiastic support in its early stages. This is just one of many debts that I owe to these remarkable people and excellent scholars. Another excellent scholar, Robert Allison, offered his support and advice at a crucial point in the project, for which I am very grateful.

Numerous individuals in the Reference Division and the Dean's Office of Mullins Library at the University of Arkansas were immensely supportive. Anne Marie Candido, Stephen Chism, Jan Dixon, Martha Guirl, and Beth Juhl all steered me in the right direction at one time or another. I am especially grateful for the patience and professionalism of Michele Tabler, Robin Roggio, and others on the staff of the Interlibrary Loan division of Mullins Library.

Staff members at other libraries and collections were equally helpful. Particular thanks to Jan Hilley and Eric Robinson of the New-York Historical Society; Helen McLallen of the Columbia County (NY) Historical Association; William Stingone, Charles J. Liebman Curator of Manuscripts in the Manuscripts and Archives Division of the New York Public Library; and Travis Westly of the Reference Division of the Library of Congress. Thanks also to the staffs of the National Archives and Records Administration, New York Regional Collection; the British Public Records Office in Kew; and the Rare Books and Music Reading Room of the British Library.

ACKNOWLEDGMENTS

Dean Donald Bobbitt of the J. William Fulbright College of Arts and Sciences at the University of Arkansas provided financial support and, even more important, allowed me time away from my associate dean's duties to complete this volume. I am grateful for his understanding. Thanks also to Vincent Cornell, Professor of Islamic History and Director of the King Fahd Center for Middle East and Islamic Studies at the University of Arkansas, for his encouragement and support. Both Vincent and his wife, Rkia Elaroui Cornell, Professor of Arabic at the University of Arkansas, offered invaluable assistance at several stages of this project.

Several friends in the University of Arkansas community lent their time and expertise. Robert Cochran, Fiona Davidson, David Frederick, Thomas Kennedy, Stephen and Christine Sheppard, Elliot West, and Randall Woods all gave thoughtful advice that I appreciate whether or not they find it incorporated into the finished product. David Parette provided superb computer support, and Jacque Fifer helped greatly with scanning, printing, and other technical matters.

The map (Fig. 1) was designed by Professor Thomas Paradise of the University of Arkansas Department of Geosciences. It locates places named in the *Narrative* or the Preface, however uncertain may be their precise location (e.g., "Woled D'leim," "Woled Adrialla," and the other nomadic encampments) or even their existence (e.g., "Soudenny").

Thanks also to Frank Smith of Cambridge University Press for his support and to Alia Winters, formerly of the Press, who took an early interest in the project and offered lots of good advice. Ken Karpinski shepherded me through the production process with skill and understanding, while the suggestions and corrections of the best copy editor I've worked with, Joanne Leary, saved me from not a few embarrassments.

My greatest debt is to my wife, Rhonda, who let Robert Adams and the African Company live with us for a while. Her sharp eye, keen ear, and thoughtful questions improved this volume at every turn – just as her good humor and generous spirit have improved me through our many years together.

THE NARRATIVE OF
ROBERT ADAMS

THE

NARRATIVE OF ROBERT ADAMS,

A SAILOR,

WHO WAS WRECKED ON THE WESTERN COAST OF

AFRICA,

IN THE YEAR 1810,

WAS DETAINED THREE YEARS IN SLAVERY BY

THE ARABS OF THE GREAT DESERT,

AND RESIDED SEVERAL MONTHS IN THE CITY OF

TOMBUCTOO.

WITH

A MAP, NOTES, AND AN APPENDIX.

LONDON:

PRINTED FOR JOHN MURRAY, ALBEMARLE-STREET,
BY WILLIAM BULMER AND CO. CLEVELAND-ROW.

1816.

COMMITTEE OF THE COMPANY OF MERCHANTS

TRADING TO AFRICA.

GENTLEMEN,

I beg leave to present to you the NARRATIVE of the Sailor, ROBERT ADAMS, in the form which I conceive will be most interesting to you and to the public, and most useful to the poor man himself, for whose benefit it has been committed to the press.

I have the honour to be,

GENTLEMEN,

your faithful and obedient Servant,

S. COCK.

African Office, April 30*th,* 1816.

CONTENTS

Introductory Details Respecting Adams

Discovered in London. – examined by the African Committee respecting his travels in Africa. – his answers satisfactory. – Notes of his story laid before the African Committee, – their belief in its truth. – Mode of interrogating Adams, – his method of reckoning bearings, distances, and rate of travelling, through the Desert. – Examined by several Members of the Government, – receives a Gratuity from the Lords of the Treasury. – Sir Willoughby Gordon's opinion of his statements, – Reasons for publishing the following Narrative. – Departure of Adams for America. – Arrival in England of Mr. Dupuis, British Vice-Consul at Mogadore, – his confirmation of the whole of Adams's story in a Letter to the Editor, with other interesting particulars relating to him on his arrival and during his stay at Mogadore.

Page 8

Advertisement to the Map

Explanations respecting the data on which the Map is constructed. – Information on the route, and nature of the country, between Haoussa and Lagos on the Coast of the Bight of Benin, – probability of Europeans being able to penetrate from Lagos in the direction of the Niger.

Page 22

CONTENTS

NARRATIVE

Chapter 1

Departure from New York on board the "Charles." – Names of the Crew. – Arrival at Gibraltar. – Voyage to the Isle of Mayo – ignorance of the Captain – the Ship is wrecked on the Western coast of Africa – the Crew saved, but are enslaved by the Moors. – El Gazie. – Description of the Moors, and their proceedings. – French Renegade. – Sufferings of the Crew. – Death of Captain Horton. – Separation of the Crew, and departure of the Moors from El Gazie. – Adams is conveyed eastward into the Desert – mode of travelling – arrival at the encampment of the Moors. – Employment there. – Expedition to steal Negro slaves at Soudenny. – Sufferings in traversing the Desert. – Arrival near Soudenny. – The Moors seize a Woman and two Children – are themselves surprised by the Negroes; taken prisoners; and confined in the town. – Soudenny, and its inhabitants. – The prisoners are conveyed by a party of armed Negroes to Tombuctoo. – Journey thither; during which fourteen of the Moors are put to death. – Arrival at Tombuctoo.

Page 26

Chapter 2

Imprisonment of the Moors at Tombuctoo – Adams an object of curiosity, and kindly treated. – King and Queen; Woollo and Fatima. – Their Dress, Ceremonies, Residence, and Attendants. – Muskets. – Curiosity of the natives to see Adams. – Tombuctoo – La Mar Zarah – Canoes – Fish – Fruits – Vegetables – Grain. – Food prepared from the Guinea-corn – Animals. – Heirie – Elephant-hunt. – Birds: Ostriches. – Sulphur – Poisonous preparation of the Negroes for their Arrows. – Persons and Habits of the Negroes – Incisions in their Faces – Dress – Ornaments – and Customs – Musical Instruments – Dancing – Military Excursions against Bambarra – Slaves – Criminal Punishments – Articles of Trade – Jealous precautions of the Negroes against the Moors; their kindness to Adams. – Rain. – Names of Countries – Words in the Language of Tombuctoo.

Page 35

Chapter 3

Ransom of the imprisoned Moors and of Adams. – Departure from Tombuctoo. – Journey eastward along the River; then northward to Taudeny – Traders in salt. – Taudeny – mixed Population of Moors and Negroes – Beds of Rock Salt – Preparations and Departure to cross the Sandy Desert. – Sufferings in the Desert. – Arrival at Woled D'leim – employment, and long detention there. – Refusal of Adams to attend to his tasks – He is punished for it; but perseveres – seizes an opportunity of escaping – is pursued; but reaches El Kabla – He is purchased by the Chief – Employed to tend the flocks of his Master's Wives – Negotiates with Aisha, the younger wife, on the subject of Wages – their bargain, and its consequences – Adams flies and conceals himself – is purchased by a Trader; and conveyed to Woled Aboussebàh – Woled Adrialla – Aiata Mouessa Ali. – He attempts to escape – is retaken; and conveyed to Wed-Noon.

Page 49

Chapter 4

Description of Wed-Noon – where Adams finds three of the crew of the "Charles" – He is purchased by Bel-Cossim-Abdallah. – French Renegade. – Wreck of the Montezuma. – Gunpowder Manufacture. – Curious Relation of a Negro Slave from Kanno. – Severe labours and cruel treatment of the Christian Slaves at Wed-Noon. – Adams is re-quired to plough on the Sabbath day; refuses; is cruelly beaten, and put in irons – his firmness; – Inhuman treatment and death of Dolbie. – Williams and Davison, worn out by their sufferings, renounce their Religion – Adams perseveres. – Letter from the British Vice-Consul at Mogadore, addressed to the Christian Slaves. – Ransom of Adams – Departure from Wed-Noon – Akkadia – Bled Cidi Heshem – Market of Cidi Hamet a Moussa – Agadeer, or Santa Cruz – Mogadore. – Adams is sent to the Moorish Emperor. – Fez – Mequinez – Tangier – Cadiz – Gibraltar – London.

Page 59

CONTENTS

Notes and Illustrations

El Gazie. – Shipwrecks. – French Renegade. – Agadeer Doma. – Soudenny. – Woollo and Fatima. – Dress of the inhabitants of Tombuctoo, Houses, &c. – La Mar Zarah. – Canoes. – Fruits. – Quadrupeds. – Heiries. – Elephant hunting. – Alligators. – Courcoo. – Wild Beasts. – Birds. – Poisons. – Polygamy. – Religion. – Physicians. – Sorcery. – Dancing. – Bambarra. – Slaves. – Punishments. – Shops and Trade at Tombuctoo. – Cowries. – Moors. – Negroes. – Crossing the Desert. – Joliba river. – Negro Language. – Taudenny. – Woled D'leim. – El Kabla. – Aisha. – Woled Aboussebàh. – Kanno. – Christian Slaves. – Reckonings of Time and Distance.

Page 68

Concluding Remarks

Page 106

Appendix No. I

Information obtained in the year 1764, respecting Tombuctoo, and the course and navigation of the Niger. – Park. – Major Rennell. – Sources of the Senegal and Gambia, – Remarks on the rivers passed by Park. – Kong mountains. – Expediency of exploring the furthest western navigation of the Niger.

Page 125

Appendix No. II

Sketch of the Population of Western Barbary. – Berrebbers – Arabs – Moors. – Distinguishing occupations.

Page 136

INTRODUCTORY DETAILS
RESPECTING ROBERT
ADAMS

In the month of October, 1815, the Editor of the following pages was informed by a friend, that a Gentleman of his acquaintance, recently arrived from Cadiz, had accidentally recognised an American seaman, in the streets of London, whom he had seen, only a few months before, in the service of an English merchant in Cadiz, where his extraordinary history had excited considerable interest; *the man having been a long time in slavery in the interior of Africa, and having resided several months at Tombuctoo.*

Such a report was too curious not to have attracted the peculiar attention of the Editor at all times; but the interest of the story was much heightened at that particular moment, by the circumstance of the recent embarkation of Major Peddie and his companions,* to explore those very parts of Africa which this person was said to have visited: and the Editor entreated his friend to assist him by all the means in his power, to find the seaman in question, in order to ascertain whether he really had been where it was reported, and in the hope that, either by his information or his personal services, the man might be rendered useful to the views of Government in the exploratory expedition then on its way to Africa.

Through the intervention of the Gentleman who had originally recognized the seaman, he was again found, and immediately brought to

---

* [An expedition under the command of Major John Peddie was sent in 1816 by the Colonial Office to continue Mungo Park's effort to discover the true course of the Niger. The company arrived on the Windward Coast early in 1817, but Peddie died shortly after striking into the interior. Peddie's successor, Captain Campbell, also died, and the expedition was finally commanded by Major William Gray, whose *Travels in Western Africa* (1825) describes the effort. The expedition was recalled in 1821.]

the office of the African Committee. The poor man, whose name was *Robert Adams*, was in very ill plight both from hunger and nakedness. Scarcely recovered from a fit of sickness, he had, in that condition, begged his way from Holyhead to London, for the purpose of obtaining through the American Consul, a passage to his native country; and he had already passed several nights in the open streets amongst many other distressed seamen, with whom the metropolis was at that period unfortunately crowded.

No time was lost in questioning him respecting the length of his residence in Africa, the circumstances which led him thither, the places he had visited, and the means by which he had escaped. His answers disclosed so extraordinary a series of adventures and sufferings, as at first to excite a suspicion that his story was an invention; and the gentlemen by whom he was accompanied to the office, and who were present at his first examination, were decidedly of that opinion, when they considered how widely his account of Tombuctoo differed from the notions generally entertained of the magnificence of that city, and of the civilization of its inhabitants. The Editor, however, received from this short examination, and from the plain and unpretending answers which the man returned to every question, a strong impression in favour of his veracity. He accordingly took notes of the leading facts of his statement, particularly of the places he had visited, the distances according to his computations, and the direction in which his several journeys lay; and having relieved his immediate necessities, and furnished him with a trifle for his future subsistence, he desired the man to attend him again in the course of a few days.

It was nearly a week before Adams again made his appearance: but upon his return, being immediately interrogated upon all the leading points of his story, the Editor had the gratification to find, upon comparing his answers with the account which he had given on his first examination, that they were in substance the same, and repeated almost in the same terms. Thus strengthened in his previous opinion that the man's veracity was to be depended upon, the Editor resolved to take down in writing (the man himself being unable either to write or read) a full account of his travels and adventures, from the period of his departure from America in the ship "Charles" in which he was wrecked on the coast of Africa, until that of his return to Cadiz, from whence he had just arrived.

With this intention, the Editor took measures to render Adams's situation more comfortable, by equipping him with decent clothes, of which he stood peculiarly in need. He was also supplied with a trifle in money, as an earnest of the future recompense which was promised to him, provided he would attend regularly every day until the whole of his story should be taken down. It was not, however, without considerable difficulty that the man could be persuaded to remain during the period thus required. He was anxious to return to his friends after so long and perilous an absence, and had been recommended by the Consul of the United States to join a transport of American seamen which was then on the point of sailing. His desire to be gone was increased by some rumours then in circulation, of a probable renewal of hostilities between Great Britain and the United States.* But his objections were at length overcome on receiving an engagement, that even if war should break out, and he, by any accident, be impressed, his discharge, either by purchase or substitute, should be immediately effected. Upon this understanding, he consented to remain as long as his presence should be required.

The Editor has been induced to enter into this detail for the satisfaction of those who might be disposed to believe that Adams had obtruded his story upon his hearers, for the purpose either of exciting their compassion, or of profiting by their credulity. To obviate such a suspicion, it is sufficient to shew with what difficulty he was induced to remain in the country to tell his story; and to state, that he was never known to solicit relief from any of the numerous gentlemen by whom he was seen and examined.

Previous, however, to Adams's agreement to stay, a Committee of the African Company having met, the Editor laid before them the notes

---

* [The Anglo-American War of 1812 officially ended on 17 February 1815, though American grievances, particularly regarding the treatment of prisoners, filled the popular press well into the autumn of the year. Consular records from this period make no mention of Adams, although they do indicate that the matter of destitute American seamen in London was a contentious one. A letter from Lord Castlereagh, the Secretary of State for Foreign Affairs, to Consul R. G. Beasley, dated 29 November 1815, complains that "a number of American seamen have been found wandering about the streets of London in a most wretched and distressed condition," and that they are being maintained by the police and the hospitals of the city "at a very considerable expense." Consul Beasley responded on 15 December, reminding His Majesty's Government that almost all of them were formerly impressed seamen now discharged without means by the Royal Navy.]

he had taken of the heads of his story, expressing at the same time his firm belief that the man had really been at Tombuctoo; and he had the satisfaction to find that the Members of the Committee concurred in his opinion of the credibility of the man's statements; in which belief they were afterwards confirmed by their personal examination of him. They strongly encouraged the Editor to proceed in the course which he had begun; and recommended him to omit no practicable means of securing the residence of Adams in this country, until all the information he could possibly give, had been obtained from him, – whether for the purpose of increasing our general knowledge of the interior of Africa, or of obtaining information on particular points which might be useful to the expedition actually on foot.

After this arrangement was completed, Adams attended the Editor for a few hours daily during the following fortnight or three weeks, for the purpose of answering his inquiries. During these examinations upwards of fifty gentlemen saw and interrogated him at different times; among whom there was not one who was not struck with the artlessness and good sense of Adams's replies, or who did not feel persuaded that he was relating simply the facts which he had seen, to the best of his recollection and belief.

The Narrative now presented to the public is the fruit of these interrogatories.

It is proper to mention in this place, that all the information contained in the Narrative was drawn from Adams, not as a continuous and strait-forward story, but in answer to the detached, and often unconnected, questions of the Editor, or of any gentlemen who happened to be present at his examinations; for he related scarcely any thing without his attention being directed to the subject by a special inquiry. This explanation will be necessary, to account for the very large portion of his Narrative devoted to the description of Tombuctoo; for it might otherwise appear extraordinary to some of Adams's readers, that his details respecting a place which occurs so early in his adventures, and of which his recollection might be presumed to be less vivid, should be so much more minute than those respecting any other place which he has visited: but the fact is, that Tombuctoo being the point to which the curiosity and inquiries of all his examiners were mainly directed, his answers on that subject were thus swelled to the prominence which they possess in the Narrative.

It has already been stated, that the first inquiries of the Editor related to the places which Adams had visited, and the courses and distances of the journeys between them. Having obtained these particulars, he communicated them to a friend, who was desirous of examining their pretensions to accuracy by tracing them upon a map of Africa, from the point where Adams appears to have been wrecked. The result of this test, as may be seen in the Map prefixed to the Narrative, at the same time that it afforded a most convincing corroboration of the truth of his story, proved that the man possessed an accuracy of observation and memory that was quite astonishing.

Being questioned how he came to have so minute a recollection of the exact number of *days* occupied in his long journeys from place to place, he answered, that being obliged to travel almost naked under a burning sun, he always inquired, before setting out on a journey, how long it was expected to last. In the progress of it he kept an exact account; and when it was finished, he never failed to notice whether it had occupied a greater or lesser number of days than he had been taught to expect, or whether it had been completed exactly in the stated time.

On asking him how he could venture to speak with confidence of the precise number of *miles* which he travelled on each day; he replied, that he could easily recollect whether the camels on any particular journey, travelled well or ill; and knowing that when they are heavily laden and badly supplied with provisions, they will not go more than from ten to fifteen miles a day; but that, on the other hand, when they are fresh and lightly laden, they will travel from eighteen to twenty-five miles a day, he had reckoned the length of his journeys accordingly.

When asked how he came to observe so minutely the *directions* in which he travelled; he replied, that he always noticed in a morning whether the sun rose in his face, or not: and that his thoughts being for ever turned to the consideration of how he should escape, he never omit-ted to remark, and as much as possible to impress on his recollection, the course he was travelling, and had travelled, and to make inquiries on the subject. Being a sailor, he observed, he had the habit of noticing the course he was steering at sea; and therefore found no difficulty in doing so, when traversing the Deserts of Africa, which looked like the sea in a calm.

Enough, it is hoped, has been said to satisfy the Reader that the Narrative is genuine. But the Editor, aware that it might be difficult to obtain credit for so extraordinary a story, was anxious that Adams, before he left the country, should be seen and examined by every gentleman who might wish it, or whose opinions would be most conclusive with the public. Fortunately this wish was fully accomplished: for the story having come to the knowledge of Earl Bathurst, the Right Honourable the Chancellor of the Exchequer, Major General Sir Willoughby Gordon, the Right Hon. Sir Joseph Banks, John Barrow, Esq.,[*] George Harrison, Esq., Henry Goulburn, Esq. M. P., and other members of the Government who interest themselves in African affairs, and they having expressed a desire to see Adams, he waited upon them in person, and the Narrative was at the same time transmitted to them for their perusal.[†] It is unnecessary to give stronger evidence of the general impression derived from this investigation than is afforded by the fact, that the Lords of the Treasury were pleased to order to the poor man a handsome gratuity for his equipment and passage home: and Sir Willoughby Gordon, in a Letter which the Editor had subsequently the honour to receive from him, expressed his opinion in the following words: "the perusal of his Statement, and the personal examination of Adams, have entirely satisfied me of the truth of his deposition. If he should be proved an impostor, he will be second only to Psalmanazar."[‡]

---

[*] In mentioning the names of Sir *Joseph Banks* and *Mr. Barrow*, the Editor ought not to conceal that Adams had the misfortune, at his first interviews with these gentlemen, and previous to the conclusive corroborations which his story has since received, to excite some doubts in their minds by his account of Tombuctoo, and by his mistakes on some subjects of natural history, (see Notes 15, 18, and 20), but of the *general* truth of his Narrative they did not, even at that early period, entertain any doubts.

[†] [Henry Bathurst, Third Earl of Bathurst (1762–1834), was Secretary of State for War and Colonies during Lord Liverpool's long premiership (1812–1827). The Chancellor of the Exchequer at this date was Nicholas Vansittart, later the first Baron Bexley (1766–1851). Major General Sir James Willoughby Gordon (1773–1851) was, in 1816, Quartermaster General of the Horse Guards. Sir Joseph Banks (1743–1820) was the President of the Royal Society, founder of the Association for Promoting the Discovery of the Interior Parts of Africa, and one of the most eminent men of science in Britain. John (later Sir John) Barrow (1764–1848) was at this time Second Secretary of the Admiralty. George (later Sir George) Harrison (d. 1841) was a prominent lawyer and Assistant Secretary to the Treasury. Henry Goulburn (1784–1856), Tory M.P. for various constituencies for nearly fifty years, was Under-Secretary for War and Colonies; in 1821, he would introduce the bill that dissolved the Company of Merchants Trading to Africa.]

[‡] [George Psalmanazar (1679?–1763) was the pseudonym of a Frenchman who, between 1703 and 1708, persuaded many among the English literary and scientific establishment that he was a native of Formosa. He never revealed his true name.]

Although the information thus obtained from Adams did not, in strictness, answer the specific object for which it was sought, that of assisting Major Peddie; yet as his extraordinary adventures, and his details of Tombuctoo, were too curious to be suppressed, it was resolved, with a view to the gratification of the public, and in some respects in justice to Adams, that the Narrative should be printed for his sole benefit. It was accordingly about to be sent to the press in December last, unsupported by any external evidence beyond the considerations and opinions, contained in the preceding part of this Preface, which was written at that time. And as no sufficient reason then existed for any longer opposing Adams's wish to revisit his home, he embarked on board a vessel bound to New York; leaving until his return, (which he promised should take place in the Spring), a large balance of the bounty of the Lords of the Treasury, and the expected profits of his Book; but before his departure he communicated to the Editor such particulars of his family as might lead to the verification of his, and their, identity, if his return to this country should be prevented by his death.

At this conjuncture an opportunity unexpectedly presented itself, of putting Adams's veracity to a decisive test on many important details of his Narrative; and the intended publication was consequently suspended until the result of this investigation should be ascertained.

The circumstance which produced this fortunate delay, was notice of the arrival in England of Mr. Dupuis, the British Vice-Consul at Mogadore;* to whose interference Adams had ascribed his ransom; and to whom, consequently, the truth or falsehood, of many of his statements must of necessity be known. No time was lost in obtaining an interview with this Gentleman: and the satisfactory answers returned by him to the Editor's first inquiries, led to further trespasses on his kindness and his leisure, which terminated in his consenting, at the earnest solicitation of the Editor, to undertake the perusal of the entire Narrative, and to communicate in writing whatever observations, whether confirmatory or otherwise, might occur to him in the course of its examination.

The general result of this scrutiny, so satisfactory to the previous believers of Adams, is contained in the following Letter from Mr. Dupuis, which is too interesting and important to admit of any abridgement.

---

* [Mogadore (also called Suerra in the narrative) is now Essaouira, Morocco.]

London, 31st January, 1816

In compliance with your request, I have great pleasure in communicating to you all the particulars with which I am acquainted respecting the American seaman who is supposed to have been at *Timbuctoo*; of whom I have a distinct recollection.

In the latter end of the year 1810, I was informed at Mogadore, that the ship Charles, of New York, to which that seaman belonged, was wrecked on the Western Coast of Africa, near the latitude of Cape Blanco: and about three months after her loss, I was fortunate enough to ransom three of her crew; who informed me that their Captain was dead, that the rest of the crew were in slavery, and that two of them, in particular, had been carried away by the Arabs in an easterly direction across the Desert, and would probably never be heard of again. Some time after this, I heard that the mate and one seaman were at *Wed-Noon*;* and I accordingly tried to effect their liberation; but after a considerable time spent in this endeavour, I could neither succeed in that object, nor in obtaining any information respecting the rest of the crew. At length, nearly two years after the wreck of the Charles, I accidentally heard that a Christian was at *El Kabla*, a remote Douar in the Desert, in a south-east direction from Mogadore; and subsequently I heard of the arrival of the same individual at *Wed-Noon*; from whence, after a tedious negociation, I ultimately obtained his release about a year afterwards.

The appearance, features and dress of this man upon his arrival at Mogadore, so perfectly resembled those of an Arab, or rather of a Shilluh,[†] his head being shaved, and his beard scanty and black, that I had difficulty at first in believing him to be a Christian. When I spoke to him in English, he answered me in a mixture of Arabic and broken English, and sometimes in Arabic only. At this early period I could not help remarking that his pronunciation of Arabic resembled that of a Negro, but concluded that it was occasioned by his intercourse with Negro slaves.

Like most other Christians after a long captivity and severe treatment among the Arabs, he appeared upon his first arrival exceedingly stupid and insensible; and he scarcely spoke to any one: but he soon began to show great thankfulness for his ransom, and willingly assisted in arranging and cultivating a small garden, and in other employment, which I gave him with a view of diverting his thoughts. About ten or twelve days afterwards his faculties seemed pretty well restored, and his reserve had in a great measure

---

* [The region of Wadinoon (or Wednoon, or Oued Noun) is roughly 100 miles south along the Moroccan coast from Agadir (called Santa Cruz in 1815). The town of Wednoon is on the wadi about forty miles from the coast.]

[†] [See Dupuis's Appendix II for his description of this group.]

worn off; and about this period, having been informed by a person with whom he conversed, that he had visited the Negro country, I began to inquire of him the extent of his travels in the Desert; suppressing every appearance of peculiar curiosity, or of expecting any thing extraordinary from his answers. He then related to me, with the greatest simplicity, the manner in which he had been wrecked, and afterwards carried away to the eastward, and to *Timbuctoo*; the misfortunes and sufferings of the party which he accompanied, his return across the Desert, and his ultimate arrival at Wed-Noon. What he dwelt upon with most force and earnestness during this recital, were the particulars of the brutal treatment which he experienced from the Arabs at El Kabla and Wed-Noon. He did not appear to attach any importance to the fact of his having been at Timbuctoo: and the only strong feeling which he expressed respecting it, was that of dread, with which some of the Negroes had inspired him, who, he said, were sorcerers, and possessed the power of destroying their enemies by witchcraft.

The probability of the events, the manner of his relating them, and the correspondence of his description of places with what information I possessed respecting them, led me to attach a considerable degree of credit to his Narrative. After repeated examinations, in which I found him uniformly clear and consistent in his accounts, I sent for several respectable traders who had been at Timbuctoo; and these persons, after examining him respecting the situation of that city and of other places, and respecting the objects which he had seen there, assured me that they had no doubt of his having been where he described. So strongly was my belief in the truth and accuracy of his recital now confirmed, that I wrote a detail of the circumstances to Mr. Simpson, Consul-General of the United States at Tangier:* I made a chart, on which I traced his course; and observed that it extended eastward nearly to the supposed situation of Timbuctoo: I also took down in writing an account of his travels, which I regret that I left amongst my papers at Mogadore; and although in doing this I had occasion to make him repeat his story several times, I never found that he differed in any important particular from the tale he told at first.

The Narrative which you have transmitted to me appears, after a minute examination, and to the best of my recollection, to be the same, in substance, as that which I received from him at Mogadore. The chain of events is

---

* [James Simpson was an English merchant who had begun his diplomatic career as the Russian Consul at Gibraltar. After receiving an appointment as U.S. Consul at Gibraltar, he skillfully negotiated Sultan Moulay Suliman's crucial reaffirmation in 1795 of the American–Moroccan Treaty of Marrakech of 1786, and was appointed U.S. Consul to Morocco at Tangier in 1797. He served there until his death in 1820.]

uniformly the same; but I think he entered more into detail on many points, in the relation which he gave to me. I do not enlarge upon this subject here, having pointed out in the Notes which I have made on the Narrative, the few passages in which I found it differ materially from what I recollect of his statements at Mogadore. I have also mentioned such circumstances as corroborated any part of his statements; and I have added, according to your desire, such illustrations or incidental information, as occurred to me in perusing the Narrative.

Being quite satisfied from your description of the person of the American seaman, and from the internal evidence of the Narrative, that *"Robert Adams"* is the identical individual who was with me at Mogadore, I must not, however, omit to inform you, that the name by which he went in Africa was *Benjamin Rose*; by which name also he was known to those of the crew of the Charles who were ransomed.

I cannot say that I am much surprised at this circumstance, because I recollect that he once hinted during his residence at Mogadore that "Benjamin Rose" was not his real name: and from the great apprehensions which he always discovered, lest he should fall in with, or be impressed by a British Man of War, as well as from the anxiety which he shewed on being sent to Tangier, so near to Gibraltar, I could not help suspecting that he might have some reasons of his own, connected with the British Naval service, for going under a feigned name. This conjecture was in some degree confirmed by an acknowledgement which he made, that he had once been on board a British Man of War, either on service, or detained as a prisoner.

There is another circumstance which he mentioned to me at Mogadore, which may possibly have led to this change of name. He told me that he had quitted America to avoid a prosecution with which he was threatened for the consequences of an amour, which he was unwilling to make good by marriage. But on the whole, I am disposed to think that the former was the real cause; since he never expressed any reluctance to go to America, but always seemed to dread the idea of visiting Europe. I never doubted at Mogadore that he was an American, as he stated; and on one occasion, he discovered an involuntary exultation at the sight of the American flag, which seemed quite convincing. He told me that he was born up the river of New York, where his father lived when he quitted America; and I learnt, either from himself or from some other of the Charles's crew, that his mother was a Mulatto, which circumstance his features and complexion seemed to confirm.

On the whole, as I consider it not improbable that *Adams* may be his real name, and being at all events quite satisfied, that he is the person whom I knew at Mogadore, I have, (to avoid confusion) adopted the name which he bears in the Narrative, when I speak of him in my Notes.

I shall be very happy if this explanation, and the details into which I have entered in the Notes, prove of any interest: if you think them of sufficient importance, I can have no possible ground for objecting to their being made public.

Joseph Dupuis

Fortified by this important testimony, the Narrative is now presented to the public, with a guarantee for its substantial veracity, which happily supercedes, though it does not render the less interesting, the presumptive and internal evidence to which the Reader's attention has already been directed.

The Editor reserves for another place, a brief review of the extent to which Mr. Dupuis' communications thus confirm the Narrative; together with an examination of those parts of it which still rest on the unsupported authority of the Narrator. But he cannot omit this, the earliest, opportunity, of publicly acknowledging his great personal obligations to that Gentleman, not merely for his examination of the Narrative, and for the confirmation which his Letter and Notes have lent to it, but peculiarly for the ready kindness with which he has yielded to the Editor's request, in extending his interesting Remarks on some particular occasions, further than the mere confirmation of Adams's Narrative in strictness seemed to require.

To this additional encroachment on the leisure of Mr. Dupuis, the Editor was impelled by information, that few persons were better qualified to give original and accurate details respecting the natives of Barbary and the Desert; a residence of eight years in the dominions of the Emperor of Morocco, (more than half of which period in an official character), and an eminent proficiency in the Arabic language, and in its very difficult pronunciation, having afforded to him facilities of accurate communication with the natives, to which very few of our countrymen have ever attained.

The Editor's particular acknowledgements are also due to two Gentlemen, Members of the African Committee (whom he should have been glad to have had permission to name), whose contributions will be found in this publication: to the one, for a Dissertation of great practical importance on the Upper Regions of the Niger, inserted in the Appendix, No. 1.; and to the other, for the Map already alluded to, and for various Notes and Remarks with which, during the Editor's temporary absence, from ill health, he has had the kindness to illustrate the Narrative.*

In conclusion, the Editor has only to add the assurance (which however he trusts is hardly necessary), that the Narrative itself is precisely in the same state now, as when it was read at the offices of the Colonial Secretary of State, and of the Quarter-Master-General; not a single liberty either of addition or suppression having been taken with the plain statements of Adams: even the imperfect orthography of the names of places, as they were first written to imitate Adams's pronunciation, remains uncorrected; in order that the Reader may judge for himself of Adams's approach to accuracy, in this respect, by comparing his recollections of the names of places and persons, with those accurately furnished by Mr. Dupuis.

April 30th, 1816

---

* [According to Cock's Minutes of the meeting of the African Committee on 3 November 1815 – the same meeting in which he first told the Committee about Robert Adams – he had been "advised by his physician to leave London during the winter months, and requested a leave of absence," which was granted. He was, presumably, back in London by April overseeing the publication of the *Narrative*.]

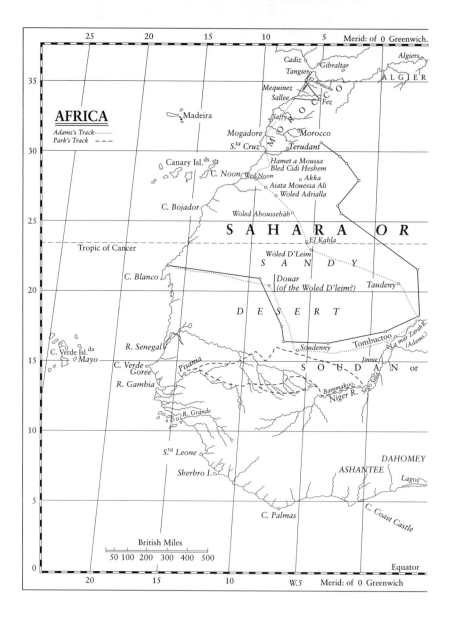

Figure 6. Map of Adams's travels from the original (1816) edition of *The Narrative of Robert Adams.*

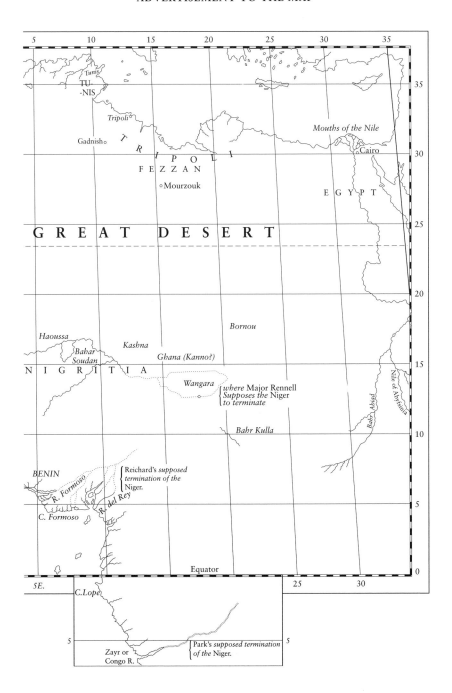

ADVERTISEMENT
TO THE MAP

In conformity with the reported computation of the master of the "Charles," the scene of the shipwreck has been placed in the Map four hundred miles north of the Senegal, or about the 22d. degree of north latitude.

The *ruled line* drawn from this point represents Adams's recollected courses to Tombuctoo and Wed-Noon, extracted from the Narrative at his highest estimates of distance.* The *dotted line* from the same point is given as the assumed real track of these journeys: being an adaptation of the former line to the positions assigned by the best authorities to the cities of Tombuctoo and Wed-Noon; and the difference between these two lines will shew the extent of allowance for errors in reckoning which Adams's statements appear to require.

It is evident, however, that the accuracy of the first part of these journeys (from the coast to Tombuctoo) must depend altogether upon the correctness of the assumed point of departure from which it is traced; and it will probably be remarked, that as the fact of the shipwreck proves the master to have been mistaken in his estimate of longitude, we may fairly presume that he was at least equally mistaken in his latitude; since the known directions of the currents which prevail on this part of the African coast (by which he was probably misled) would doubtless carry the ship at least as far to the *southward* of her reckoning, as the fact of the wreck proves that she was carried to the *eastward*.

Admitting the force of this consideration, we may observe, that in the degree in which it tends to invalidate the accuracy of the master's estimate, it corroborates the precision of Adams's recollections – his line

* See the Table at p. 104 [in Note 60].

of journey (as now traced from the master's position of the shipwreck) lying actually a little further to the *north* than is requisite to bring him to the supposed situation of Tombuctoo.

There is not, however, any sufficient ground for believing that Captain Harrison's* estimates, after the loss of his ship, did not include all the allowances for the effect of the currents, which we are now contemplating, and which that misfortune was calculated to suggest; and we are, consequently, not at liberty to deviate from his opinion merely to fit the circumstances to Adams's story. Nevertheless, this opinion (which *may* be erroneous) must be taken in conjunction with Adams's description of the place where they were cast away; and the only certain conclusion thus deducible from the Narrative appears to be, – that the "Charles" was wrecked on a ledge of low rocks, projecting from a level sandy coast, not far from the latitude of Cape Blanco.[†]

With respect to other positions in the Map, we have only to explain, – that the latitude of Park's lines of journey from the Gambia to Silla is adjusted from the data afforded by his last Mission; but that Major Rennell's[‡] situation of Tombuctoo has been retained.

A conjectural junction has been suggested between Adams's river La Mar Zarah and the Niger; and a suppositious course has also been assigned to the latter river, above the point to which Park's personal observation extended, in order to illustrate the question discussed in the Appendix, No. I.

In a publication professedly intended to promote, in however trifling a degree, our acquaintance with the interior of Africa, it has not appeared improper to advert to the question of the termination of the *Niger*; and the outline of the Map has accordingly been extended to the *Zaire* and the *Nile*, in order to afford a glance at the great points of this much agitated question. It is not, however, our intention to mix further in this discussion. The problem which has excited so strong an interest, is now, we trust, in a fair way of being satisfactorily solved, by the joint labours

---

* [Horton is the name given to the ship's captain elsewhere in the narrative. Harrison is the name of the captain of the *Montezuma*.]

† [Cape Blanco is now Ras Nouâdhibou.]

‡ [Major James Rennell (1742–1830) was the preeminent British geographer of the day. His essay providing "Geographical Illustrations of Africa," including maps of Mungo Park's course and of Africa above the equator, was published as part of the *Travels* in 1799. "Park's last mission" was the explorer's disastrous second expedition, described in *A Journal of a Mission to the Interior of Africa in the Year 1805* (1815).]

of the double expedition which is actually on foot;* and it has been, in the mean time, so ably illustrated in all its parts, by Major Rennell in his Geographical Illustrations of Park's first Travels, – by the Editor of Park's Second Mission, – *and* by the most respectable of our periodical publications, that it would appear a little presumptuous in us to expect that we could throw any new interest into the discussion. But desirous of contributing our mite of information to the *facts* upon which the discussion itself is founded, we shall offer no apology for inserting, in this place, the substance of a communication with which we have been favoured by a gentleman upon whose statements we can rely, and who has resided, at different intervals, a considerable time at the settlement of *Lagos* and at other stations on the coast of the *Bight of Benin.*

We learn from our informant that the *Haoussa*† traders who, previous to the abolition of the slave trade, were continually to be met with at Lagos, still come down to that mart, though in smaller bodies. The result of his frequent communications with them respecting the journey to their own country and the Negro nations through which it lay, has strongly persuaded him of the practicability of a body of Europeans penetrating in that direction to the Niger, with proper precautions, under the protection of the Haoussa merchants; and of insuring their safe return by certain arrangements to be made between the adventurers, themselves (countenanced by the authority of the Governors of the neighbouring forts), – their Haoussa conductors, and the settled native traders on the coast. The principal Negro nation on the journey are the *Joos*,‡ a powerful and not ill-disposed people; and, nearer the coast, (avoiding the Dahomey territories), the *Anagoos* and the *Mahees*; the latter of whom are stated to be an industrious people and good planters. Cowries alone would be necessary, for sustenance or presents, during the whole of the journey.

---

* ["Double expedition" because the Peddie–Campbell–Gray expedition was one of two sent out in 1816 to follow up Park's explorations. While Peddie's group was to approach the Niger from the west, a group under the command of Captain Tuckey, R.N., was sent to explore the rivers of the Bight of Biafra to see if any of them might be the Niger's mouth.]

† Pronounced by the Negroes as if it were written *A-Houssa.*

‡ *Yos*, or *Ayos* in D'Anville's maps. [The Oyos, or Yoruba, now in southwestern Nigeria and Benin: according to Robin Hallett, "the Yoruba kingdom of Oyo was at the height of its power at the end of the eighteenth century and the greatest of the forest kingdoms of West Africa" (194). The 1749 map of Africa by Jean-Baptiste Bourgignon D'Anville (1697–1782) was the standard image before Rennell revised it according to Park's discoveries.]

But it is principally with reference to the nature of the country which lies between the coast and Haoussa that we notice this communication. The traders describe their journey to the coast as occupying between three and four months, which is as much time as they require for the journey from Haoussa to the Gambia; the difficulties and delays incidental to the former journey counterbalancing its shorter distance. These difficulties are invariably described as resulting from the numerous *rivers, morasses*, and *large lakes* which intersect the countries between Haoussa and the coast. Some of these lakes are crossed by the traders on rafts of a large size capable of transporting many passengers and much merchandize at one passage; and here the travellers are often detained a considerable time until a sufficiently large freight of passengers and goods happens to be collected. On no occasion does our informant recollect that the Haoussa traders have spoken of a range of *mountains* which they had to cross in coming down from their own country, and he has no idea that any such range exists in that direction, as the traders spoke only of morasses and other impediments from *water*.

We hardly need to observe that these statements appear to remove some of the difficulties which have been objected to the prolongation of the course of the Niger to the southward, either to the kingdom of Congo or to the Gulf of Guinea, in consequence of the supposed barrier of the *Jibbel Kumri*, or mountains of the moon; but the details are of course too vague to supply any argument in favour of either of the particular systems here alluded to respecting the termination of the Niger, – either of the conjectural theory of Reichard, or of the more reasoned system which Park adopted, and which is so ably illustrated and inforced in one of the publications* to which we have already alluded.

---

* See the Quarterly Review for April 1815, Art. VI. [The mystery of the true course of the Niger was not settled until the explorations of Richard and John Lander in 1830, which also put to rest the supposition that a high range of mountains (called Kong in the west and Komri, or lunar, in the east) stretched across Africa at about the tenth parallel and made any southerly course for the Niger impossible. Christian Gottlieb Reichard (1758–1837) was actually the first to correctly surmise the course of the Niger. His theory that the Oil Rivers in the Bight of Benin were the river's mouth first appeared in Germany in 1802. It was not published in England until 1815, when it was incorporated into a discussion of various theories of the Niger's course in the *Journal* of Park's second mission (cxxi–cxxiii; see Curtin 203–5).]

Departure from New York on board the "Charles." – Names of the Crew. – Arrival at Gibraltar. – Voyage to the Isle of Mayo – ignorance of the Captain – the ship is wrecked on the Western coast of Africa – the Crew saved, but are enslaved by the Moors. – El Gazie. – Description of the Moors, and their proceedings. – French Renegade. – Sufferings of the Crew. – Death of Captain Horton. – Separation of the Crew, and departure of the Moors from El Gazie. – Adams is conveyed eastward into the Desert – mode of travelling – arrival at the encampment of the Moors. – Employment there. – Expedition to steal Negro slaves at Soudenny. – Sufferings in traversing the Desert. – Arrival near Soudenny. – The Moors seize a Woman and two Children – are themselves surprised by the Negroes; taken prisoners; and confined in the town. – Soudenny, and its inhabitants. – The prisoners are conveyed by a party of armed Negroes to Tombuctoo. – Journey thither; during which fourteen of the Moors are put to death. – Arrival at Tombuctoo. –

Robert Adams, aged 25, born at *Hudson*, about one hundred miles up the North River,* from New York, where his father was a sail maker, was brought up to the seafaring line, and made several voyages to Lisbon, Cadiz, Seville, and Liverpool.

On the 17th of June 1810, he sailed from New York in the ship Charles, John Horton master, of 280 tons, Charles Stillwell owner; laden with flour, rice, and salted provisions, bound to Gibraltar.

The crew consisted of the following persons:

Stephen Dolbie, mate,
Thomas Williams,

---

* [The Hudson River.]

CHAPTER 1

Martin Clarke,
Unis Newsham,
Nicholas (a Swede),
John Stephens,
John Matthews,
James Davison,
Robert Adams,

shipped at New York.

The vessel arrived in twenty-six days at Gibraltar, where the cargo was discharged. Here she was joined by Unis Nelson, another sailor: she lay at Gibraltar about a month, and after taking in sand ballast, 68 pipes of wine, some blue nankeens, and old iron, proceeded on her voyage, the Captain stating that he was bound to the Isle of May, for salt, but afterwards it appeared that he was going on a trading voyage down the coast.[1]* When they had been at sea about three weeks, Adams heard two of the crew, Newsham and Matthews, who were old sailors, and had been on the coast before, speaking to the mate, stating their opinion that the Captain did not know where he was steering: the ship's course was then south south-west: they said he ought to have steered to the northward of west.[†] They had to beat against contrary winds for eight or nine days afterwards; and on the 11th of October, about 3 o'clock in the morning, they heard breakers; when Matthews, the man at the helm, told the mate who was keeping watch, that he was sure they were near the shore; to which the mate replied, that "he had better mind the helm, or his wages would be stopped." An hour afterwards the vessel struck, but there was so much fog that the shore could not be seen. The boat was immediately hoisted out, and the mate and three seamen got into it, but it instantly swamped. The four persons who were in it, swam, or were cast ashore by the surf: soon after a sea washed off

---

* [Numbered notes refer to the extensive "Notes and Illustrations" of the text provided by Joseph Dupuis (marked *D.*), Simon Cock, and/or the unnamed member of the African Committee referred to at the end of Cock's introduction. This may have been James Swanzey, a merchant with extensive experience along the Gold Coast. Cock's apparent absence from London during the winter of 1816 makes unclear the extent of his contributions, if any, to the notes. The Isle of May, or, Mayo, is one of the Cape Verde Islands.]

[†] These courses, whether from the fault of Adams's memory, or of the judgement of the "old sailors," hardly seem to warrant the consequences here ascribed to them.

four or five more of the crew, including Adams; but as all of the ship's company could swim, except Nicholas, and the mate, they reached the shore without much difficulty; the latter two were nearly exhausted, but no lives were lost. When morning came, it appeared that the ship had struck on a reef of rocks that extended about three quarters of a mile into the sea, and were more than twelve feet above the surface at low water. The place, according to the Captain's reckoning, was about four hundred miles to the northward of Senegal.

Soon after break of day they were surrounded by thirty or forty Moors, who were engaged in fishing on that coast, by whom Captain Horton and the ship's company were made prisoners. The vessel bilged: the cargo was almost entirely lost; and what remained of the wreck was burnt by the Moors, for the copper bolts and sheathing; but as they had no tools wherewith to take off the copper, they saved little more than the bolts. The place, which was called *El Gazie*,[2] was a low sandy beach, having no trees in sight, nor any verdure. There was no appearance of mountain or hill; nor (excepting only the rock on which the ship was wrecked) any thing but sand as far as the eye could reach.

The Moors* were straight haired, but quite black; their dress consisted of little more than a rug or a skin round their waist, their upper parts and from their knees downwards, being wholly naked. The men had neither shoes nor hats, but wore their hair very long: the women had a little dirty rag round their heads by way of turban. They were living in tents made of stuff like a coarse blanket, of goat's hair, and sheep's wool interwoven; but some of them were without tents, until they were enabled to make them of the sails of the ship; out of which they also made themselves clothes. The men were circumcised. They appeared to be provided with no cooking utensil whatever. Their mode of dressing fish was by drying it in the sun, cutting it into thin pieces,

---

* [L. C. Briggs argues that these "Moors" are the Imraguen (or Hawata) people, an Arabized Berber group that survives by fishing, and that Adams's is the first recorded description of them (116). If this is the case, it is unlikely that the coastal Imraguen would have carried Adams as far into the interior as he claims to have gone. Adams indicates that he and his Moorish captors are ransomed at Timbuctoo by members of the "Woled D'leim" (Oulad Delim); if so, he may have been transferred to this group by the Imraguen. In Dupuis's Note 6, he mentions that Adams's shipmates told him at Mogador that Adams had been purchased from their initial captors by other Arabs "from the eastward." For more on these tribes, see Pazzanita and Hodges, *Historical Dictionary of Western Sahara* (331–4).]

and letting it broil on the hot sand; but they were better off after the wreck, as they secured several pots, saucepans, &c. So extremely indigent were these people, that when unable to catch fish, they were in danger of starving; and in the course of fourteen days, or thereabouts, that they remained at El Gazie, they were three or four days without fish, owing to the want of proper tackle. Among the articles in a chest that floated ashore, was fishing tackle, which the crew of the Charles offered to shew the Moors how to use, and to assist them in fishing; but they refused to be instructed, or to receive any assistance. At length, having accumulated enough to load a camel, they raised their tents and departed, taking with them their prisoners.

Besides the Moors there was a young man in appearance a Frenchman, but dressed like a Moor. As Captain Horton spoke French, he conversed with this man, who told him that about a year before he had made his escape from Santa Cruz, in the Canary Islands, in a small vessel, with some other Frenchmen;* and that having approached the shore to procure goats, they had found it impossible to get the vessel off again, on account of the surf, and were taken prisoners; his companions had been sent up the country. As he associated, and ate and slept with the Moors, Adams was of opinion that he had turned Mohammedan, although he assured Captain Horton that he had not done so.[3]

On the landing of the Captain and crew, the Moors stripped all of them naked, and hid the clothes under ground, as well as the articles which they had collected from the ship, or which had floated ashore. Being thus exposed to a scorching sun, their skins became dreadfully blistered, and at night they were obliged to dig holes in the sand to sleep in, for the sake of coolness.

This was not the only evil they had to encounter, for as the Moors swarmed with lice, Adams and his companions soon became covered with them.

About a week after landing, the Captain became extremely ill, and having expressed himself violently on the occasion of his being stripped, and frequently afterwards using loud and coarse language, and menacing gestures, he was at length seized by the Moors and put to death. The

* [This was the period of the Spanish War of Independence against Napoleonic France, 1804–1814; the Canary Islands were Spanish territory.]

instrument they used on the occasion was a sword, which they found in the cabin: the Captain used no resistance; he was in fact so reduced by sickness, and was in such a state of despondency, that he frequently declared he wished for death. It was the manner of the Captain that gave offence, as the Moors could not understand what he said, any more than he could understand them. One thing in particular, about which Adams understood the Moors to quarrel with him was, that as he was extremely dirty, and (like all the party) covered with vermin, they wished him to go down to the sea to wash, and made signs for him to do so. But partly from an obstinacy of disposition, and partly from the lassitude brought on by sickness and despair, he refused to do as desired; and whenever pressed to do so, used the most threatening looks, actions, and words.[4]

When the vessel struck, the Captain gave orders that the heads of the wine casks should be knocked in, in the hope of thereby making her float; and when he found that did not succeed, he ordered that the guns, flour, anchors, &c. should be thrown overboard, and the water started. In the confusion and alarm, the muskets and powder were also thrown overboard; otherwise the party might have had the means of defending themselves against the Moors who appeared on their first landing, the number of whom did not exceed forty or fifty people; but though the Captain was a man of courage, he appeared to be utterly deprived of reflection after the vessel had struck. He was also an excellent navigator, but relied too much upon the mate.

After they had remained about ten or twelve days, until the ship and materials had quite disappeared, the Moors made preparation to depart, and divided the prisoners among them, carefully hiding in the sand every thing they had saved from the wreck. Adams, the mate, and Newsham were left in the possession of about twenty Moors, (men, women, and children), who quitted the sea coast, having four camels, three of which they loaded with water, and the other with fish and baggage. They travelled very irregularly, sometimes going only ten or twelve miles a day, but often considerably more, making upon an average about fifteen miles a day; occasionally going two or three days without stopping, except at night, at others resting a day or two; on which occasions they pitched the tents to recruit the camels.

Except one woman, who had an infant, which she carried on her back, the whole of the party went on foot. The route was to the eastward, but inclining rather to the south than to the north of east, across a desert sandy plain, with occasional low hills and stones. At the end of about thirty days, during which they did not see any human being, they arrived at a place, the name of which Adams did not hear, where they found about thirty or forty tents, and a pool of water, surrounded by a few shrubs, which was the only water they had met with since quitting the coast.

In the first week after their arrival, Adams and his companions being greatly fatigued, were not required to do any work, but at the end of that time they were put to tend some goats and sheep, which were the first they had seen. About this time John Stevens* arrived, under charge of a Moor, and was sent to work in company with Adams. Stevens was a Portuguese, about eighteen years of age. At this place they remained about a month.

The mate offered the Moors one hundred dollars to take the party to Senegal, which was called by the Moors Agadeer Bomba,† which they refused; but, as Adams understood, they were willing to take them to a place called Suerra.⁽⁵⁾ Not being acquainted with this place, they objected to go thither; but when they began to learn the language, they found that what was called *Suerra*, meant *Mogadore*. The mate and Newsham remained only a few days at the place at which they were stopping, when they went away with some of the Moors in a northerly direction. It was very much the desire of Adams and Stevens to continue in company with the mate and the others, but they were not permitted.⁽⁶⁾

Some days after, it was proposed by the Moors to Adams and Stevens to accompany them in an expedition to Soudenny to procure slaves. It was with great difficulty they could understand this proposal, but the Moors made themselves intelligible by pointing to some Negro boys who were employed in taking care of sheep and goats; and as they frequently mentioned the word "Suerra," Adams at last made out, that if he and Stevens would join in the expedition, they should be taken to that place. Being in the power of the Moors, they had no option, and

---

* [Presumably the "John Stephens" on the *Charles*'s crew list.]

† "Agadeer Doma." D. [Heinrich Barth wrote in 1857 that "Ághadír Dóme, or, as it is called by the Arabs, E' Dákhela.... is said to contain from 50 to 60 huts of reed, inhabited by the Imrághen..." (719). This supports L. C. Briggs's argument that Adams's captors were Imrauguen.]

having therefore signified their consent, the party, consisting of about eighteen Moors and the two whites, set off for Soudenny, taking with them nine camels, laden with water and barley flour, procured at the place at which they had stopped. After proceeding two days, they were joined by twelve other Moors, and three more camels, and then the whole party set off to cross the Desert,* proceeding south southeast; travelling at first at the rate of from fifteen to twenty miles a day. It was the expectation of the Moors, that by travelling at that rate for ten days, they should come to a place where water was to be procured; but the weather having been exceedingly hot, and the season dry, when they arrived at the spot (which they did in ten days) where the water was expected, which seemed to be a well about eight or nine feet deep, it was found quite dry. By this time their water running very short, they resorted to the expedient of mixing the remainder of their stock with the camel's urine, and then set out again on their journey to Soudenny, pursuing a course rather more southerly, in the neighbourhood of which they arrived in about four days more. About two days journey from this place they appeared to have left the Desert, the country began to be hilly, and they met with some small trees.

Soudenny is a small negro village, having grass and shrubs growing about it, and a small brook of water. The houses are built of clay, the roofs being composed of sticks laid flat, with clay on the top. For a week or thereabouts, after arriving in the neighbourhood of this place, the party concealed themselves amongst the hills and bushes, lying in wait for the inhabitants; when they seized upon a woman with a child in her arms, and two children (boys), whom they found walking in the evening near the town.[7]

During the next four or five days the party remained concealed, when one evening, as they were all lying on the ground, a large party of Negroes, (consisting of forty or fifty men,) made their appearance, armed with daggers and bows and arrows, who surrounded and took them all prisoners, without the least resistance being attempted, and carried them into the town; tying the hands of some, and driving the whole party before them. During the night, above one hundred Negroes kept watch over them. The next day they were taken before the Governor,

---

* Adams calls "the Desert" only those parts of the great Sahara, which consist of loose sand, without any traces of vegetation.

or chief person, named Mahamoud, a remarkably ugly Negro, who ordered that they should all be imprisoned. The place of confinement was a mere mud wall, about six feet high, from whence they might readily have escaped (though strongly guarded), if the Moors had been enterprising; but they were a cowardly set. Here they were kept three or four days, for the purpose, as it afterwards appeared, of being sent forward to Tombuctoo, which Adams concluded to be the residence of the king of the country.

The better order of natives at Soudenny wear blue nankeen, in the manner of a frock; but are entirely without shoes, hats, or turbans, except the Chief, who at times wears a blue turban. The distinguishing ornament of the Chief is some gold worked on the shoulder of his frock, in the manner of an epaulette; some of the officers about him were ornamented in a similar manner, but with smaller epaulettes. Their arms were bows and arrows; the former about four feet long, with strings made of the skin of some animal; the arrows were about a foot and a half long, not feathered. The Negroes frequently practised shooting at small marks of clay, which they scarcely ever missed at fifteen or twenty yards distance.

The houses have only a ground floor; and are without furniture or utensils, except wooden bowls, and mats made of grass. They never make fires in their houses. The lower order of people wear blankets, which they buy from the Moors. After remaining about four days at Soudenny, the prisoners were sent to Tombuctoo, under an escort of about sixty armed men, having about eighteen camels and dromedaries.

During the first ten days, they proceeded eastward at the rate of about fifteen to twenty miles a day, the prisoners and most of the Negroes walking, the officers riding, two upon each camel or dromedary. As the prisoners were all impressed with the belief that they were going to execution, several of the Moors attempted to escape; and in consequence, after a short consultation, fourteen were put to death, by being beheaded at a small village at which they then arrived; and as a terror to the rest, the head of one of them was hung round the neck of a camel for three days, until it became so putrid that they were obliged to remove it. At this village the natives wore gold rings in their ears, sometimes two rings in each ear. They had a hole through the cartilage of the nose, wide enough to admit a thick quill, in which Adams saw some of the natives wear a large ring of an oval shape, that hung down to the mouth.

They waited only one day at this place, and then proceeded towards Tombuctoo, shaping their course to the northward of East: and quickening their pace to the rate of twenty miles a day, they completed their journey in fifteen days.

2

Imprisonment of the Moors at Tombuctoo – Adams an object of curiosity, and kindly treated. – King and Queen; Woollo and Fatima. – Their
Dress, Ceremonies, Residence, and Attendants. – Muskets. – Curiosity
of the natives to see Adams. – Tombuctoo – La Mar Zarah – Canoes –
Fish – Fruits – Vegetables – Grain. – Food prepared from the Guinea-
corn – Animals. – Heirie – Elephant-hunt. – Birds: Ostriches. – Sulphur –
Poisonous preparation of the Negroes for their Arrows. – Persons and
Habits of the Negroes – Incisions in their Faces – Dress – Ornaments –
and Customs – Musical Instruments – Dancing – Military Excursions
against Bambarra – Slaves – Criminal Punishments – Articles of Trade –
Jealous precautions of the Negroes against the Moors; their kindness
to Adams. – Rain. – Names of Countries. – Words in the Language of
Tombuctoo.

Upon their arrival at Tombuctoo, the whole party was immediately
taken before the King, who ordered the Moors into prison, but treated
Adams and the Portuguese boy as curiosities; taking them to his house,
where they remained during their residence at Tombuctoo.

For some time after their arrival, the Queen and her female attendants
used to sit and look at Adams and his companion for hours together.
She treated them with great kindness, and at the first interview offered
them some bread baked under ashes.

The King and Queen, the former of whom was named *Woollo*, the
latter *Fatima*,[8] were very old grey-headed people. The Queen was extremely fat. Her dress was of blue nankeen, edged with gold lace round
the bosom and on the shoulder, and having a belt or stripe of the same
material half way down the dress, which came only a few inches below
the knees. The dress of the other females of Tombuctoo, though less ornamented than that of the Queen, was in the same short fashion; so that

as they wore no close under garments, they might, when sitting on the ground, as far as decency was concerned, as well have had no covering at all. The Queen's head-dress consisted of a blue nankeen turban; but this was worn only upon occasions of ceremony, or when she walked out. Besides the turban, she had her hair stuck full of bone ornaments of a square shape about the size of dice, extremely white; she had large gold hoop ear-rings, and many necklaces, some of them of gold, the others made of beads of various colours. She wore no shoes; and, in consequence, her feet appeared to be as hard and dry "as the hoofs of an ass."*

Besides the blue nankeen dress just described, the Queen sometimes wore an under dress of white muslin; at other times a red one. This colour was produced by the juice of a red root which grows in the neighbourhood, about a foot and a half long. Adams never saw any silks worn by the Queen or any other inhabitant of Tombuctoo; for, although they have some silks brought by the Moors, they appeared to be used entirely for purposes of external trade.

The dress of the King was a blue nankeen frock decorated with gold, having gold epaulettes, and a broad wristband of the same metal. He sometimes wore a turban; but often went bare-headed.(9) When he walked through the town he was generally a little in advance of his party. His subjects saluted him by inclinations of the head and body; or by touching his head with their hands, and then kissing their hands. When he received his subjects in his palace, it was his custom to sit on the ground, and their mode of saluting him on such occasions was by kissing his head.

The King's house, or palace, which is built of clay and grass (not white-washed), consists of eight or ten small rooms on the ground floor; and is surrounded by a wall of the same materials, against part of which the house is built. The space within the wall is about half an acre. Whenever a trader arrives, he is required to bring his merchandize into this space for the inspection of the King, for the purpose, Adams thinks, (but is not certain,) of duties being charged upon it.(10) The King's attendants, who are with him all the day, generally consist of about thirty persons, several of whom are armed with daggers and bows and arrows. Adams does not know if he had any family.

* Adams's expression.

36

In a store-room of the King's house Adams observed about twenty muskets, apparently of French manufacture, one of them double-barrelled; but he never saw them made use of.[11]

For a considerable time after the arrival of Adams and his companion, the people used to come in crowds to stare at them; and he afterwards understood that many persons came several day's journey on purpose. The Moors remained closely confined in prison; but Adams and the Portuguese boy had permission to visit them. At the end of about six months, there arrived a company of trading Moors with tobacco, who after some weeks ransomed the whole party. Adams does not know the precise quantity of tobacco which was paid for them, but it consisted of the lading of five camels, with the exception of about fifty pounds weight reserved by the Moors. These Moors seemed to be well known at Tombuctoo, which place, he understood, they were accustomed to visit every year during the rainy season.

Tombuctoo is situated on a level plain, having a river about two hundred yards from the town, on the south-east side, named *La Mar Zarah*.* The town appeared to Adams to cover as much ground as Lisbon. He is unable to give any idea of the number of its inhabitants; but as the houses are not built in streets, or with any regularity, its population, compared with that of European towns, is by no means in proportion to its size.† It has no walls, nor any thing resembling fortification. The houses are square, built of sticks, clay, and grass, with flat roofs of the same materials. The rooms are all on the ground floor, and are without any article of furniture, except earthen jars, wooden bowls, and mats made of grass, upon which the people sleep. He did not observe any houses, or any other buildings, constructed of stone.[12]

The river *La Mar Zarah* is about three quarters of a mile wide at Tombuctoo, and appears to have, in this place, but little current, flowing to the south-west. About two miles from the town to the southward it

---

* Or *La Mar Zahr*. It was not easy to fix the probable orthography of African names, from Adams's indistinct pronunciation.
† [Lisbon's population in 1815 has been estimated to be at least 160,000, down from over 200,000 before the start of the Napoleonic war (see Ferro 52). Caillié estimated Timbuctoo's population in 1828 to be ten to twelve thousand, though even this figure is probably too high.]

runs between two high mountains, apparently as high as the mountains which Adams saw in Barbary: here it is about half a mile wide. The water of La Mar Zarah is rather brackish, but is commonly drunk by the natives; there not being, as Adams believes, any wells at Tombuctoo.[13] The vessels used by the natives are small canoes for fishing, the largest of which is about ten feet long, capable of carrying three men: they are built of fig-trees hollowed out, and caulked with grass, and are worked with paddles about six feet long.[14] The river is well stored with fish, chiefly of a sort which Adams took for the red mullet: there is also a large red fish, in shape somewhat like a salmon, and having teeth; he thinks it is the same fish which is known in New York by the name of "sheep's-head." The common mode of cooking the fish is by boiling; but they never take out the entrails.

The principal fruits at Tombuctoo are cocoa-nuts, dates, figs, pineapples, and a sweet fruit about as large as an apple, with a stone about the size of a plum stone. This latter was greatly esteemed; and being scarce, was preserved with care for the Royal Family. The leaves of this fruit resembled those of a peach.[15]

The vegetables are carrots, turnips, sweet potatoes, negro beans, and cabbages; but the latter are eaten very small, and never grow to a solid head.

The grain is principally rice and guinea-corn.* The cultivation of the soil at Tombuctoo requires very little labour, and is chiefly performed with a kind of hoe which the natives procure from the Moors, and which appears to be their only implement of husbandry. Adams never observed any cattle used in agriculture.

The guinea-corn grows five or six feet high, with a bushy head as large as a pint bottle, the grain being about the size of a mustard seed, of which each head contains about a double handful. This they beat upon a stone until they extract all the seed, and then they put it between two flat stones and grind it. These operations are performed by one person. The meal, when ground, is sifted through a small sieve made of grass. The coarse stuff is boiled for some time, after which the flour is mixed with it, and when well boiled together it makes a thick mess like burgoo. This is put into a wooden dish, and a hole being made in the

* [Sorghum.]

middle of the mess, some goats' milk is poured into it. The natives then sit on the ground, men, women and children, indiscriminately round the mess thus prepared, and eat it with their fingers. Even the King and Queen do the same, having neither spoons, knives, nor forks. In the preparation of this food for the King and Queen, they sometimes use butter, which is produced from goats' milk; and though soft and mixed with hair, it appeared to be considered a great dainty. Some of the bowls out of which the natives eat are made of cocoa-nut shells; but most of them are of the trunk of the fig-tree hollowed out with chisels.

The animals are elephants, cows, goats, (no horses),[16] asses, camels, dromedaries, dogs, rabbits, antelopes, and an animal called heirie, of the shape of a camel, but much smaller.* These latter are only used by the Negroes for riding, as they are stubborn, and unfit to carry other burdens: they are excessively fleet, and will travel for days together at the rate of fifty miles a day. The Moors were very desirous of purchasing these animals, but the Negroes refused to sell them.[17]

The elephants are taken by shooting with arrows pointed with a metal like steel, about a foot long, and exceedingly sharp. These arrows are steeped in a liquid of a black colour; and when the animal is wounded they let him go, but keep him in sight for three or four days, at the end of which he expires from the effects of the wound. Adams never saw more than one killed, which was at the distance of about two miles from the town. He was one evening speaking to a Negro, when they heard a whistling noise at a distance: as soon as it was heard, the Negro said it was an elephant, and next morning at day-light he set off with his bow and arrows in pursuit of him. Adams, the Portuguese boy, and many of the town's people accompanied him, until they came within about three quarters of a mile of the elephant, but were afraid to go any nearer on account of his prodigious size. The Negro being mounted on a heirie, went close to him, riding at speed past his head: as he passed him he discharged an arrow, which struck the elephant near the shoulder, which instantly started, and went in pursuit of the man,

---

* [Almost certainly a corruption of *mahri* (plural *mahārī*), which Richard Bulliet calls "the North African camel of purest lineage,... a slender riding camel prized by the Tuaregs and other desert tribes" (113; see Note 17).]

striking his trunk against the ground with violence, and making a most tremendous roaring, which "might have been heard three miles off." Owing to the fleetness of the heirie, which ran the faster from fear, the elephant was soon left at a distance; and three days afterwards was found lying on the ground in a dying state, about a mile from the spot where it was shot. According to the best of Adams's recollection, it was at least twenty feet high; and though of such an immense size, the natives said it was a young one. The legs were as thick as Adams's body.[18] The first operation of the Negroes was to take out the *four* tusks, the two largest of which were about five feet long. They then cut off the legs, and pieces of lean from the hinder parts of the body, and carried them home; where they skinned the flesh, and then exposed it to dry in the sun for two days. It was afterwards boiled, but proved to Adams's taste very coarse food, the grain of the meat being as thick as a straw, and of a very strong flavour. The only thing eaten with it was salt, which is procured from a place called Tudenny wells, which will be spoken of hereafter. Upon the occasion of the elephant being killed, the Negroes were greatly delighted: and Adams frequently laughed with them, at the recollection of their appearance as they stood round the dead carcase, all laughing and shewing their white teeth at once, which formed a ridiculous contrast with their black faces.

The other wild animals which Adams saw were foxes, porcupines, baboons, wolves, and a large species of rat which frequents the river. He does not appear to have seen either hippopotami or alligators.[19]

Besides these, there is in the vicinity of Tombuctoo a most extraordinary animal named *courcoo*, somewhat resembling a very large dog, but having an opening or hollow on its back like a pocket, in which it carries its prey.[20] It has short pointed ears and a short tail. Its skin is of an uniform reddish-brown on its back, like a fox, but its belly is of a light-grey colour. It will ascend trees with great agility and gather cocoa-nuts, which Adams supposes to be a part of its food. But it also devours goats and even young children, and the Negroes were greatly afraid of it. Its cry is like that of an owl.

The wolves are destructive to asses as well as goats. The foxes frequently carry off young goats and guinea-fowls, particularly the former. Although he never saw either lions, tigers, or wild cats; yet the roaring of animals of these descriptions was heard every night in the neighbouring mountains.[21]

The domestic birds are guinea-fowls. The wild birds are ostriches, eagles, crows, owls, green parrots, a large brown bird that lives upon fish, and several smaller birds. He does not recollect to have seen any swallows.[22]

The ostriches are about double the size of a turkey, quite wild, and go in flocks. When any are observed in the day time, the place where they resort is marked, and they are caught at night by men mounted on heiries, who strike them with sticks. When they are first caught their feathers are very beautiful. The flesh of the ostrich is cooked without being previously dried in the sun, and is good eating, as well as the eggs, which are boiled: in fact, almost every thing which the Negroes of Tombuctoo eat is boiled.

The principal animal food eaten by the Negroes is goats' flesh. Adams did not see more than one cow killed during his stay; and then, he thinks, it was on account of the animal's being in a declining state. The cows are very small, and but few in number: some of them are milk-white; but the colour of the greater part is red.

There are two sorts of ants at Tombuctoo; the largest black, the smallest red; which appear at times in prodigious numbers. He has also seen bees there; but he has no recollection of having seen any honey.

Having occasionally at night, seen a light like fire on the mountains to the southward of the town, Adams had the curiosity to visit them, and found a considerable quantity of sulphur, which the natives collected. The only use to which he has seen them apply this mineral, was to mix it with a substance in black lumps which looked like opium,[23] for the purpose of making a liquid into which they dipped the heads of their arrows. It was with an arrow so prepared that the elephant, before spoken of, was killed.

The natives of Tombuctoo are a stout, healthy race, and are seldom sick, although they expose themselves by lying out in the sun at mid-day, when the heat is almost insupportable to a white man. It is the universal practice of both sexes to grease themselves all over with butter produced from goat's milk, which makes the skin smooth, and gives it a shining appearance.[24] This is usually renewed every day; when neglected, the skin becomes rough, greyish, and extremely ugly. They usually sleep under cover at night; but sometimes, in the hottest weather, they will be exposed to the night air with little or no covering, notwithstanding that the fog which rises from the river descends like dew, and in fact, at that season, supplies the want of rain.

All the males of Tombuctoo have an incision on their faces from the top of the forehead down to the nose, from which proceed other lateral incisions over the eyebrows, into all of which is inserted a blue dye, produced from a kind of ore which is found in the neighbouring mountains. The women have also incisions on their faces, but in a different fashion; the lines being from two to five in number, cut on each cheek bone, from the temple straight downwards: they are also stained with blue. These incisions being made on the faces of both sexes when they are about twelve months old, the dyeing material which is inserted in them becomes scarcely visible as they grow up.[25]

Except the King and Queen and their companions, who had a change of dress about once a week, the people were in general very dirty, sometimes not washing themselves for twelve or fourteen days together. Besides the Queen, who, as has been already stated, wore a profusion of ivory and bone ornaments in her hair, some of a square shape and others about as thick as a shilling, but rather smaller, (strings of which she also wore about her wrists and ankles) many of the women were decorated in a similar manner; and they seemed to consider hardly any favour too great to be conferred on the person who would make them a present of these precious ornaments. Gold ear-rings were much worn. Some of the women had also rings on their fingers; but these appeared to Adams to be of brass; and as many of the latter had letters upon them (but whether in the Roman or Arabic characters Adams cannot tell) he concluded both from this circumstance, and from their workmanship, that they were not made by the Negroes, but obtained from the Moorish traders.

The ceremony of marriage amongst the upper ranks at Tombuctoo, is for the bride to go in the day time to the King's house, and to remain there until after sunset, when the man who is to be her husband goes to fetch her away. This is usually followed by a feast the same night, and a dance. Adams did not observe what ceremonies were used in the marriages of the lower classes.

As it is common to have several concubines besides a wife, the women are continually quarrelling and fighting. But there is a marked difference in the degree of respect with which they are each treated by the husband;

the wife always having a decided pre-eminence.[26] The Negroes, however, appeared to Adams to be jealous and severe with all their women,
frequently beating them for apparently very little cause.

The women appear to suffer very little from child-birth, and they will
be seen walking about as usual the day after such an event. It is their
practice to grease a child all over soon after its birth, and to expose it
for about an hour to the sun: the infants are at first of a reddish colour,
but become black in three or four days.

Illicit intercourse appeared to be but little regarded amongst the lower
orders; and chastity amongst the women seemed to be preserved only
so far as their situations or circumstances rendered it necessary for their
personal safety or convenience. In the higher ranks, if a woman prove
with child the man is punished with slavery, unless he will take the
woman for his wife and maintain her. Adams knew an instance of
a young man, who, having refused to marry a woman by whom he
had a child, was on that account condemned to slavery. He afterwards
repented; but was not then permitted to retract his refusal, and was sent
away to be sold.

The practice of procuring abortion is very common. Adams was informed that in cases of pregnancy from illicit intercourse, where the
woman would not submit to this alternative, it was no unusual thing
for the father secretly to poison her.

The Negroes of Tombuctoo are very vehement in their quarrels. When
they strike with their fists they use the under part of the hand, as if
knocking with a hammer; but their principal mode of offence is by
biting. On the whole, however, they are a good natured people; and
always treated Adams with the greatest kindness.

It does not appear that they have any public religion, as they have
no house of worship, no priest, and as far as Adams could discover,
never meet together to pray. He has seen some of the Negroes who were
circumcised; but concluded, that they had been in the possession of the
Moors, or had been resident at Tudenny.[27]

The only ceremony that appeared like the act of prayer was on the
occasion of the death of any of the inhabitants, when their relatives
assembled and sat round the corpse. The burial is unattended with any
ceremony. The deceased are buried in the clothes in which they die, at
a small distance to the south-west of the town.

Adams does not believe that any of the Negroes could write, as he never saw any of them attempt it; their accounts appeared to be kept by notching sticks. Almost all the Moors, on the contrary, are able to write.

Their only physicians are old women, who cure diseases and wounds by the application of simples. Adams had a wen on the back of his right hand, the size of a large egg; which one of the women cured in about a month by rubbing it and applying a plaister of herbs.[28] They cure the tooth-ache by the application of a liquid prepared from roots; which frequently causes not only the defective tooth to fall out, but one or two others.

He never saw any of the Negroes blind but such as were very old; of these, judging from their appearance, he thinks he has seen some upwards of one hundred years of age. Children are obliged to support their parents in their old age; but when old people are childless, there is a house for their reception, in which they live, four or five in a room, at the cost of the King.

The only tools which the Negroes appeared to possess (besides the hoes and chisels previously mentioned) were knives and small hatchets with which they cut their timber, and a few other rough instruments of iron which they procured from the Moors. Adams does not remember ever to have seen a saw.

Their musical instruments are, 1st, a sort of fife made of reeds; 2d, a kind of tambourine covered with goat skin, within which are ostrich quills laid across in such a manner that when the skin is struck with the hand the quills jar against it; 3d, an instrument which they call *bandera*, made of several cocoa-nut shells tied together with thongs of goat-skin, and covered with the same material; a hole at the top of the instrument is covered with strings of leather or tendons, drawn tightly across it, on which the performer plays with the fingers in the manner of a guitar.

Their principal and favourite amusement is dancing, which takes place about once a week in the town, when a hundred dancers or more assemble, men, women and, children, but the greater number men. Whilst they are engaged in the dance they sing extremely loud to the music of the tambourine, fife, and bandera: so that the noise they make may be heard all over the town. They dance in a circle, and (when this amusement continues till the night) generally round a fire. Their usual time of beginning is about two hours before sun-set, and the dance not unfrequently lasts all night. The men have the most of the exercise in these sports whilst daylight lasts, the women continuing nearly in one spot and the men dancing to and from them.[29] During this time the dance is conducted with some decency; but when night approaches, and the women take a more active part in the amusement, their thin and short dresses, and the agility of their actions, are little calculated to admit of the preservation of any decorum.

It has been already stated, that Adams can form no idea of the population of Tombuctoo; but he thinks that once he saw as many as two thousand persons assembled at one place. This was on the occasion of a party of five hundred men going out to make war in Bambarra.[30] The day after their departure they were followed by a great number of camels, dromedaries, and heiries, laden with provisions. Such of these people as afterwards returned, came back in parties of forty or fifty; many of them did not return at all whilst Adams remained at Tombuctoo: but he never heard that any of them had been killed.

About once a month a party of a hundred or more armed men marched out in a similar manner to procure slaves. These armed parties were all on foot except the officers; they were usually absent from one week to a month, and at times brought in considerable numbers. The slaves were generally a different race of people from those of Tombuctoo, and differently clothed, their dress being for the most part of coarse white linen or cotton. He once saw amongst them a woman who had her teeth filed round, he supposes by way of ornament; and as they were very long they resembled crow-quills. The greatest number of slaves that he recollects to have seen brought in at one time, were about twenty, and these he was informed were from the place called Bambarra, lying to the southward and westward of Tombuctoo; which he understood to be the country whither the aforesaid parties generally went out in quest of them.

The slaves thus brought in were chiefly women and children, who, after being detained a day or two at the King's house, were sent away to other parts for sale.[31] The returns for them consisted of blue nankeens, blankets, barley, tobacco, and sometimes gunpowder. This latter article appeared to be more valuable than gold, of which double the weight was given in barter for gunpowder. Their manner of preserving it was in skins. It was however never used at Tombuctoo, except as an article of trade.

Although the King was despotic, and could compel his subjects to take up arms when he required it, yet it did not appear that they were slaves whom he might sell, or employ as such generally; the only actual slaves being such as were brought from other countries, or condemned criminals. Of the latter class only twelve persons were condemned to slavery during the six months of Adams's residence at Tombuctoo. The offences of which they had been guilty were poisoning, theft, and refusing to join a party sent out to procure slaves from foreign countries.

Adams never saw any individual put to death at Tombuctoo,[32] the punishment for heavy offences being, as has just been stated, slavery; for slighter misdemeanours the offenders are punished with beating with a stick; but in no case is this punishment very severe, seldom exceeding two dozen blows, with a stick of the thickness of a small walking cane.

Adams did not observe any shops at Tombuctoo.[33] The goods brought for sale, which consisted chiefly of tobacco, tar, gunpowder, blue nankeens, blankets, earthen jars, and some silks, are obtained from the Moors, and remain in the King's house, until they are disposed of. The only other objects of trade appeared to be slaves.

The principal articles given in exchange in trade by the people of Tombuctoo, are gold-dust, ivory, gum, cowries, ostrich feathers, and goat skins; which latter they stain red and yellow. Adams has seen a full-grown slave bought for forty or fifty cowries.[34] He never saw the Negroes find any gold, but he understood that it was procured out of the mountains, and on the banks of the rivers, to the southward of Tombuctoo.

The Negroes consume the tobacco both in snuff and for smoking; for the latter purpose they use pipes, the tubes of which are made of the leg bones of ostriches.

The chief use to which they apply the tar brought by the Moors, is to protect the camels and other animals from the attacks of large green flies, which are very numerous, and greatly distress them. Adams has sometimes seen tar-water mixed with the food of the natives as medicine, which made it so nauseous to his taste that he could not eat it. The Negroes, however, did not appear to have the same dislike to it; from which he infers, that the use of tar-water in their food, was frequent, though he only saw it four or five times. None of the persons whom he saw using it were in bad health at the time.

During the whole of Adams's residence at Tombuctoo, he never saw any other Moors than those whom he accompanied thither, and the ten by whom they were ransomed: and he understood from the Moors themselves, that they were not allowed to go in large bodies to Tombuctoo.[35] He did not see any mosque or large place of worship there; and he does not think that they had any.

Neither Adams nor the Portuguese boy were ever subjected to any restraint whilst they remained at Tombuctoo. They were allowed as much food, and as often as they pleased; and were never required to work. In short, they never experienced any act of incivility or unkindness from any of the Negroes, except when they were taken prisoners in company with the Moors engaged in stealing them.[36] Adams could not hear that any white man but themselves had ever been seen in the place; and he believes, as well from what he was told by the Moors, as from the uncommon curiosity which he excited (though himself a very dark man, with short curly black hair), that they never had seen one before.[37]

There was no fall of rain during his residence at Tombuctoo, except a few drops just before his departure: and he understood from the Negroes that they had usually little or none, except during the three months of winter, which is the only season when the desert can be crossed, on account of the heat.[38] In some years, Adams was informed, when the season had been unusually dry, there was great distress at Tombuctoo for want of provisions: but no such want was felt whilst he was there.

He never proceeded to the southward of Tombuctoo, further than about two miles from the town, to the mountains before spoken of; and he never saw the river Joliba:* but he had heard it mentioned; and was told at Tudenny, that it lay between that place and Bambarra.[39]

Being asked the names of any other places which he had heard mentioned, he recollected that the people of Tombuctoo spoke of *Mutnougo*, and of a very considerable place to the eastward called *Tuarick*, to which they traded. He had also often heard them mention *Mandingo*, and *Bondou*; but he cannot recollect what was said respecting these places.†

* [The Niger River.]
† Adams mentioned *Jinnie* [Djenné] to me, amongst the towns that he had heard named by the Negroes of Tombuctoo. D.

The following is a list of some of the words which Adams recollects in the language of Tombuctoo.[40]‡

Man,	– *Jungo.*
Woman,	– *Jumpsa.*
Camel,	– *So.*
Dog,	– *Killab.*
Cow,	– *Fallee.*
Goat,	– *Luganam*
Sheep,	– *Naidsh.*
Elephant,	– *Elfeel.*
House,	– *Dah.*
Water,	– *Boca.*
Mountain,	– *Kaddear.*
Tree,	– *Carna.*
Date Tree,	– *Carna Tomar.*
Fig Tree,	– *Carna Carmoos.*
Gold,	– *Or.*
A Moor,	– *Seckar.*

‡ [As Dupuis says in Note 40, some of these words are related to Arabic. Jomard (1830) noted that while eight of them are from Songhai, they are given incorrect meanings here. None appear to be related to Bambarran or Tamashek.]

3

Ransom of the imprisoned Moors and of Adams. – Departure from Tombuctoo. – Journey eastward along the River; then northward to Taudeny – Traders in salt. – Taudeny – mixed Population of Moors and Negroes – Beds of Rock Salt – Preparations and Departure to cross the Sandy Desert. – Sufferings in the Desert. – Arrival at Woled D'leim – employment, and long detention there. – Refusal of Adams to attend to his tasks – He is punished for it; but perseveres – seizes an opportunity of escaping – is pursued; but reaches El Kabla – He is purchased by the Chief – Employed to tend the flocks of his Master's Wives – Negotiates with Aisha, the younger wife, on the subject of Wages – their bargain, and its consequences – Adams flies and conceals himself – is purchased by a Trader; and conveyed to Woled Aboussebàh – Woled Adrialla – Aiata Mouessa Ali. – He attempts to escape – is retaken; and conveyed to Wed-noon.

The ten Moors who had arrived with the five camels laden with tobacco, had been three weeks at Tombuctoo before Adams learnt that the ransom of himself, the boy, and the Moors his former companions, had been agreed upon. At the end of the first week he was given to understand, that himself and the boy would be released, but that the Moors would be condemned to die; it appeared, however, afterwards, that in consideration of all the tobacco being given for the Moors, except about fifty pounds weight, which was expended for a man slave, the King had agreed to release all the prisoners.

Two days after their release, the whole party, consisting of the

10 Moorish traders
14 Moorish prisoners
2 white men, and
1 slave

quitted Tombuctoo, having only the five camels which belonged to the traders; those which were seized when Adams and his party were made prisoners not having been restored. As they had no means left of purchasing any other article, the only food they took with them was a little Guinea-corn flour.

On quitting the town they proceeded in an easterly course, inclining to the north, going along the border of the river, of which they sometimes lost sight for two days together. They did not meet with any high trees; but on the banks of the river, which were covered with high grass, were a few low trees, and some shrubs of no great variety. Occasionally they came to a Negro hut. Except the two mountains before spoken of, to the southward, between which the river runs, there are none in the immediate neighbourhood of Tombuctoo; but at a little distance there are some small ones.

They had travelled eastward about ten days, at the rate of about fifteen to eighteen miles a day, when they saw the river for the last time: it then appeared rather narrower than at Tombuctoo. They then loaded the camels with water, and striking off in a northerly direction, travelled twelve or thirteen days, at about the same pace. In the course of this journey they saw a great number of antelopes, rabbits, foxes, and wolves, and a bird somewhat larger than a fowl, which the Moors called *Jize*;* it appeared to Adams to be the same kind of bird known in America by the name of cuckoo.

The soil was generally covered with shrubs, and a low kind of grass like moss. Trees were seldom seen, and those not large. From the time of quitting the river, the only persons whom they saw were Negro travellers carrying salt to Tombuctoo; of whom they met parties of about ten or twelve almost every day with dromedaries, camels, and asses.

At the end of the thirteen days they arrived at a place called *Tudenny*,† a large village inhabited by Moors and Negroes, in which there are four wells of very excellent water. At this place there are large ponds or beds of salt, which both the Moors and Negroes come in great numbers to purchase, and date and fig-trees of a large size: in the neighbourhood the ground is cultivated in the same manner as at Tombuctoo. From the

---

* *Djez*, is the Arabic name for the common domestic fowl. *D.*
† *Taudeny. D.*

number of Moors, many if not all of whom were residents, it appeared that the restriction respecting them, existing at Tombuctoo, did not extend to Tudenny.[41]

The salt beds which Adams saw were about five or six feet deep, and from twenty to thirty yards in circumference. The salt comes up in hard lumps mixed with earth, and part of it is red.

The Moors here are perfectly black; the only personal distinction between them and the Negroes being, that the Moors had long black hair, and had no scars on their faces. The Negroes are in general marked in the same manner as those of Tombuctoo. Here the party staid fourteen days, to give the ransomed Moors, whose long confinement had made them weak, time to recruit their strength; and having sold one of the camels for two sacks of dates and a small ass, and loaded the four remaining camels with water, the dates, and the flour, (in the proportion of eight goat skins of water, or six skins of water and two bags of dates or flour, to each camel) they set out to cross the Desert,* taking a north-west direction.

They commenced their journey from Tudenny about four o'clock in the morning, and having travelled the first day about twenty miles, they unloaded the camels, and lay down by the side of them to sleep.

The next day they entered the Desert; over which they continued to travel in the same direction, nine and twenty days, without meeting a single human being. The whole way was a sandy plain, like a sea, without either tree, shrub or grass. After travelling in this manner about fourteen days at the rate of sixteen or eighteen miles a day, the people began to grow very weak; their stock of water began to run short; and their provisions were nearly exhausted. The ass died of fatigue; and its carcase was immediately cut up and laden on the camel, where it dried in the sun, and served for food; and had it not been for this supply, some of the party must have died of hunger. Being asked if asses' flesh was good eating, Adams replied; "It was as good to my taste then, as a goose would be now."

In six days afterwards, during which their pace was slackened to not more than twelve miles a day, they arrived at a place where it was expected water would be found; but to their great disappointment,

* See Note, p. [44].

owing to the dryness of the season, the hollow place, of about thirty yards in circumference, was found quite dry.

All their stock of water at this time consisted of four goat skins, and those not full, holding from one to two gallons each; and it was known to the Moors that they had then ten days further to travel before they could obtain a supply.

In this distressing dilemma, it was resolved to mix the remaining water with camels' urine. The allowance of this mixture to each camel was only about a quart for the whole ten days: each man was allowed not more than about half a pint a day.

The Moors who had been in confinement at Tombuctoo becoming every day weaker, three of them in the four following days lay down, unable to proceed. They were then placed upon the camels: but continual exposure to the excessive heat of the sun, and the uneasy motion of the camels, soon rendered them unable to support themselves, and towards the end of the second day they made another attempt to pursue their journey on foot, but could not. The next morning at day break they were found dead on the sand, in the place where they had lain down at night, and were left behind without being buried. The next day another of them lay down; and, like his late unfortunate companions, was left to perish: but on the following day one of the Moors determined to remain behind, in the hope that he who had dropped the day before might still come up, and be able to follow the party: some provisions were left with him. At this time it was expected, what proved to be the fact, that they were within a day's march of their town: but neither of the men ever afterwards made his appearance; and Adams has no doubt that they perished.

*Vled Duleim** (the place at which they now arrived) was a village of tents inhabited entirely by Moors, who from their dress, manners, and general appearance, seemed to be of the same tribe as those of the encampment to which Adams was conveyed from El Gazie.[42] They had numerous flocks of sheep and goats, and two watering places, near one of which their tents were pitched; but the other lay nearly five miles off.

---

* *Woled D'leim. D.* [The Oulad Delim ("Sons of the Gun") are a tribe of the Beni Hassan who possess, according to Pazzanita and Hodges, "probably the purest Arab ancestry" of the Western Saharan tribes claiming descent from the Maqil (331).]

The first fortnight after the arrival of the party, was devoted to their recovery from the fatigues of the journey; but as soon as their strength was re-established, Adams and his companion were employed in taking care of goats and sheep. Having now begun to acquire a knowledge of the Moorish tongue, they frequently urged their masters to take them to Suerra; which the latter promised they would do, provided they continued attentive to their duty.

Things, however, remained in this state for ten or eleven months, during which time they were continually occupied in tending the flocks of the Moors. They suffered severely from exposure to the scorching sun, in a state of almost utter nakedness; and the miseries of their situation were aggravated by despair of ever being released from slavery.

The only food allowed to them was barley-flour, and camels' and goats' milk; but of the latter they had abundance. Sometimes they were treated with a few dates, which were a great rarity; there being neither date-trees nor trees of any other kind in the whole country round. But as the flock of goats and sheep consisted of a great number (from one hundred and fifty to two hundred), and as they were at a distance from the town, Adams and his companion sometimes ventured to kill a kid for their own eating; and to prevent discovery of the fire used in cooking it, they dug a cave, in which the fire was made, covering the ashes with grass and sand.

At length Adams, after much reflection on the miserable state in which he had been so long kept, and was likely to pass the remainder of his life, determined to remonstrate upon the subject. His master, whose name was *Hamet Laubed*, frankly replied to him, that as he had not been successful in procuring slaves, it was now his intention to keep him, and not, as he had before led him to expect, to take him to Suerra or Mogadore. Upon hearing this, Adams resolved not to attend any longer to the duty of watching the goats and sheep; and in consequence, the next day, several of the young goats were found to have been killed by the foxes.

This led to an inquiry, whether Adams or the boy was in fault; when it appearing that the missing goats were a part of Adams's flock, his master proceeded to beat him with a thick stick; which he resisted, and took away the stick; upon which a dozen Moors, principally women, attacked him, and gave him a severe beating.

As, notwithstanding what had occurred, Adams persisted in his determination not to resume his task of tending the goats and sheep, his master was advised to put him to death;[43] but this he was not inclined to do, observing to his advisers, that he should thereby sustain a loss, and that if Adams would not work, it would be better to sell him. In the mean time he remained idle in the tent for about three days; when he was asked by his master's wife, if he would go to the distant well to fetch a couple of skins of water, that being of a better quality; to which he signified his consent, and went off the next morning on a camel with two skins to fetch the water.

On his arrival at the other well, instead of procuring water, he determined to make his escape; and understanding that the course to a place called Wadinoon, lay in a direction to the northward of west,* he passed the well, and pushing on in a northerly course, travelled the whole of that day; when the camel, which had been used to rest at night, and had not been well broke in, would not proceed any further; and in spite of all the efforts Adams could make, it lay down with fatigue, having gone upwards of twenty miles without stopping. Finding there was no remedy, Adams took off the rope with which his clothes were fastened round his body, and as the camel lay with his fore-knee bent, he tied the rope round it in a way to prevent its rising, and then lay down by the side of it. This rope, which Adams had brought from Tombuctoo, was made of grass, collected on the banks of the river. The saddles of camels are made of the same material, interwoven between a frame of sticks placed together in the form of a St. Andrew's cross, so as to fit the back of the animal.

The next morning at day light he mounted again, and pushed on till about nine o'clock, when he perceived a smoke a-head, which he approached. There was a small hillock between him and this place, ascending which, he discovered about forty or fifty tents pitched, and on looking back he saw two camels coming towards him, with a rider on each. Not knowing whether these were pursuers, or strangers going to the place in view, but being greatly alarmed, he made the best of his way forwards. On drawing near to the town, a number of women came out, and he observed about a hundred Moors standing in a row in the act of prayer, having their faces towards the east, and at times kneeling

---

* This account of the relative bearings of Woled D'leim and Wed Noon is rather at variance with the details of Adams's recollected course between those two places; but it accords very nearly with what is assumed in the map, on other grounds, to have been his real route.

down, and leaning their heads to the ground. On the women discovering Adams, they expressed great surprise at seeing a white man. He inquired of them the name of the place, and they told him it was Hilla Gibla. Soon afterwards the two camels, before spoken of, arriving, the rider of one of them proved to be the owner of the camel on which Adams had escaped, and the other his master. At this time Adams was sitting under a tent speaking to the Governor, whose name was *Mahomet*, telling him his story; they were soon joined by his two pursuers, accompanied by a crowd of people.

Upon his master claiming him, Adams protested that he would not go back; that his master had frequently promised to take him to Suerra, but had broken his promises; and that he had made up his mind either to obtain his liberty or die. Upon hearing both sides, the Governor determined in favour of Adams; and gave his master to understand, that if he was willing to exchange him for a bushel of dates and a camel, he should have them; but if not, he should have nothing. As Adams's master did not approve of these conditions, a violent altercation arose: but at length finding the Governor determined, and that better terms were not to be had, he accepted the first offer, and Adams became the slave of Mahomet.[44]

The natives of *Hilla Gibla** appeared to be better clothed, and a less savage race, than those of Vled Duleim, between whom there appeared to be great enmity; the Governor therefore readily interfered in favour of Adams, and at one time threatened to take away the camel and to put Mahomet Laubed himself to death. Another consideration by which the Governor was probably influenced, was, a knowledge of the value of a Christian slave, as an object of ransom, of which Mahomet Laubed seemed to be wholly ignorant.

On entering the service of his new master, Adams was sent to tend camels, and had been so employed about a fortnight, when this duty was exchanged for that of taking care of goats. Mahomet had two wives who dwelt in separate tents, one of them an old woman, the other young:

---

* *El Kabla. D.* [Archibald Robbins, enslaved after the wreck of the American brig *Commerce*, was traded along much the same route as Adams in 1816–1817. He provides an extended description of Oulad El Kabla, including the observation that they were, "in every respect, the most wealthy" he had seen in the desert (167–72). Their unwillingness to cooperate with the Oulad Delim in Adams's narrative is explained by the fact that they are a tribe of the Oulad Bou Sbaa, a rival Beni Hassan group (see Dupuis's Note 44).]

the goats which Adams was set to take care of, were of the property of the elder one.

Some days after he had been so employed, the younger wife, whose name was *Isha*,* proposed to him, that he should also take charge of her goats, for which she would pay him; and as there was no more trouble in tending two flocks than one, he readily consented. Having had charge of the two flocks for several days, without receiving the promised additional reward, he at length remonstrated; and after some negotiation on the subject of his claim, the matter was compromised, by the young woman's desiring him, when he returned from tending the goats at night, to go to rest in her tent. It was the custom of Mahomet to sleep two nights with the elder woman, and one with the other, and this was one of the nights devoted to the former. Adams accordingly kept the appointment; and about nine o'clock Isha came and gave him supper, and he remained in her tent all night. This was an arrangement which was afterwards continued on those nights which she did not pass with her husband.

Things continued in this state about six months, and as his work was light, and he experienced nothing but kind treatment, his time passed pleasantly enough. One night his master's son coming into the tent, discovered Adams with his mother-in-law, and informed his father, when a great disturbance took place: but upon the husband charging his wife with her misconduct, she protested that Adams had laid down in her tent without her knowledge or consent; and as she cried bitterly, the old man appeared to be convinced that she was not to blame.

The old lady, however, declared her belief that the young one was guilty, and expressed her conviction that she should be able to detect her at some future time.

For some days after, Adams kept away from the lady; but at the end of that time, the former affair appearing to be forgotten, he resumed his visits. One night the old woman lifted up the corner of the tent and discovered Adams with Isha; and having reported it to her husband, he came with a thick stick, threatening to put him to death: Adams being alarmed, made his escape; and the affair having made a great deal of noise, an acquaintance proposed to Adams to conceal him in his tent, and to endeavour to buy him of the Governor. Some laughed at the

---

* *Aisha.* D.

adventure; others, and they by far the greater part, treated the matter as an offence of the most atrocious nature, Adams being "a Christian, who never prayed."[45]

As his acquaintance promised, in the event of becoming his purchaser, to take him to Wadinoon, Adams adopted his advice and concealed himself in his tent. For several days the old Governor rejected every overture; but at last he agreed to part with Adams for fifty dollars worth of goods, consisting of blankets and dates; and thus he became the property of *Boerick*, a trader, whose usual residence was at Hilla Gibbila.

The girl (Isha) ran away to her mother.

The next day, Boerick set out with a party of six men and four camels for a place called *Villa de Bousbach*,*[46] which they reached after travelling nine days at the rate of about eighteen miles a day; their course was north-east. On the route they saw neither houses nor trees, but the ground was covered with grass and shrubs. At this place they found about forty or fifty tents inhabited by Moors, and remained five or six days; when there arrived a Moor from a place called Hieta Mouessa Ali, named *Abdallah Houssa*, a friend of Boerick, who informed him that it was usual for the British Consul at Mogadore to send to Wadinoon (where this man resided), to purchase the Christians who were prisoners in that country; and, that as he was about to proceed thither, he was willing to take charge of Adams, to sell him for account of Boerick; at the same time he informed Adams that there were other Christians at Wadinoon. This being agreed to by Boerick, his friend set out in a few days after, for Hieta Mouessa Ali, taking Adams with him. Instead, however, of going to that place, which lay due north,† they proceeded north-north-West, and as they had a camel each, and travelled very fast, the path being good, they went at the rate of twenty-five miles a day, and in six days reached a place called *Villa Adrialla*,‡ where there were about twenty tents. This place appeared to be inhabited entirely by traders, who had at least five hundred camels, a great number of goats and sheep, and a few horses. The cattle were tended by Negro slaves.

---

* *Woled Aboussebàh. D.* [That is, the Oulad Bou Sbaa ("Sons of the Fathers of Lions"); for a summary of their history, see Pazzanita and Hodges (327–31).]

† This bearing is not reconcilable with Adams's subsequent course.

‡ This should probably be *Woled Adrialla*; but I have no knowledge of the place. *D.* [Robbins mentions a fight between the Oulad Bou Sbaa and the Oulad Adrialla that occurred while he was held by the former (202).]

Here they remained about three weeks, until Abdallah had finished his business; and then set out for Hieta Mouessa Ali, where they arrived in three days. Adams believes that the reason of their travelling so fast during the last stage was, that Abdallah was afraid of being robbed, of which he seemed to have no apprehension after he had arrived at Villa Adrialla, and therefore they travelled from that place to Hieta Mouessa Ali at the rate of only about sixteen or eighteen miles a day; their course being due north-west.

*Hieta Mouessa Ali** was the largest place Adams had seen in which there were no houses, there being not less than a hundred tents. Here was a small brook issuing from a mountain, being the only one he had seen except that at Soudenny; but the vegetation was not more abundant than at other places. They remained here about a month; during which Adams was as usual employed in tending camels. As the time hung very heavy on his hands, and he saw no preparation for their departure for Wadinoon, and his anxiety to reach that place had been very much excited by the intelligence that there were other Christians there, he took every opportunity of making inquiry respecting the course and distance; and being at length of opinion that he might find his way thither, he one evening determined to desert; and accordingly he set out on foot alone, with a small supply of dried goats' flesh, relying upon getting a further supply at the villages, which he understood were on the road. He had travelled the whole of that night, and until about noon the next day without stopping; when he was overtaken by a party of three or four men on camels, who had been sent in pursuit of him. It seems they expected that Adams had been persuaded to leave Hieta Mouessa Ali, by some persons who wished to take him to Wadinoon for sale; and they were therefore greatly pleased to find him on foot, and alone. Instead of ill treating him as he apprehended they would do, they merely conducted him back to Hieta Mouessa Ali; from whence, in three or four days afterwards, Abdallah and a small party departed, taking him with them. They travelled five days in a north-west direction at about sixteen miles a day, and at the end of the fifth day, reached Wadinoon; having seen no habitations on their route except a few scattered tents within a day's journey of the town.

---

* *Aiata Mouessa Ali. D.* [*Ait* is the Berber equivalent of the Arabic *Beni* or *Oulad* ("sons of").]

4

Description of Wed-Noon – where Adams finds three of the crew of the "Charles:" – He is purchased by Bel-Cossim-Abdallah. – French Renegade. – Wreck of the Montezuma. – Gunpowder Manufacture. – Curious Relation of a Negro Slave from Kanno. – Severe labours and cruel treatment of the Christian Slaves at Wed-Noon. – Adams is required to plough on the Sabbath day; refuses; is cruelly beaten, and put in irons – his firmness; – Inhuman treatment and death of Dolbie – Williams and Davison, worn out by their sufferings, renounce their Religion – Adams perseveres. – Letter from the British Vice-Consul at Mogadore, addressed to the Christian Slaves. – Ransom of Adams – Departure from Wed-Noon – Akkadia – Bled Cidi Heshem – Market of Cidi Hamet a Moussa – Agadeer, or Santa Cruz – Mogadore. – Adams is sent to the Moorish Emperor. – Fez – Mequinez – Tangier – Cadiz – Gibraltar – London.

*Wadinoon** was the first place at which Adams had seen houses after he quitted Tudeny. It is a small town, consisting of about forty houses, and some tents. The former are built chiefly of clay, intermixed with stone in some parts; and several of them have a story above the ground floor. The soil in the neighbourhood of the town was better cultivated than any he had yet seen in Africa, and appeared to produce plenty of corn and tobacco. There were also date and fig-trees in the vicinity, as well as a few grapes, apples, pears, and pomegranates. Prickly pears flourished in great abundance.

The Christians whom Adams had heard of, whilst residing at Hieta Mouessa Ali, and whom he found at Wadinoon, proved to be, to his great satisfaction, his old companions *Stephen Dolbie*, the mate, and

* Wed-Noon. *D.*

James Davison and *Thomas Williams*, two of the seamen of the Charles. They informed him that they had been in that town upwards of twelve months, and that they were the property of the sons of the Governor.[47]

Soon after Adams's arrival at Wadinoon, Abdallah offered him for sale to the Governor, or Shieck, called *Amedallah Salem*, who consented to take him upon trial; but after remaining about a week at the Governor's house, Adams was returned to his old master, as the parties could not agree about the price. He was at length, however, sold to *Belcassam Abdallah** for seventy dollars in trade, payable in blankets, gunpowder and dates.[48]

The only other white resident at Wadinoon was a Frenchman, who informed Adams that he had been wrecked about twelve years before, on the neighbouring coast, and that the whole of the crew except himself, had been redeemed. He further stated, that a vessel called (as Adams understood him) the *Agezuma*† from Liverpool, commanded by Captain Harrison, had been wrecked about four years before, and that the Captain and nearly the whole of the crew had been murdered.[49] This man had turned Mohammedan, and was named *Absalom*; he had a wife and child and three slaves, and gained a good living by the manufacture of gunpowder. Adams has often seen him employed in making it, by pounding brimstone in a wooden mortar, and grinding charcoal by hand between two stones, in the manner of grinding grain. The final process of mixing he performed in a room by himself, not being willing to let any person see how it was done. He lived in the same house as the person who had been his master, who, upon his renouncing his religion, gave him his liberty.[50]

Among the Negro slaves at Wadinoon was a woman, who said she came from a place called *Kanno*,‡ a long way across the Desert, and that she had seen in her own country, white men, as white as "bather," meaning the wall, and in a large boat with two high sticks in it, with cloth upon them, and that they rowed this boat in a manner different

---

* *Bel-Cossim-Abdallah.* D. [This is, apparently, the same Abdallah bel Cossim who in April 1816 (just as Adams's narrative was being published in London) purchased Archibald Robbins. Robbins received similarly brutal treatment from bel Cossim and his son (see King 331).]

† *Montezuma.*

‡ [Kano, in what is now northern Nigeria, was in the fifteenth century the greatest of the Hausa states.]

from the custom of the Negroes, who use paddles: in stating this, she made the motion of rowing with oars, so as to leave no doubt that she had seen a vessel in the European fashion, manned by white people.[51]

The work in which Adams was employed at Wadinoon, was building walls, cutting down shrubs to make fences, and working in the corn lands or in the plantations of tobacco, of which great quantities are grown in the neighbourhood. It was in the month of August that he arrived there, as he was told by the Frenchman before spoken of; the grain had been gathered; but the tobacco was then getting in, at which he was required to assist. His labour at this place was extremely severe. On the Moorish sabbath, which was also their market-day, the Christian slaves were not required to labour, unless on extraordinary occasions, when there was any particular work to do which could not be delayed. In these intervals of repose, they had opportunities of meeting and conversing together; and Adams had the melancholy consolation of finding that the lot of his companions had been even more severe than his own. It appeared that on their arrival, the Frenchman before mentioned, from some unexplained motive, had advised them to refuse to work; and the consequence was, that they had been cruelly beaten and punished, and had been made to work hard and live hard, their only scanty food being barley flour, and Indian-corn flour. However, on extraordinary occasions, and as a great indulgence, they sometimes obtained a few dates.

In this wretched manner Adams and his fellow captives lived until the June following; when a circumstance occurred which had nearly cost the former his life. His master's son, *Hameda Bel Cossim*, having, one sabbath day, ordered Adams to take the horse and go to plough, the latter refused to obey him, urging that it was not the custom of any slaves to work on the sabbath day, and that he was entitled to the same indulgence as the rest. Upon which Hameda went into the house and fetched a cutlass, and then demanded of Adams, whether he would go to plough or not. Upon his reply that he would not, Hameda struck him on the forehead with the cutlass, and gave him a severe wound over the right eye, and immediately Adams knocked him down with his fist. This was no sooner done than Adams was set upon by a number of Moors, who beat him with sticks in so violent a manner that the blood came out of his mouth, two of his double teeth were knocked out, and he was almost killed; and he thinks they would have entirely killed him had it not been for the interference of *Boadick*, the Shieck's son, who reproached them for their cruelty, declaring that they had no right to compel Adams to work on a market-day. The next morning Hameda's mother, named *Moghtari*, came to him, and asked him how he dared to lift his hand against a Moor? to which Adams, being driven to desperation by the ill treatment he had received, replied that he would even take his life if it were in his power. Moghtari then said, that unless he would kiss Hameda's hands and feet, he should be put in irons; which he peremptorily refused to do. Soon after Hameda's father came to Adams and told him, unless he did kiss his son's feet and hands, he must be put in irons. Adams then stated to him, that he could not submit to do so; that it was "contrary to his religion"* to kiss the hands and feet of any person; that in his own country he had never been required to do it; and that whatever might be the consequence, he would not do it. Finding he would not submit, the old man ordered that he should be put in irons, and accordingly they fastened his feet together with iron chains, and did the same by his hands. After he had remained in this state about ten days, Moghtari came to him again, urging him to do as required, and declaring that if he did not, he should never see the Christian country again: Adams, however, persevered in turning a deaf ear to her entreaties and threats. Some time afterwards, finding that close confinement was destructive of his health, Hameda came to him, and took the irons from his hands. The following three weeks he remained with the irons on his legs, during which time, repeated and pressing entreaties, and the most dreadful threats, were used to induce him to submit; but all to no purpose. He was also frequently advised by the mate and the other Christians (who used to be sent to him for the purpose of persuading him), to submit, as he must otherwise inevitably lose his life. At length, finding that neither threats nor entreaties would avail, and Adams having remained in irons from June till the beginning of August, and his sufferings having reduced him almost to a skeleton, his master was advised to sell him, as if longer confined, he would certainly die, and thus prove a total loss. Influenced by this consideration, his master at last determined to release him from his confinement; but though very weak, the moment he was liberated he was set to gathering in the corn.[52]

* Adams's expression.

About a week afterwards, *Dolbie*, the mate, fell sick. Adams had called to see him, when Dolbie's master (named *Brahim*, a son of the Shieck) ordered him to get up and go to work; and upon Dolbie declaring that he was unable, Brahim beat him with a stick to compel him to go; but as he still did not obey, Brahim threatened that he would kill him; and upon Dolbie's replying that he had better do so at once than kill him by inches, Brahim stabbed him in the side with a dagger, and he died in a few minutes. As soon he was dead, he was taken by some slaves a short distance from the town, where a hole was dug, into which he was thrown without ceremony. As the grave was not deep, and as it frequently happened that corpses after burial were dug out of the ground by the foxes, Adams and his two surviving companions went the next day and covered the grave with stones.[53]

As the Moors were constantly urging them to become Mohammedans, and they were unceasingly treated with the greatest brutality, the fortitude of *Williams* and *Davison* being exhausted, they at last unhappily consented to renounce their religion, and were circumcised; and thus obtained their liberty; after which they were presented with a horse, a musket, and a blanket each, and permitted to marry; no *Christian* being allowed at any of the places inhabited by Moors, to take a wife, or to cohabit with a Moorish woman.

As Adams was the only remaining Christian at Wadinoon, he became in a more especial manner an object of the derision and persecution of the Moors, who were constantly upbraiding and reviling him, and telling him that his soul would be lost unless he became a Mohammedan, insomuch that his life was becoming intolerable;[54] when, only three days after Williams and Davison had renounced their religion, a letter was received from *Mr. Joseph Dupuis*, British Consul at Mogadore, addressed to the Christian prisoners at Wadinoon, under cover to the Governor; in which the Consul, after exhorting them most earnestly not to give up their religion, whatever might befal them, assured them that within a month, he should be able to procure their liberty. Davison heard the letter read apparently without emotion, but Williams became so agitated, that he let it drop out of his hands, and burst into a flood of tears.[55]

From this time Adams experienced no particular ill treatment; but he was required to work as usual. About a month more elapsed, when the man who brought the letter, who was a servant of the British Consul, disguised as a trader, made known to Adams that he had succeeded in procuring his release; and the next day they set out together for Mogadore.

On quitting Wadinoon, (where Adams is confident he stayed more than twelve months; the second year's crop of tobacco having been completely got in before his departure) they proceeded in a northerly direction, travelling on mules at the rate of thirty miles a day, and in fifteen days* arrived at Mogadore. The first night they stopped at a village called *Akkadia*, situated at the foot of a high mountain. Here, for the first time, Adams saw olive trees, and palm trees from the nuts of which oil is extracted. The place consisted of about twenty houses; some of them two stories high. Having slept there, they set out the next morning at four o'clock, and the following day about sun-set reached another village, the name of which he does not remember. Here were only a few houses, but a great many tents, and in the neighbourhood large fields of wheat, Indian-corn, and barley. Adams thinks this place was all the property of one man.

The place at which they next stopped, having travelled that day in a north-east direction, was the residence of a great warrior named *Cidi Heshem*, who had with him upwards of six hundred black men and Moors, most of them armed with muskets, which they kept in excellent order. Adams was informed that he admitted into his service any runaway Negroes or Moors; to whom he gave liberty on condition of their entering into his service. He appeared to be very rich: having numerous camels, goats, sheep, and horned cattle, and abundance of piece goods of various kinds, as also shoes and other manufactures which were exposed for sale in shops kept by Jews. The place was called after its owner, *Bled de Cidi Heshem*, in the district of Suz, and to the best of Adams's recollection, contained from twenty to thirty houses. Here he saw a great quantity of silver money, principally dollars. Cidi Heshem was at war with the Emperor of Morocco.[56]

After staying one night and part of the next day, Adams and his companion proceeded on their journey; and the following night slept at a place where there were only two huts. The next day they arrived at a place of a similar description, and then set out, expecting to arrive at a large town, situate on a high hill by the sea side named in English *Santa Cruz*, (where he was told, formerly a British Consul resided), but

* The details of Adams's course from Wed-Noon to Mogadore, makes only *thirteen* days.

called by the Moors *Agadeer*. They did not, however, get so far; but reached a place called *Cidi Mahomeda Moussa** situate in a wide sandy plain, where the harvest being just got in, the inhabitants were holding a market, at which there appeared to be assembled not less than four thousand persons from all quarters, who had goods of all descriptions for sale. This market, he was told, is held once a year, and lasts for five days. Here Adams's companion was met by several persons of his acquaintance, who seemed greatly delighted at his success in effecting his (Adams's) liberation: some of them spoke English.

After remaining there one day, they set out again on their journey, and by one o'clock reached *Agadeer*. As soon as they arrived, the Governor sent for Adams, and said to him in the Moorish language, "now, my lad, you may consider yourself safe." He afterwards made particular inquiry as to the treatment Adams had met with; and on being told with what inhumanity he had been used at Wadinoon, the Governor said he well knew their manner of treating Christians; but that they were savages, and not subjects of the Emperor: he added, that having the good fortune now to be in the dominions of the Emperor, Adams might rest satisfied that he was perfectly safe, and would meet with nothing but good treatment; an assurance that afforded him the greatest satisfaction, although ever since his departure from Wadinoon he had felt a confident belief that his complete deliverance was at hand. The next day they resumed their journey, and from this time travelled northerly for five days without meeting with any other habitation than occasional huts. About twelve o'clock on the fifth day, ascending a hill, they discovered the town of Mogadore beneath them, and square rigged vessels lying in the harbour; the sight of which, says Adams, "I can no otherwise describe than by saying, I felt as if a new life had been given to me." In about half an hour afterwards they entered the town, and immediately went to the house of the Governor, who sent Adams to Mr. Dupuis, the British Consul; by whom he was received into his house, and treated with the utmost kindness. "Never," says Adams, "shall I forget the kindness of this good gentleman, who seemed to study how to make me comfortable and happy."

---

* There is a sanctuary near Santa Cruz, called *Cidi Mohammed Monsoul*, but Adams appears to have confounded it, (probably from the similarity of names) with *Cidi Hamet a Moussa*. See Note 56. D.

On the arrival of Adams at *Mogadore*, it appeared to be the wish of the Governor to send him to the Emperor; but to this Mr. Dupuis objected, and Adams remained with him the following eight months; in the course of which time, Mr. Dupuis frequently interrogated him upon the subject of the several places at which he had been in Africa, and sent for travellers for the purpose of comparing their statements with those given by him;[57] after which he expressed a strong desire that Adams should come to England for the purpose of giving an account of his travels, as he said many gentlemen would be glad to receive it. But as England and America were then at war, Adams was apprehensive lest he might be made a prisoner, and therefore declined the pressing offers and solicitations of the Consul that he should take his passage in an English vessel, bound to London. Finding Adams thus averse from going to England, and the only vessels which were lying at Mogadore being bound thither, Mr. Dupuis wrote to the Emperor of Morocco, and also to Mr. Simpson the British* Consul at Tangier with the view of procuring permission for Adams to go to Tangier, from whence he hoped he might get a passage by some Spanish vessel to Cadiz. This being at length agreed to, Adams took leave of Mr. Dupuis in the month of April, 1814, who sent him under the protection of two Moorish soldiers, to *Fez*, the residence of the Emperor.[58]

They travelled on mules; but as they stopped two days at *L'Arrache*,† and travelled but slowly, it was eighteen days before they arrived at Fez. On their arrival the Emperor was absent at *Mequinez*, and they accordingly proceeded thither the next day, and went to the house of Doctor Manuel, a Portuguese physician, who informed the Emperor of Adams's arrival. Adams was then ordered into the presence of the Emperor, who first asked him of what country he was; he replied, "an Englishman." He then inquired into the treatment he had met with, and whether he liked the Moors as well as the Europeans, to which Adams answered, "No." The Emperor then ordered that Adams should be taken to the Governor; who, the next day, sent him in the charge of two soldiers to Tangier, where, travelling on mules, they arrived in three days.

---

* Mr. Simpson was *American* Consul. D.

† Adams has evidently forgotten the situation of *El Araische*. He could not have touched there on his journey from Mogadore to Fez; though he might very probably pass through it on his way from Mequinez to Tangier. The place to which he alludes must be either *Rhabatt* or *Sallee*. D.

Immediately upon his arrival at *Tangier*, Adams was presented to the Governor, and then conveyed to the Consul, Mr. Simpson; who two days afterwards procured him a passage on board a Spanish schooner bound to Cadiz,[59] where he arrived the next day, being the 17th of May, 1814, making *three years and seven months*,[60] since he was wrecked in the Charles; during which period, except from the effect of the severe beating he received at Wadinoon, and the weakness produced by his long confinement at that place in irons, he never was sick a single day.

After remaining about fourteen months at Cadiz as a servant or groom, in the service of Mr. Hall, an English merchant there; peace having in the mean time been restored; Adams was informed by the American Consul that he had now an opportunity of returning to his native country with a cartel, or transport of American seamen, which was on the point of sailing from Gibraltar. He accordingly proceeded thither; but arrived two days after the vessel had sailed. Soon afterwards he engaged himself on board a Welsh brig lying at Gibraltar, in which he sailed to Bilboa, from whence the brig took a cargo of wool to Bristol; and, after discharging it there, was proceeding in ballast to Liverpool. But having been driven into Holyhead by contrary winds, Adams there fell sick, and was put on shore. From this place he begged his way up to London, where he arrived about the middle of October, completely destitute; and had slept two or three nights in the open streets, before he was accidentally met by a gentleman, who had seen him in Mr. Hall's service at Cadiz, and was acquainted with his history; by whom he was directed to the office of the African Committee.

End of the Narrative

NOTES AND
ILLUSTRATIONS OF
ADAMS'S NARRATIVE

Note 1, p. 27: I do not recollect to have heard any suspicion stated either by Adams or others of the crew of the "Charles," that the Captain was really bound to any other place than the Isle of May, or some other of the Cape de Verd Islands; but the ship's name, the owners, captain, crew and cargo, agree precisely with the statements which were made to me at Mogadore. *D.*

Note 2, p. 28: *El Gazie* (the *g* strongly guttural) has been described to me by Arabs who have occasionally visited that part of the coast, chiefly for the purpose of sharing or purchasing the plunder of such vessels as may be cast on shore: – which misfortune but too frequently happens to those who do not use the precaution of keeping a good *offing*; for most parts of this desert coast are so low, and the weather is here in general so hazy, as to preclude a distant view of the shore.

The *Douar* (by which word I mean a village of tents, and which I shall accordingly so use hereafter, in speaking, of the encamped residences of the Arabs) is here scarcely deserving of the name; consisting, as I have been told, only of a few scattered tents, inhabited by a small community of poor and miserable Arabs, whose manner of living, dress and appearance, are doubtless such as Adams here describes; and who, residing chiefly, if not entirely, on the sea-coast, become the first possessors of the valuables and surviving crews of such vessels as here suffer shipwreck.

As soon as such an event is known in the Desert, their Douar becomes a mart, to which Arabs from all parts of the interior resort for trade; and it even not unfrequently happens, that when the news of such a catastrophe reaches the southern provinces of Barbary, the native traders of Santa Cruz, Mogadore, and their districts, make long journeys for the same purpose, and frequently bring back valuable articles saved from the wreck, which they purchase from the ignorant natives as things of no value. In this manner, I have been informed of superfine cloths being bought at half-a-dollar the cubit measure. Occasionally also I have seen Bank of England notes, which I was assured cost a mere trifle; the purchaser only knowing their value. Watches, trinkets, wearing apparel, muslins, silks, linens, &c. are gladly disposed of for dates, horses, camels, their favourite blue linens (baftas) or any of the few articles which are felt by these poor people to be immediately serviceable in their wretched way of living. They are, however, more tenacious of the fire-arms, cutlasses, pikes, cordage, bits of old iron, spike nails, and copper, upon which they set great value, and therefore seldom part with them.

This is the common mode of transacting the *trade of a wreck*. However, it not unfrequently happens that when the crew and cargo fall into the possession of any tribe of insignificant note, the latter are invaded by one of their more powerful neighbours, who either strip them by force of all their collected plunder, or compel them, through fear, to barter it at rates far beneath its estimated value. In either case, whether obtained by purchase or by force, the Arabs load their camels with the spoil, and return to their homes in the Desert, driving the unfortunate Christians before them. The latter, according to the interest of their new masters, are sold again or bartered to others; often to Arabs of a different tribe, and are thus conveyed in various directions across the Desert, suffering every degree of hardship and severity, which the cruelty, caprice or self-interest of their purchasers may dictate. *D.*

Note 3, p. 29: At the very time that Adams was making this statement relative to the Frenchman who had escaped from the Canary Islands, Mr. John Barry, a merchant of Teneriffe, accidentally entered the room: and upon being asked whether he had ever heard of such a circumstance, he stated that between four and five years ago, some French prisoners did make their escape from Santa Cruz in a boat belonging to Canary, and that it was afterwards reported they had run their vessel on shore on the Coast of Africa, and had been seized and carried into captivity by the Moors.

It can hardly be doubted that the man of whom Adams speaks, was one of them.

Note 4, p. 30: I perfectly recollect that the fact of the Captain's death, was mentioned to me by others of the Charles's crew who were ransomed at Mogadore, as well as by Adams; but I do not think that I was told he was murdered; only that he died from disease, want of nourishment, and severe treatment. *D.*

Note 5, p. 31: Adams should have said *Agadeer Doma.* This proposition made by the mate to the Arabs, to convey the Christians to Senegal, was related to me, as well by Adams, as by others of the crew who were ransomed. The Arabs, I was told, had frequent consultations together; apparently to determine how they should dispose of their prisoners: after which, as if to raise the spirits of the sailors, they would point with their fingers to the north, or north-northeast; saying many words, which they (the sailors) did not understand, and frequently repeating the words *Suerra* and *Sultan. D.*

Note 6, p. 31: In the spring of 1811, at which time, and until the breaking out of the war between Great Britain and the United States, I held the commission of Agent for the American Consulate at Mogadore, (under James Simpson Esq. Consul General of the United States at Tangier), three of the Charles's crew, named *Nicholas, Newsham,* and *Nelson,* were brought to me at Mogadore by an Arab of the tribe of *Woled Aboussebàh,* for the purpose of bargaining for their ransom; which, after some difficulties described in a subsequent Note, I effected. These men related to me the circumstances of their shipwreck, almost precisely in the same terms in which they were afterwards described to me by Adams, and as they are described in the Narrative. They also informed me that Adams (or *Rose*) and another of the crew had been purchased from the Arabs, who first made them prisoners, by a party who came from the eastward, and who had carried him into the Desert in that direction. *D.*

Note 7, p. 32: Soudenny has been described to me as a Negro town or village bordering on the Desert: and I am credibly informed by traders, that it is a practice of the neighbouring Arabs to resort to the habitations of the Negroes on the confines of the Desert, for the purpose of stealing and carrying them away into slavery. This, however, is not the common method of procuring slaves; for it is attended with great personal risk, as Adams here relates. During my residence in South Barbary, I have frequently inquired of different Negro slaves the manner of their falling into the hands of the Arabs; and many have assured me that they were stolen by them from their own country, and not regularly purchased at the slave marts. *D.*

According to Adams's statement of his route, Soudenny may be supposed to lie about the 6th degree of west longitude and the 16th of north latitude. This situation will fall very near the northern confines of Bambarra, where they approach, (if they do not actually touch) the Desert, on the eastern borders of Ludamar. It also approaches close to the line of Park's route in his first journey, when endeavouring to escape from the Moors of Benown: and we are consequently enabled to derive from Park's descriptions, materials for estimating in some degree, the probability of what Adams says respecting Soudenny.*

Referring therefore to Park's account of this part of Africa, we find him drawing a melancholy picture of the sufferings of its Negro inhabitants from the plundering incursions of Moorish Banditti; on which excursions he says, (4to. Ed. p. 159), "they will seize upon the Negroes' cattle, and even on the inhabitants themselves." On arriving at *Sampaka*, in Ludamar, he says, p. 119, "the townspeople informed us that a party of Moors had attempted to steal some cattle from the town in the morning, but had been repulsed." He describes the Foulahs of *Wassiboo*, who are extensive cultivators of corn, as "obliged for fear of the Moors to carry their arms with them to the fields." See page 350. And in the next page he says, on approaching *Satilé*, "the people, who were employed in the corn-fields, took us for Moors, and ran screaming away from us. When we arrived at the town, we found the gates shut and the people all under arms."

The places here mentioned are in the immediate vicinity of each other; and occur in that part of the line of Park's travels, which lies nearest to the presumed situation of Soudenny. The details, therefore, afford the nearest evidence which can at present be obtained, by which to

---

* [There is a village in western Mali called Sidoni, located at approximately 8°W, 13°N, that may be connected with the place that Dupuis had been told of. On the other hand, the name *Soudenny* is suspiciously close to the generic *Soudan*.]

estimate the probability of this part of Adams's story; and it is presumed that stronger circumstantial corroboration of it, will hardly be thought necessary.

Note 8, p. 35: *Woollo*, which is a Negro, and not a Moorish appellative, occurs in a Note on Isaaco's Journal (4to. p. 203)* as the name of a former King of Bambarra, the father of Mansong: but the probability of Adams's statement in this passage is more immediately corroborated by Mr. Jackson; who assures his readers that there was a King Woollo, actually reigning at Tombuctoo in the year 1800. Mr. Jackson further states, that this same King of Tombuctoo was also sovereign of Bambarra; in which respect, however, (as in many other instances where he relies on *African authority*) it is apparent that he was misinformed; for the name of the sovereign of Bambarra from the year 1795 to 1805 inclusive, (the dates of Park's journeys) was certainly *Mansong*. Nevertheless it is very possible that Woollo, of whom Mr. Jackson heard in 1800, and whom Adams saw in 1811, as King of Tombuctoo, was one of the numerous tributaries of the sovereign of Bambarra; and that this connection between the two states may have led to the report that they had jointly, but one King.[†]

The name of *Fatima* affords, in itself, no proof that its possessor was a Moorish or even a Mohammedan woman: for Park, in speaking of another Negro sovereign, (the King of Bondou), says "this monarch was called Almami, a Moorish name; although I was told that he was not a Mahomedan, but a Kafir or Pagan." 1st. Journey, 4to. p. 53.

Note 9, p. 36: I have always understood the articles of dress at *Timbuctoo*[‡] to be much the same as Adams here describes. I have also been told,

---

[*] [Isaaco was an African sent by the Governor of Senegal in 1810 to discover Park's fate; his account, including a narrative of the circumstances of Park's death by Amadi Fatouma, a guide who accompanied Park on his journey down the Niger, was included in the published report of the "second mission," *The Journal of a Mission to the Interior of Africa, in the Year 1805.*]

[†] [See Jackson, *An Account of the Empire of Marocco* (299). Also, Elias Saad discusses the "stories later current in Morocco which claimed that Timbuktu fell under the sovereignty of one of the Bambara states" in the early eighteenth century, and which Jackson was surely repeating. The origin of these stories, Saad contends, was the use of troops from Bambara in a prolonged civil war fought among factions of the city's ruling class during the first half of the century (203).]

[‡] This city was invariably called Timbuctoo, by all the traders and slaves with whom I have conversed respecting it. *D.*

that the inhabitants occasionally wear the *alhaik* of Barbary (with which they are supplied by the Moorish and Arab traders), after the fashion of the inhabitants of the Barbary states; but that this mode of dress is not very prevalent. I have been assured that the cotton tree grows spontaneously in many parts of Soudan, and that the clothes of the natives generally, are of that material, manufactured by themselves. Judging from the specimens of their cottons which I have seen, they must be good spinners and weavers. Their shirts, which are of a fine texture, are imported by the caravans into the Barbary states, and are much valued by the Arabs and Moors on account of the regularity and strength of the thread. Many of them are interwoven in particular parts with silk. These shirts, which I have frequently seen, are much in the shape of a waggoner's frock, supposing it to be longer, fuller, and without sleeves: they are either white, or simply blue, or blue and white in various shades.

This I have always understood to be the principal dress of what may be termed the middle class of Negroes; possibly of the Chiefs also: but the poor are represented to be clothed simply round the waist with a cotton wrapper, more or less coarse, according to the means of the wearer, which either hangs down loose, or is twisted between their legs and girt round their loins. *D.*

Note 10, p. 36: With respect to the enclosure of the King's palace, into which Adams says the foreign merchandize is carried, for the payment (as he thinks) of duties, what I have heard from Moorish traders with reference to such a place, is briefly this; that the palace of the King of Timbuctoo is situated in what they call the *kusba*, or citadel, in the centre of the town; which being a place of security, the traders naturally deposit their effects therein, and even inhabit a part of it; and that duties, (the nature and rate of which I do not recollect) are exacted by the King on all merchandize brought by strangers.

With respect to the King's palace, and the houses generally, I have been informed that they are only one story high. It has also been stated to me that there are shops in the city, which the Negroes frequent for the purchase of foreign and domestic commodities; and that natives of all parts of Soudan may be seen there, many of them entirely naked.

The country, without the gates of the enclosure or citadel noticed above, is represented to be thickly covered with the hovels or huts of the natives as far as the eye can reach; especially in the direction of the river, to the banks of which these habitations extend, deserving, in fact, the name of a town. *D.*

From Park's description (1st Journey, 4to. p. 22) the palace of the King of Bondou appears to be a structure very much resembling that described by Adams at Tombuctoo.

"All the houses," he says, "belonging to the King and his family, are surrounded by a lofty mud wall, which converts the whole into a kind of citadel. The interior is subdivided into different courts."

Note 11, p. 37: I perfectly recollect that Adams told me at Mogadore of these muskets which he had seen in the King's house at Timbuctoo: and at the same time that fire arms were not used by the inhabitants; which agrees with what I have heard from other quarters.

In the northern regions of the Desert, I have always understood that double-barrelled guns are in common use; and Park mentions them even on the south and southwestern confines of the Desert: but the arms of the Arabs bordering on the Negroes of Timbuctoo, have been described to me by the traders, to consist of javelins, swords and daggers. *D.*

Note 12, p. 37: As far as I can recollect, the description, which I received from Adams in Barbary of the houses of Timbuctoo, was more detailed than that in the Narrative. There were, he said, two distinct sorts of habitations; the houses of the Chiefs and wealthier Negroes, and the huts of the poor. The former (as well as the palace of the King,) he described as having walls of clay, or clay and sand, rammed into a wooden case or frame, and placed in layers one above another until they attained the height required; the roof being composed of poles or rafters laid horizontally, and covered with a cement or plaister of clay and sand. The huts of the poorer people are constructed merely of the branches of trees stuck into the ground in circles, bent, and lashed together at the top. This frame is then covered with a sort of matting made of a vegetable substance which he called grass, but which from his description appeared to be the *palmeta* (called *dome* by the Arabs), and the hut, I think he told me, was afterwards covered with clay.

This description corresponds in all respects with those which I have received from the Arab and Moorish traders. *D.*

Note 13, p. 38: I do not at all recollect either by what name Adams spoke of the river of Timbuctoo, when he mentioned it to me at Mogadore, or that I have ever heard it called *La Mar Zarah*, by any of the traders with whom I have conversed. If I were to hazard a conjecture on so uncertain a subject, I might suppose that Adams had made a slight mistake in repeating this name: and that he should have said, *El Bakar Sahara*, which in Arabic would mean the *Desert Sea*, or the *River of the Desert*. His pronunciation of Arabic was at all times indistinct, and often quite incorrect: and I remember other words in which he interchanged the sound of different consonants in the manner that I have here supposed. However, *La Mar Zarah* may very possibly be the name of the river in the language of the Negroes.

Another question here suggests itself, whether the river mentioned by Adams is really the great river Niger; or whether it is only a branch of it flowing from the southeast parts of the Desert, and falling into the principal stream not far from Timbuctoo?

The river of Timbuctoo (which I have always supposed to be the Niger itself) is called by the traders of Barbary, indiscriminately by the several names of *Wed-Nile*, *Bahar-Nile*, or *Bahar-Abide*. The same people have described it to me in a situation corresponding with that in the Narrative; at a very short distance from the town, and as pursuing its course through fertile countries on the east and south-east borders of the Desert; after which it is generally supposed in Barbary to fall into the Nile of Egypt.

According to these statements of the Moorish traders, Adams would seem to have mistaken the *course of the stream* at Timbuctoo. In fact, I do not recollect that he told me at Mogadore, that it flowed in a westerly direction: but I think I am correct in saying, that he discovered some uncertainty in speaking upon this subject, (and almost upon this subject alone), observing, in answer to my inquiries, that he had not taken very particular notice, and that the river was steady, without any appearance of a strong current.

The mountains near Timbuctoo, between which, Adams describes the river to flow, have also been mentioned to me by the traders from Barbary. *D.*

It is certain that Adams spoke with apparently less confidence of the direction of the stream of the *La Mar Zarah*, than of any other point of his Narrative. Nevertheless, although he was repeatedly questioned upon the subject, and might easily perceive that the fact of a stream flowing in that direction, in that place, was considered extremely improbable, he invariably stated his preponderating belief that it did flow to the south-west.

We shall reserve for our concluding Note, a few further remarks on this point of the Narrative; and shall only add in this place (to Mr. Dupuis' very probable conjecture on the subject) that the Spanish geographer *Marmol*,* who describes himself to have spent twenty years of warfare and slavery in Africa, about the middle of the 16th century, mentions the river *Lahamar* as a branch of the Niger; having muddy and unpalateable waters. By the same authority the Niger itself is called *Yça* or *Issa* at Tombuctoo; a name which D'Anville has adopted in his maps of Africa.

Note 14, p. 38: The description which Adams gives of the vessels or canoes at Timbuctoo, is, as far as it goes, consistent with what I recollect of his statement to me at Mogadore. But I think he described them to me as being more numerous; adding, that he had seen them navigate the river in fleets of from ten to twenty canoes together; that he had been informed that they were absent occasionally a month or more, and that frequently they returned to Timbuctoo, laden with slaves and merchandize. He also mentioned *Jinnie* to me, as a place to which, as he understood, the inhabitants of Timbuctoo resorted for trade; and that the communication between the two cities was by water.

I ought to observe, moreover, that these particulars correspond in substance with the information which I have obtained from Arab and Moorish traders respecting Timbuctoo, and the *Nile-Abide*. The same persons have told me that *Jinnie* lay fifteen days journey to the south-west of Timbuctoo. *D.*

Note 15, p. 38: I do not recollect to have heard *dates* or *pine apples* mentioned by any of the natives of Barbary who have visited Timbuctoo; but I have heard that both *figs* and *cocoa-nuts* grow there. The other vegetables enumerated by Adams in the Narrative, and which he also mentioned to me, are described by traders as being produced, generally speaking, throughout the Soudan. *D.*

With respect to *dates*, Park in his first Journey, mentions two occasions on which he met with them in Soudan: first at Gangadi near the Senegal

---

* [Luis del Mármol Carvajal, 1520?–1600?, a native of Granada: his principal work was the *Descripción General de Áffrica* (1573–99).]

above Galam, where he "observed a number of date trees," 4to. p. 71: and, secondly, dates were part of the food set before him by the Foulah shepherd on the northern confines of Bambarra, mentioned in p. 182.

Speaking generally of the vegetable productions of Soudan, Park says p. 250: "Although many species of the edible roots which grow in the West India Islands are found in Africa, yet I never saw in any part of my journey, either the sugar-cane, the coffee, or the cacao tree; nor could I learn on inquiry, that they were known to the natives. The pine-apple, and the thousand other delicious fruits which the industry of civilized man has brought to so great perfection in the tropical climates of America, are here equally unknown."

The *pine-apple*, however, is well known upon the Gold Coast, and in the Bight of Benin, and there appears to be no sufficient reason for doubting that it grows at Tombuctoo. We have not heard that Africa produces the *cacao-tree*; but the *sugar-cane* and the *coffee plant* are both amongst its products. Both are found upon the coasts just mentioned; and coffee has long been known to grow in abundance in Abyssinia.

With respect to the *cocoa-nut tree*, (not the cacao), which Adams names amongst the vegetable productions of Tombuctoo, some doubts of his accuracy in this respect have arisen; first, in consequence of the opinion that this tree flourishes only near the shores of the sea; and, secondly, because Adams was unable to describe its appearance. But as we are not disposed, on the one hand, to attach much value to the botanical recollections of a common sailor, neither do we think, on the other, that much stress ought to be laid either upon the fact of his having forgotten, or upon his inability to describe the appearance of any plants, which he may have seen. It would be by the *fruit* which it bore, that we should expect such a person to recollect any particular tree; and before we reject his assertion respecting he latter, we ought to consider that he mentions the former, incidentally, not less than three times in the course of his Narrative.

Although these circumstances entitle Adams's statement to considerable attention, yet we shall not be much surprised if he should be found to have mistaken the shell of the *calabash* (which is known to be much in use amongst the Mandingoes to the westward) for that of the cocoa-nut, when he speaks of the latter as a common domestic utensil at Tombuctoo, and as employed by the natives in the composition of one of their musical instruments.

Note 16, p. 39: In speaking of the quadrupeds at Timbuctoo, Adams says there are *no horses.* I do not recollect that he told me this at Mogadore, but I am disposed to give credit to the statement, from the corresponding accounts which I have received from traders. The same opinion prevails among the resident Moors of Barbary, who, in deriding and reviling their Negro slaves, frequently use a proverbial expression, implying, that "God who had blessed the Moors with horses, had cursed the Negroes with asses." The other animals which Adams here mentions are, in general, the same as are described by the Arab and Moorish traders. *D.*

Note 17, p. 39: The *Heiries,* of which Adams speaks, are doubtless the species of camel which is known by that name in the Desert. What I can learn with certainty respecting this extraordinary animal (one of which I have seen at Morocco, brought by the Arabs of Aboussebàh as a present to the Emperor) is, that though there is scarcely any visible difference between it and the common camel, its speed, patience, and abstinence, are much greater; and, that it is, on these accounts, highly prized by the Arabs. *D.*

There can be no doubt that Adams's *heirie* is the animal described by Leo Africanus in the following passage, which we quote from the Latin translation before us; "Tertium genus (camelorum) patriâ linguâ *ragnahil* dictum, gracilibus exiguaeque staturae camelis, constat; qui sarcinis gerendis inferiores, reliquos tanta sui pernicitate superant, ut diei unius spatio centum passuum millia conficiant, iter modico viatico ad dies octo vel decem perpetuantes."* And Pennant's description of the animal accords still more minutely with the details given by Adams. (See Pennant's Zool. 4to. vol. i. p. 131.) "There are varieties among the camels; what is called the dromedary, *Maihary,* and raguahl is very swift. The latter has a less hunch, is much inferior in size, never carries burdens, but is used to ride on."†

---

* [Leo Africanus, or "Giovanni Leone," was born El-Hasan ben Muhammed el-Wazzan-ez-Zayyati in Moorish Granada in 1485, and died in Tunis in 1584. John Pory's English translation (1600) of this passage is as follows: "The thirde kinde called Raguahill, are camels of a slender and low stature, which albeit they are unfit to carry burthens, yet do they so excell the two other kindes in swiftnes, that in the space of one day they will travell an hundred miles, and will so continue over the deserts for eight or ten days togither with very little provender" (338).]

† [Thomas Pennant's *History of Quadrupeds* (London: B. White, 1781).]

Note 18, p. 40: I have been frequently informed that *elephant-hunting* is common at Timbuctoo as well as in most parts of Soudan: and it is certain that great numbers of their teeth are brought by the caravans into Barbary. The manner in which Adams describes the hunting in the Narrative, corresponds exactly with what he related to me at Mogadore; as well as with the accounts which I had previously heard from traders, of the mode of hunting practised by the Negroes of Timbuctoo.

I do not recollect the exact dimensions of the elephant which Adams described to me; and I am confident that no such phenomenon as the *"four* tusks" was mentioned to me at Mogadore. In fact, I do not think that I asked him any question whatever on the subject of the teeth, or that they were mentioned by him at all. *D.*

It must be admitted that Adams has attributed dimensions to his elephant, which considerably surpass the limits of any previous authorities respecting this most bulky of animals; but without attempting to maintain the possibility of his accuracy, by quoting the authorities of Buffon and others, who have represented the breed of elephants in the *interior* and *eastern* parts of Africa, as greatly exceeding in size those of the western coast, and even as being larger than the elephants of the East Indies; all that we shall here contend for is, the probability that Adams, in this instance relates no more than he honestly *believes* he saw. He did not approach the animal nearer than three-quarters of a mile whilst it was alive; and it is not surprising that the sight for the first time of so huge a body, when lying dead on the ground, should impress him with an exaggerated idea of its dimensions.

However, we will not deny that the strange novelty of this stupendous creature seems to have disturbed Adams's usual accuracy of observation: we allude to his subsequent mistake about the animal's "four tusks."

It would be dealing rather unreasonably with a rude sailor cast upon the wilds of Africa, to expect that he should in that situation, whilst every thing was strange and new around him, minutely observe, – or could at a long interval afterwards, correctly describe, – the details of the plants* or animals which he had there an opportunity of seeing; and it would be unjust indeed, to make his accuracy on these points the standard of his veracity.

* See Note 15.

The same objects which would be full of interest to a tutored eye, and would be scanned in all their parts with eager and systematic curiosity, might pass almost unobserved before the vague and indifferent glance of an uncultivated individual like Adams; and his recollection of them, if he recollected them at all, would only extend to a rude and indistinct idea of their general appearance. The details in the text leave no room to doubt that it was an elephant which Adams saw; and with respect to the teeth it must not be forgotten, that he was questioned about them, apparently *for the first time*, more than four years after he saw the animal. If his observation of it might be expected to be vague and indistinct even at first, it would not be very extraordinary that his recollection of it, after so long an interval, should be far from accurate; and we cannot feel much surprise that, though he remembered that the animal *had* teeth, he should not be very well able to recollect whether it had *two* or *four*.

Note 19, p. 40: Alligators I have been informed are met with in the river near Timbuctoo: but I never heard the *hippopotamus* mentioned. *D.*

Note 20, p. 40: I never before heard of this extraordinary animal, either from Adams or any one else. *D.*

It would be unfair to Adams not to explain that when questioned as to his *personal knowledge* of the "courcoo," it appeared that he had never seen the animal nearer than at thirty or forty yards distance. It was from the Negroes he learnt that it had on its back "a hollow place like a pouch, which they called '*coo*,'" in which it pocketed its prey; and having once seen the creature carrying a branch of cocoa-nut with its fruit, "which as the courcoo ran swiftly away, seemed to lie on its back," Adams concluded of course that the pocket *must* be there; and further, that the animal fed on cocoa-nuts, as well as goats and children.

In many respects Adams's description of the animal, (about which the Narrative shews that he was closely questioned), answers to the lynx.

Note 21, p. 40: Lions, tigers, wolves, hyenas, foxes, and *wild-cats*, have been described to me as natives of most parts of Soudan; and are hunted by the Negroes on account of the ravages which they frequently make amongst their flocks and domestic animals. *D.*

Note 22, p. 41: The birds, both wild and tame, are, to the best of my recollection, the same as he previously described to me. The *ostriches* he told me were hunted both for their flesh and feathers, the latter not being used by the Negroes, except in trade with the Moors: who occasionally bring them to Barbary. *D.*

Note 23, p. 41: The poisonous liquid prepared from "black lumps like opium," into which the Negroes of Tombuctoo dip their arrows, appears to be the same as that which Park describes the Mandingoes to use, for a similar purpose.

"The poison, which is very deadly, is prepared from a shrub called *kooma,* (a species of echites); the leaves of which, when boiled in a small quantity of water, yield a thick, black juice." 1st Journey, 4to. p. 281.

Note 24, p. 41: Park observed a similar custom of anointing their persons among the Negroes of Bondou. See 1st. Journey, 4to. p. 62. "The cream (of cow's milk) is converted into butter by stirring it violently in a large calabash. This butter forms a part of most of their dishes; it serves likewise to anoint their heads; and is bestowed very liberally on their faces and arms."

Note 25, p. 42: This account of the marks on the faces of the inhabitants of Timbuctoo, agrees with that which Adams gave at Mogadore.

I have occasionally seen Negroes with similar incisions on their faces, but I cannot state with any confidence that they came from Timbuctoo. However, I have certainly heard from some of the traders that these marks are a prevalent, if not universal, ornament of the male Negroes of that country.

Many of the Negro slaves brought up to Barbary by the Arabs, have the cartilage of the nose bored through, in which, it is said, they wear in their own countries, a large gold ring, in the manner described by Adams of the Negroes between Soudenny and Timbuctoo. I have frequently seen female slaves with perforations in the lobes of their ears, which had the appearance of having been distended by wearing heavy ornaments. *D.*

Note 26, p. 43: Here again Adams, in his assertion of the existence of polygamy amongst the Negroes, and in his shrewd observation of the feuds which it excited amongst the ladies, may be illustrated and corroborated by a parallel passage from Park.

"As the Kafirs (Pagan Negroes) are not restricted in the number of their wives, every one marries as many as he can conveniently maintain; and as it frequently happens that the ladies disagree amongst themselves, family quarrels sometimes rise to such a height that the authority of the husband can no longer preserve peace in his household." 1st. Journey, 4to. pp. 39, 40.

Note 27, p. 43: I cannot speak with any confidence of the religion of the Negroes of Timbuctoo.

However, I have certainly heard, and entertain little doubt, that many of the inhabitants are Mohammedans: it is also generally believed in Barbary, that there are mosques at Timbuctoo. But on the other hand, I am pretty confident that the King is neither an Arab nor a Moor; especially as the traders from whom I have collected these accounts have been either the one, or the other, and I might consequently presume, that if they did give me erroneous information on any points, it would at least not be to the prejudice both of their national self-conceit, and of the credit and honour of their religion.

I think Adams told me that circumcision is not unfrequent there; and I have been informed by traders that it is common, though not universal, throughout Soudan; but without necessarily implying Mohammedanism in those who undergo the practice. *D.*

Park has stated circumcision to be common amongst the Negroes nearer the coast; and Barrow and other travellers describe the custom to be prevalent amongst the natives of some of the countries of southern Africa; but it does not appear in either of these cases to be practised exclusively as a Mohammedan rite.

With respect to the religious ceremonies in general, of the Pagan natives of Soudan, Park says, that on the first appearance of the new moon they say a short prayer, which is pronounced in a whisper, the party holding up his hands before his face; and that this "seems to be the only visible adoration which the Kafirs offer up to the Supreme Being." (1st. Journey, 4to. p. 272.) Thus far Adams's observation appears to have been perfectly accurate, that they have "no public religion, no house of worship, no priest, and never meet together to pray." But it is difficult to suppose that there are not Mohammedan converts amongst the Negroes of Tombuctoo, who publicly exercise the ceremonies of their religion: and we apprehend that Adams will be suspected of careless observation on that subject, notwithstanding the confidence with which he speaks of it. Indeed we should have said, that he had himself borne testimony to some of the externals of Islamism, when he mentions the *turbans* which the Chiefs of Soudenny and Tombuctoo occasionally wore, did we not learn from Park, that the Kafirs are in the habit of adopting the customs, names, and even in some instances, the prayers* of the Mohammedans, without adopting their religious ceremonies or creed.

Note 28, p. 44: Adams gave me a particular description of the wen or swelling on the back of his hand, and of its cure at Timbuctoo, in the manner here related.

I may take this opportunity of observing, that he recounted at Mogadore, (what I do not find in the Narrative,) several miraculous stories of the supernatural powers, or charms possessed by some of the Negroes, and which they practised both defensively to protect their own persons from harm, and offensively against their enemies. Of these details I do not distinctly remember more than the following circumstance, which I think he told me happened in his presence.

A Negro slave, the property of a Desert Arab, having been threatened by his master with severe punishment for some offence, defied his power to hurt him, in consequence of a charm by which he was protected. Upon this the Arab seized a gun, which he loaded with ball, and fired at only a few paces distance from the Negro's breast: but the Negro, instead of being injured by the shot, stooped to the ground, and picked up the ball which had fallen inoffensive at his feet!

It seems strange that Adams should have omitted these extraordinary stories (and almost these alone) in his Narrative; for he frequently expressed to me, a firm belief that the Negroes were capable of injuring their enemies by witchcraft; and he once pointed out to me a slave at Mogadore, of whom, on that account he stood peculiarly in awe. He doubtless imbibed this belief, and learnt the other absurd stories which he related, from the Arabs; some of whom profess to be acquainted with the art themselves, and all of whom, I believe, are firmly persuaded of its existence, and of the peculiar proficiency of the Negroes in it. *D.*

Is it unreasonable to suppose, that having found his miraculous stories, and his belief in witchcraft, discredited and laughed at, both at Mogadore and Cadiz, Adams should at length have grown ashamed of repeating them, or even have outlived his superstitious credulity? This

---

* See Park's 1st Journey, 4to. p. 37.

solitary instance of suppression (the particular stories suppressed being of so absurd a nature), may rather be considered as a proof of his good sense, and as the exercise of a very allowable discretion, than as evidence of an artfulness, of which not a trace has been detected in any other part of his conduct.

Note 29, p. 45: The dancing of the people of Timbuctoo has been frequently described to me by Adams; and on one occasion particularly, when some Negro slaves were enjoying this their favourite amusement, at Mogadore, he brought me to the spot, telling me that their dance was similar to those in Soudan which he had described to me. The following was the nature of the dance: – six or seven men, joining hands, surrounded one in the centre of the ring, who was dressed in a ludicrous manner, wearing a large black wig stuck full of cowries. This man at intervals repeated verses which, from the astonishment and admiration expressed at them by those in the ring, appeared to be extempore. Two performers were playing on the outside of the ring; one on a large drum, the other on a sort of guitar. They did not interrupt the singer in the ring during his recitations; but at the end of every verse the instruments struck up, and the whole party joined in loud chorus, dancing round the man in the circle, stooping to the ground and throwing up their legs alternately. Towards the end of the dance, the man in the middle of the ring was released from his enclosure, and danced alone, occasionally reciting verses; whilst the other dancers begged money from the bystanders.

I do not recollect to have seen any of the female slaves join in these dances; but I have observed them very much interested whilst attending the diversion; sometimes appearing extravagantly delighted, and at others exhibiting signs of mourning and sorrow.

These dances were prohibited soon after the accession of the present Emperor; but they have been occasionally permitted of late years. Whether the prohibition arose from some connection either real or supposed, which the dances had with any of the religious ceremonies of the Negroes, offensive to the Mohammedans, I was never able to ascertain. *D.*

The dancing of the Negroes at Joag in Kajaaga, as described by Mr. Park, corresponds very remarkably with Adams's description of the same amusement at Tombuctoo.

"I found," he says, 1st Journey 4to. p. 68, "a great crowd surrounding a party who were dancing by the light of some large fires, to the music of four drums, which were beaten with great exactness and uniformity. The dances, however, consisted more in wanton gestures than in muscular exertion or graceful altitudes. The ladies vied with each other in displaying the most voluptuous movements imaginable. They continued to dance until midnight."

Note 30, p. 45: This statement, which is in opposition to the usual opinion that Tombuctoo is a dependency of Bambarra, receives some corroboration from a passage in Isaaco's Journal (4to. p. 205) where a "Prince of Tombuctoo" is accused by the King of Sego, of having, either personally or by his people, plundered two Bambarra caravans, and taken both merchandize and slaves. This was in September 1810, some months previous to the date of the expeditions mentioned in the Narrative.

Note 31, p. 45: The Negro slaves brought to Barbary from Timbuctoo appear to be of various nations; many of them distinguishable by the make of their persons and features, as well as by their language. I have seen slaves, who were described as coming from the remote country of *Wangara*; but the greater part of them are brought from *Bambarra*; the Negroes of that nation being most sought after, and fetching the highest prices in Barbary.

I recollect an unusually tall, stout Negress at Mogadore, whose master assured me that she belonged to a populous nation of cannibals. I do not know whether the fact was sufficiently authenticated; but it is certain that the woman herself declared it, adding some revolting accounts of her own feasts on human flesh.

Being in the habit of inquiring from Negroes at Mogadore the manner of their falling into slavery, I received, on one such occasion, from a Bambarreen Negro, a long account of his capture, (on a plundering expedition), his sale, escape, and re-capture, amongst different Negro nations before he was finally sold, at Timbuctoo, to the Arabs. His account was chiefly curious from his description of a nation which he called *Gollo*, or *Quallo*, which conveyed to me an idea of a people more advanced in the arts, and wealthier than any that I had previously heard of. The King's palace and the houses in general were described as superior structures to those of the Moors: and he even spoke of domesticated elephants trained to war, of which the King had a large force.

To this nation he was conveyed by a party of its natives, a stout race of people; who, happening to be in a town on the *Wed-Nile*, in which he and half of the plundering party to which he belonged, had been made prisoners, bought him from his captors, and carried him away to their own country. They arrived at *Gollo* after nearly a month's journey inland from the river; during which they crossed a large chain of mountains; and as far as I could judge from his account, the country lay south-east of Bambarra. Within three days journey of the capital was a large lake or river which communicated with the *Wed-Nile*, by which he eventually escaped.

Notwithstanding the reserve with which the stories of Negroes must be received, there was a circumstantiality in this man's account, which seemed very like the truth; and he bore about him ocular evidence in corroboration of one part of his story; namely, that the right ears of himself and his plundering companions were cut off, as a punishment, by the people who sold him to the Negroes of *Gollo*. D.

Note 32, p. 46: It was already evident from Park's accounts, and the fact receives a more extended confirmation from Adams, that the Negroes in the interior of Soudan are in general harmless and compassionate in their personal characters, and humane in their laws; in which respects they are remarkably distinguished from many of their neighbours to the south, who, besides the ordinary implacability of savages towards their external and public enemies, are not sparing of the blood of their own countrymen, in their quarrels, punishments, or superstitious sacrifices.

Adams's account of the punishment assigned by the laws of Tombuctoo to the principal criminal offences, is substantially the same as that given by Park, in speaking of the laws of the Mandingoes; amongst whom, he informs us, that murder, adultery, and witchcraft (which, in other words, is the administering of poison) are punished with slavery. It appears, however, that in cases of murder, the relations of the deceased have, in the first instance, power over the life of the offender.

The infrequency of the punishment of death, in a community which counts human life amongst its most valuable objects of trade, is not, however, very surprising; and considerable influence must be conceded to the operation of self-interest, as well as to the feelings of humanity, in accounting for this merciful feature (if it be indeed merciful) in the criminal code of the Negroes of Soudan.

Note 33, p. 46: I do not at present recollect whether Adams told me, that there were, or that there were not, shops at Timbuctoo; but, as I have stated in Note 10, I have been informed by some of the traders, and am disposed to believe, that there *are* shops, in which foreign merchandize, and the domestic commodities of the inhabitants, are exposed for sale. Others, however, have contradicted this account.

The articles of trade which Adams enumerates in the succeeding lines, appear to me to correspond with tolerable accuracy with those which the caravans from the Barbary states carry to Soudan, and bring from thence.

This trade from the states of Morocco, which appears to have been carried on to a considerable and uniform extent since the reign of *Mulai Ismael* (at whose death the dominion previously exercised by the Moors over the natives of Timbuctoo is reported to have been shaken off by the latter), has begun to decline of late years, in consequence of the establishment of the market of *Hamet a Mousa*, in the territory of the *Cid Heshem*, described in a subsequent note: and I do not suppose that more than a hundred of the Emperor's subjects now annually cross the Desert.

With respect to the caravans themselves, their manner of assembling and travelling, the dangers which they incur in the Desert from the *Shume* wind, from want of water, and from the marauding disposition of the Desert Arabs, have been so fully described in other places, that any further detail here would be unnecessary. *D.*

Note 34, p. 46: In quoting the price in cowries of a full grown slave, Adams must certainly have committed a great mistake. I remember he told me that the Arabs gave a considerable value in tobacco or other merchandize for a slave; and that he thought them cheaper in the Desert than at Timbuctoo. *D.*

At Sansanding Park gives forty thousand cowries, as the current price of a male slave: it is not possible that the value either of cowries or slaves can be so utterly disproportionate in two countries so near to each other. Adams must have been quite in the dark with respect to the real terms of the bargain.

Note 35, p. 47: That the people of Timbuctoo should feel some jealousy of the tribes of *Arabs* immediately in their neighbourhood, is extremely probable, considering the general marauding characters of the latter; but I do not know what particular measures of exclusion are enforced against them. With respect to the traders from Barbary, I have always been told that they are permitted to reside at Timbuctoo as long as they think proper. On the other hand, I believe, that camel-drivers, Arab guides, and those attached to the caravans, who are either not able, or not willing, to make the King a present, are excluded. *D.*

Adams's assertion, that he saw no Moors during his stay at Tombuctoo, except the aforesaid two parties, is not so improbable as it may at first sight appear.

Tombuctoo, although it is become, in consequence of its frontier situation, the *port*, as it were, of the caravans from the north (which could not return across the Desert the same season if they were to penetrate deeper into Soudan) is yet, with respect to the trade itself, probably only the point from whence it diverges to Haoussa, Tuarick, &c. on the east, and to Walet, Jinnie, and Sego, in the west and south, and not the mart where the merchandize of the caravans is sold in detail. Park was informed, that Haoussa and Walet were, both of them, larger cities than Tombuctoo. Such Moors therefore as did not return to Barbary with the returning caravan, but remained in Soudan until the following season, might be expected to follow their trade to the larger marts of the interior, and to return to Tombuctoo, only to meet the next winter's caravans. Adams, arriving at Tombuctoo in February, and departing in June, might therefore miss both the caravans themselves and the traders who remained behind in Soudan: and, in like manner, Park might find Moors carrying on an active trade in the summer at Sansanding, and yet there might not be one at Tombuctoo.

With respect to the trade actually carried on at Tombuctoo (which makes but an insignificant figure in Adams's account,) we can only regret that a person placed in his extraordinary situation, was not better qualified to collect or communicate more satisfactory information on this and many other interesting subjects. However his lists of the articles of trade, show that he was not wholly unobservant in this respect; and we cannot but think it probable that the "armed parties of a hundred men or more," which he describes at page 45, as going out once a month for slaves, and returning sometimes in a week and sometimes after a longer absence, were in reality traders.

Note 36, p. 47: I was frequently told by Adams, who appeared to take pleasure in speaking of the circumstance, that the Negroes behaved to him on all occasions with great humanity, never insulting or ill treating him on account of his religion, as the Arabs did. He was never confined at Timbuctoo, but could go where he pleased. Upon these grounds I entertain little doubt (and I was confirmed in my opinion by Timbuctoo traders with whom I conversed on the subject) that had Adams explained his story to the Negroes, and expressed any unwillingness to accompany the Arabs on their return, he would have been rescued out of their hands and left at liberty. I do not recollect whether he told me, that the idea had ever occurred to him; but, if it did, it is probable that when he came to consider his hopeless prospect of reaching the sea coast, if left to himself, and that the Arabs had promised to take him to Suerra after their expedition to Soudenny; he would prefer the chance of ultimate liberation afforded him by accompanying the Arabs, of whose severe treatment he had then had but a short experience. D.

Note 37, p. 47: I do not imagine that the curiosity of the Negroes can have been excited so much on account of Adams's colour, as because he was a Christian, and a *Christian slave*, which would naturally be to them a source of great astonishment. The Negroes must have seen, in the caravans from the Barbary states which annually visit the countries of Soudan, and Timbuctoo in particular, many Moors, especially those from Fez, of a complexion quite as light as that of Adams. D.

Note 38, p. 47: September and October are the months in which the caravans from Barbary to Timbuctoo assemble on the northern confines of the Desert. They commence their journey as soon as the first rains have cooled the ground, and arrive again from the Desert about the month of March. D.

Whilst Adams states in the text, on the one hand, that the Desert can be crossed only in winter during the rainy season, it appears on the other, that he himself must have crossed it in July. (See Note 60.) Yet upon examination, the circumstances of the Narrative will be found not only to reconcile this apparent contradiction, but even to add to the internal evidence of the truth of Adams's story. The winter is, admittedly, the only proper time for crossing the Desert, and (as Mr. Dupuis states in the preceding part of this Note), the trading caravans from Barbary never attempt the journey at any other season. But the solitary troop of Arabs from the Woled D'leim do not appear to have come to Tombuctoo for the ordinary purposes of trade. Their only object seems to have been to ransom their imprisoned comrades: and having this alone in view, they would naturally come as soon as they had ascertained the captivity of the latter and prepared the means of redeeming them; without regarding the inconveniences of travelling at an unusual season. Their extraordinary sufferings, and loss of lives, from heat and thirst in returning across the Desert, may be hence accounted for.

This explanation moreover confirms, and is corroborated by, Adams's subsequent remark, in page 52, that the Arabs of Woled D'leim (which was the home of his ransomers) to be of the same tribe as those of the douar whither he was first conveyed from the coast, and consequently, as those who were taken prisoners with him at Soudenny.

Note 39, p. 47: This apparently unimportant passage affords, on examination, a strong presumption in favour of the truth and simplicity of this part of Adams's Narrative.

In the course of his examinations, almost every new inquirer eagerly questioned him respecting the *Joliba*; and he could not fail to observe, that, because he had been at Tombuctoo, he was expected, as a matter of course, either to have seen, or at least frequently to have heard of, this celebrated river. Adams, however, fairly admits that he knows nothing about it: and, notwithstanding the surprise of many of his examiners, he cannot be brought to acknowledge that he had heard the name even once mentioned at Tombuctoo. All that he does recollect is, that a river Joliba had been spoken of at Tudenny, where it was described as lying in the direction of Bambarra.

Those who recollect Major Rennell's remarks respecting the Niger in his "Geographical Illustrations," will not be much surprised that Adams should not hear of the "Joliba" from the natives of Tombuctoo. At that point of its course, the river is doubtless known by another name: and if the Joliba were spoken of at all, it would probably be accompanied (as Adams states in the text) with some mention of Bambarra, which may be presumed to be the last country eastward in which the Niger retains its Mandingo name.

Note 40, p. 48: Some of the words mentioned in this short specimen of the Negro language are Arabic; for instance, – *killeb*, a dog; *feel*, an elephant; *dar*, a house: also the name which he has given for "date" and "fig;" but the word *carna*, which he has prefixed to the latter, signifying "tree," is not Arabic. Whether Adams, in consequence of the short opportunity which he had of hearing the language of the Negroes, and his subsequent residence amongst the Arabs, has confounded the two languages in the above instances; or whether there may not really be some mixture of the languages at Timbuctoo (as not unfrequently happens in the frontier places of adjoining countries), I cannot pretend to determine.

It is at least certain, that Adams did know something of the Negro language, for I have frequently heard him hold conversations with the slaves at Mogadore; especially with a young Negro who used to visit my house on purpose to see Adams, and (as he has himself told me) to converse with him about his own country, where, he has often assured me, Adams had been. *D.*

Note 41, p. 51: Taudeny has been frequently described to me by traders in a manner which corresponds with Adams's account; it being reported to have four wells of good water, and a number of date and fig trees: the inhabitants are represented as quite black, but without the Negro features. The salt pits consist of large beds of rock salt, in the manner that Adams describes, and of very considerable extent. Their produce is in much request at Timbuctoo, and in all Soudan, whither it is sent in large quantities; the people of Taudeny receiving in return slaves and merchandize, which they again exchange with the Arabs of Woled D'leim, and Woled Aboussebàh, for camels, horses, or tobacco; so that I should imagine Taudeny to be a place of importance, and highly interesting. *D.*

Note 42, p. 52: Woled D'leim is the douar of a tribe of Arabs inhabiting the eastern parts of the Desert from the latitude of about twenty degrees north to the tropic. I have been informed by travellers who have visited these parts, that they are a tribe of great extent and power; that they inhabit detached fertile spots of land where they find water, and pasturage for their flocks, but do not at all practise agriculture. I have occasionally seen Arabs of this tribe during my residence at Mogadore. They appear to be an extremely fine race of men. Their complexion is very dark, almost as black as that of the Negroes; but they have straight hair, which they wear in large quantities, aquiline noses, and large eyes. Their behaviour was haughty and insolent: they spoke with fluency and energy, appeared to have great powers of rhetoric; and I was told that many of them possessed the talent of making extempore compositions in verse, on any object that attracted their notice. Their arms were javelins and swords. *D.*

Note 43, p. 54: The circumstances of Adams's neglect of his employment, and of the punishment which he received in consequence, appear to have made a strong impression on him; for he frequently mentioned them to me; always adding, that he had firmly determined to persevere in his resistance, though it had cost him his life. *D.*

Note 44, p. 55: Adams described the circumstances of his escape from the *Woled D'leim* to *El Kabla,* precisely as they are here related: but he observed to me that, with respect to masters, he had scarcely bettered his condition; and at all times he shewed an inveterate animosity against any of the Arabs of the Desert whom he saw at Mogadore.

El Kabla means the *eastern* Arabs, so distinguished from those of West Barbary and the coast. In the pronunciation of a Desert Arab, the name might sound very like *El Gibla,* or *Hilla Gibla.*

These people inhabit large tracts of the Desert on the northern limits of the Woled D'leim. They are looked upon as a tribe of considerable importance, and are frequently employed by the traders in crossing the Desert, serving as guides or escorts as far as Taudeny. They have been represented to me as a haughty and ferocious race, yet scrupulously observant of the rites of hospitality. In persons they are said to resemble their Woled D'leim neighbours, being extremely dark, straight haired, and of the true Arabian feature. They are reported to be descendants from the race of Woled Aboussebàh; from whom they probably separated themselves, in consequence of some of the disputes which frequently involve the Desert tribes in domestic wars. Their large flocks of sheep and goats supply them with outer raiment as well as food; but the blue shirts of Soudan, are almost universally worn by them as under garments. *D.*

Note 45, p. 57: These details of Adams's amour with *Aisha* are the same as he gave to me at Mogadore. Of the fact itself I can entertain no doubt; from the following circumstances.

After the loss of the "Charles" it had been my constant practice, when traders went to the Desert, to commission them to make inquiries respecting the remainder of the crew, who were in the possession of the Arabs; and, in particular, respecting those who had been reported to me to be carried eastward. On the return of one of these men from El Kabla, he told me that there was a Christian slave at that place, in possession of an Arab, who would doubtless be very glad to dispose of him, in consequence of the slave having been detected in an affair with his wife. He then briefly related to me the same story, in substance, as I afterwards heard from Adams.

I also heard of it from a trader from Wed-Noon, who told me of Adams being there, some time before I effected his ransom: I was informed at the same time that this trait of his character and history was much talked of at Wed-Noon. *D.*

Note 46, p. 57: *Villa de Bousbach* should be *Woled Aboussebàh; Woled* signifying *sons* or *children*, and being commonly applied to all the tribes of Arabs.

The Woled Aboussebàh is a considerable tribe of Arabs distinct from the Woled D'leim, inhabiting large tracts of the northern and western parts of the Desert. They report themselves to be descendants from the line of *sheriffes*, or race of the Prophet. Their country is described as a Desert interspersed with spots of fertile land, where they fix their douars, and pasture their flocks of goats, sheep, and camels. Their diet is occasionally the flesh of their flocks, but chiefly the milk of the *niag*, or female camel. They trade with their northern neighbours for dates and tobacco; being immoderately fond of the latter for their own consumption in snuff and smoking, and employing it also in their trade with Soudan for slaves and blue cottons.

As this tribe is reported to reach quite down to the sea coast, and to be spread over a very extensive tract of country, there are various branches of it, who consider themselves wholly independent of each other, yet all calling themselves the "Woled Aboussebàh." Those who inhabit the sea coast are supplied with double-barrelled guns, and various implements of iron, by trading vessels from the Canary Islands, for which they give cattle in exchange. They are represented to be very expert in the management of their horses, and in the use of fire-arms, being excellent marksmen at the full speed of the horse, or of the Desert camel (*heirie*). They have frequent wars with their southern and eastern neighbours, though without any important results; the sterility of the soil through-out the whole of this region of sand affording little temptation to its inhabitants to dispossess each other of their territorial possessions.

The inhabitants of Wed-Noon are descended from this tribe, and owe their independence to its support: for the Arabs of Aboussebàh being most numerous on the northern confines of the Desert, present a barrier to the extension of the Emperor of Morocco's dominion in that direction.

During the discords and civil wars which raged in Barbary previous to the present Emperor's tranquil occupation of the throne of Morocco, a horde of these Arabs, amounting to about seven thousand armed men, seizing that opportunity of exchanging their barren Deserts for more fertile regions, over-ran the southern parts of the Empire. Mounted on horses and camels, and bearing their tents and families with them, they pursued their course, with little or no opposition, until they reached the provinces of *Abda* and *Shiedma*, which lie between Saffy and Mogadore, where they were opposed by the Arabs of those provinces, united with a powerful tribe called *Woled-el-Haje*,* who inhabit a fertile country north of the river Tensift. The Woled Aboussebàh were, however, victorious, and a dreadful slaughter of their enemies ensued; who, after being driven down to the sea were cut to pieces without mercy, neither women nor children escaping the massacre. The victors then took possession of the country, where they settled, and maintained themselves against all opposition; and they now form a part of the subjects of the Emperor of Morocco. *D.*

Note 47, p. 60: The mate and the seamen of the "Charles," whom Adams described to have found at *Wed-Noon*, were, to my knowledge, in that town a considerable time previous to his arrival.

Some explanation may not be out of place here, of the reasons why these men did not reach the Emperor's dominions at the period when the three of the Charles's crew, whom I have before named, were ransomed.

---

* [The Oulad El-Hadj Ben Demouiss, a faction of the Oulad Bou Sbaa (see Pazzanita and Hodges, 328).]

Upon the arrival of the Arab of Aboussebàh (whom I have mentioned in Note 6) at Santa Cruz on his way to Mogadore, with *Nicholas, Newsham,* and *Nelson,* the Governor of that city and district wished to take possession of the Christians in order to send them to the Emperor: but the Arab refused to part with them, not considering himself a subject of the Emperor, or under the controul of any of the rulers of Barbary; and he accordingly escaped out of the city with his property by night; but before he reached Mogadore he was overtaken by two soldiers whom the Governor had dispatched after him, and who accompanied him and the Christians to me.

The Arab then declared to me that it never was his intention to take his slaves to the Emperor, that he had bought them in the Desert in the hopes of making some profit by their ransom, and that, if he succeeded in this object, he would return, and endeavour to bring the others up to Mogadore. Upon this I bargained with him for the purchase of them; but refusing to accept the highest sum which it was in my power to offer him, he left me, pretending that he had resolved to take his slaves to Fez, where the Emperor then was. Fearful of trusting the men again in his power, I objected to his taking them from under my protection; unless they were entrusted to the care of a Moorish soldier; but the Governor of Mogadore refused to grant him a soldier for that purpose. Thus circumstanced, he was at length compelled to accept the proffered ransom.

The dissatisfaction which the Arab felt at the result of his journey, and at the interference of the Governors of Santa Cruz and Mogadore, was, I fear, the cause why the rest of the Charles's crew were not subsequently brought up to be ransomed; but it could not be helped. *D.*

Note 48, p. 60: The sale of Adams at Wed-Noon to *Bel-Cossim-Abdallah* was mentioned to me by him at Mogadore; Adams observing that he had been bought by Bel-Cossim very cheap, the latter having paid no more for him than the value of seventy dollars in barter.

This part of the Narrative was further confirmed by Bel-Cossim himself; who having arrived at Mogadore some time after Adams had been ransomed, called upon me, and requested permission to see him. Bel-Cossim then shewed a great regard for him, and told me that he had been unwilling to part with him, when he was ransomed. *D.*

Note 49, p. 60: The following is an extract of a letter from P. W. Brancker, Esq. of Liverpool, in reply to an inquiry into the truth of this part of Adams's story.

Liverpool, Nov. 28, 1815

The American seaman is correct as to the loss of a vessel from this port, but makes a small mistake in the name; for it appears that the ship *Montezuma*, belonging to Messrs. Theodore Koster and Co., and bound from hence to the Brazils, was wrecked on the 3d November, 1810, between the Capes de Noon and Bajedore on the coast of Barbary; that the master and crew were made prisoners by a party of Arabs, and that he (the master) was taken off without the knowledge of the persons in whose service he then was, and might therefore be *supposed* to be murdered; for being left in charge of a drove of camels, he was found by a party of the Emperor's cavalry and carried off to Morocco, from whence he was sent to Gibraltar.

It is also said that the crew have obtained their liberty, except one boy.

Note 50, p. 60: I have often heard of this French renegade, and of his manufacture of gun-powder; he is said to have died about two years ago. *D*.

Note 51, p. 61: It has already been stated (see Note 31) that many of the slaves purchased at Tombuctoo, and brought by the Arabs across the Desert, come from countries even as far east of that city as Wangara; it is therefore not unreasonable to suppose that *Kanno*, mentioned in the text, may be the kingdom of *Ghana*, or *Cano*, which D'Anville places on the Niger, between the tenth and fifteenth degrees of eastern longitude. Assuming this to be the fact, the curious relation of the Negro slave at Wed-Noon might afford ground to conjecture that Park had made further progress down the Niger than Amadi Fatouma's story seems to carry him; further, we mean, than the frontier of Haoussa.

In fact, the time which intervened between Park's departure from Sansanding, and his asserted death, would abundantly admit of his having reached a much more distant country even than *Ghana*: for according to Isaaco and Amadi Fatouma (see Park's Second Mission, 4to. p. 218), he had been *four months* on his voyage down the Niger before he lost his life; having never been on shore during all that time. This long period is evidently quite unnecessary for the completion of an uninterrupted voyage from Sansanding to the frontiers of Haoussa: for Park was informed by Amadi Fatouma himself, that the voyage even to *Kashna* (probably more than twice the distance, according to Major Rennell's positions of these places), did not require a longer period than *two months* for its performance.

The mention of *Kashna*, reminds us of another remarkable circumstance in Amadi Fatouma's statements. In the instance just quoted, he appears to be inconsistent with himself; but in the passages to which we allude, we find him at issue with Park.

In his last letter to Sir Joseph Banks, announcing the completion of his preparations, and written apparently only three days before he commenced his voyage from Sansanding, Park, speaking of Amadi Fatouma, says, "I have hired *a guide to go with me to Kashna*"; and again, in the same letter, "I mean to write *from Kashna by my guide*." But Amadi Fatouma, in accounting for his separation from Park before the fatal catastrophe, tells quite another story. He asserts that he was only engaged to go to *Haoussa*: and an apparently forced prominence is given to this assertion by his manner of making it. His words are these (p. 212): "Entered the country of Haoussa, and came to an anchor. Mr. Park said to me, 'Now, Amadi, you are at the end of your journey. I *engaged you to conduct me here*; you are going to leave me.'" Almost the same words are repeated a few lines afterwards; with this difference, however, that Amadi Fatouma now quotes the remark as his own. "I said to him (Mr. Park) *I have agreed to carry you to Haoussa*; we are now in Haoussa. *I have fulfilled my engagements with you*; I am therefore going to leave you, and return."

The Reader will not need to be informed, that Amadi Fatouma's account goes on to state, that Park and his party lost their lives the day but one after he (Amadi) had thus parted from them; and that they had previously thrown into the river "every thing they had in the canoe;" a proceeding for which no sufficient reason is afforded by the details in the Journal.

We are quite disposed to make all due allowances for the evidence of an African, conveyed to us through an uncertain translation; but, we really think, that the discordances which we have quoted, (joined to other improbabilities in the Narrative) warrant a suspicion that, either with respect to the circumstances of Park's death, or to the appropriation of his effects, Amadi Fatouma had something to conceal. We are not, however, very confident that the further prosecution of this inquiry could lead to any satisfactory conclusion; for whatever suspicion it might tend to throw on Amadi Fatouma's statement of the *time, place,* and *circumstances* of Park's lamented death, it could not, we fear, justify a reasonable doubt, at this distant period, of the actual occurrence, in some mode or other, of the melancholy event itself.

Note 52, p. 62: I heard from several other persons of the ill-treatment which Adams received from *Hameda-Bel-Cossim,* his master's son: and the Moors who visited Wed-Noon corroborated the account of his un-shaken resolution, and of the punishment which he suffered in conse-quence of it, having been put in irons and in prison. *D.*

Note 53, p. 63: I have no reason to doubt the truth of the circumstances here related by Adams respecting Stephen Dolbie, except as to the fact of his dying *in consequence* of a wound given by Brahim. Other accounts stated that he died at Wed-Noon of a fever only, the effects of a cold contracted by gathering in the harvest during heavy rain: and this, as far as I can recollect, was the account which Adams gave me at Mogadore. I remember that he told me he had assisted at Dolbie's interment, and that he had afterwards covered the grave with stones. *D.*

Note 54, p. 63: I can easily believe Adams's statement of the brutal treatment he experienced at *Wed-Noon.* It is consistent with the accounts I have always heard of the people of that country, who I believe to be more bigotted and cruel than even the remoter inhabitants of the Desert. The three men of the Charles's crew already mentioned, complained vehemently of the miseries they had suffered, though they had been but a comparatively short time in slavery; and one of them shewed me a scar upon his breast, which he told me was the mark of a wound given him by one of the Arabs.

In the frequent instances which have come under my observation, the general effect of the treatment of the Arabs on the minds of the Christian captives has been most deplorable. On the first arrival of these unfortunate men at Mogadore, if they have been any considerable time in slavery, they appear lost to reason and feeling, their spirits broken, and their faculties sunk in a species of stupor which I am unable adequately to describe. Habited like the meanest Arabs of the Desert they appear degraded even below the Negro slave. The succession of hardships which they endure from the caprice and tyranny of their purchasers, without any protecting law to which they can appeal for alleviation or redress, seems to destroy every spring of exertion or hope in their minds; they appear indifferent to every thing around them, – abject, servile, and brutified.

Adams alone was in some respects an exception from this description. I do not recollect any ransomed Christian slave who discovered a greater elasticity of spirit, or who sooner recovered from the indifference and stupor here described.

It is to be remarked that the Christian captives are invariably worse treated than the idolatrous or Pagan slaves whom the Arabs, either by theft or purchase, bring from the interior of Africa; and that religious bigotry is the chief cause of this distinction. The zealous disciples of Mohammed consider the Negroes merely as ignorant unconverted be-ings, upon whom, by the act of enslaving them they are conferring a benefit, by placing them within reach of instruction in the "true belief;" and the Negroes having no hopes of ransom, and being often enslaved when children, are in general, soon converted to the Mohammedan faith. The Christians, on the contrary, are looked upon as hardened infidels, and as deliberate despisers of the Prophet's call; and as they in general stedfastly reject the Mohammedan creed, and at least never embrace it whilst they have hopes of ransom, the Mooslim, consistently with the spirit of many passages in the Koran, views them with the bitterest hatred, and treats them with every insult and cruelty which a merciless bigotry can suggest.

It is not to be understood, however, that the Christian slaves, though generally ill treated and inhumanly worked by their Arab owners, are persecuted by them ostensibly on account of their religion. They, on the contrary, often encourage the Christians to resist the importunities of those who wish to convert them: for, by embracing Islamism the Christian slave obtains his freedom; and however ardent may be the zeal of the Arab to make proselytes, it seldom blinds him to the calculations of self-interest.

A curious instance of the struggle thus excited between Moham-medan zeal and worldly interest, was related to me to have occurred at Wed-Noon, in the case of a boy belonging to an English vessel which had been wrecked on the neighbouring coast a short time previous to the "Charles."

This boy had been persuaded to embrace the Mohammedan faith; but after a little while, repenting of what he had done, he publicly declared that he had renounced the doctrines of the Koran, and was again a Christian. To punish so atrocious an outrage, the Arabs of Wed-Noon resolved to burn him; and they would no doubt have punctually performed the ceremony, but for the interference of the man from whose service the boy had emancipated himself by his first conversion. This man contended, that by abjuring the Mohammedan faith, the boy had returned into his former condition of slavery, and was again his property, and in spite of the most opprobrious epithets which were heaped upon him (including even the term "infidel," the horror and abomination of all true Mooselmin) the man insisted that if they would burn the boy, they should first reimburse him for the value of a slave. Reluctant to lose their sacrifice, the Arabs now attempted to raise money by subscription to purchase the boy; and contributions were begged about the town *to burn the Christian*. But in the end, as they made slow progress towards obtaining by these means a sufficient sum to purchase the boy, they relinquished their project; the owner, however was shortly afterwards obliged to remove his slave to another part of the country, to secure him from private assassination. *D.*

Note 55, p. 63: Adams describes correctly the tenor of my Letter addressed to the survivors of the crew of the "Charles" at Wed-Noon. His account, also, of the behaviour of Williams, is confirmed by the testimony of the man whom I employed to purchase Adams, who was a Moor, – and not, as Adams supposes, an European in disguise. He informed me that he found that Adams's two companions had embraced the Mohammedan faith; but that the younger, in particular, interested him so deeply by his tears, and by his earnest supplications that he would take him to Mogadore, that he could not himself refrain from tears; and was half inclined to steal him away let the consequence be what it would. He also assured me that he gave him some money at parting, and a few rags for clothing.

Just previous to my quitting Mogadore in October, 1814, these two men contrived to make their escape as Mohammedans, from Wed-Noon, and reaching Mogadore in safety, they staid there only a few hours and then departed for Tangier. I learnt shortly afterwards that upon their arrival at the latter city, they claimed the protection of their respective Consuls there, (one of the men being an Englishman and the other an American) disclaiming the Mohammedan faith; but it was not without much difficulty and negociation, during which time the men were placed in confinement, that they were ultimately liberated and restored to the Christian world. *D.*

Note 56, p. 64: I was informed by the man who brought Adams to Mogadore, that he had passed through the country called *Bled Cidi Heshem*, on his return; having gone for the purpose of purchasing another of the Charles's crew, (*Martin Clark*, a black man), who was in slavery there, in which he could not then succeed. The country is just on the southern confines of the Emperor's dominions. It is a small independent state of *Shilluh*, and (as described by Adams) lies in lower Suse. The Chief here mentioned, the *Cid Heshem*, who has successfully resisted the endeavours of his neighbours to subvert his government, is the descendant of *Cidi Hamet a Moussa*, a reputed modern Saint, who during his life was highly venerated for his justice and piety, and whose tomb, since his death, has been resorted to by religious Mooselmin from many parts of South Barbary and the Desert. This chief has lately opened an extensive trade with Soudan, for gums, cottons, and ostrich feathers, ivory, gold-dust, and slaves, which are sold by his agents at the great annual market of *Hamet a Moussa*. The traders from Southern Barbary resort to this market in great numbers; and I have heard it asserted that they can there purchase, for money, the produce of Soudan, to more advantage than they can themselves import it, without taking into account the risks and fatigues of the journey; insomuch that but for the important object of disposing of their own commodities in barter, in the Douars of the Desert and the markets of Soudan, I apprehend that very few of the native traders of Barbary would continue to cross the Desert.

It appears by the account which Adams subsequently gives of this market, that he must have been there; and the time of his journey corresponds with the season when it is held: but I think he must have committed an error in placing it more than a day's journey from the residence of the *Cid Heshem*; as the sanctuary and market of *Cidi Hamet a Moussa* are within the small territory of this Chief, who himself presides during the market days, to preserve order and tranquillity.

The inhabitants of this district, as I have stated before, are *Shilluh*, who are a distinct race from the Arabs, and have different dress, customs, and language. They live in houses built of stone, which are generally situated on eminences and fortified, for security in their domestic wars. They are possessed of a fertile country, producing abundance of barley and some wheat. The fruits and vegetables common in South Barbary are also grown here. Their sheep and goats are of the finest breed, and are frequently brought to Mogadore as presents: and their camels are much esteemed for their patience and great power of enduring fatigue.* D.

Note 57, p. 66: I *did* frequently interrogate Adams, when at Mogadore, respecting his travels in Africa; and frequently sent for persons who had been at the places he described, in order to confront their accounts with his, and especially to ascertain the probability of his having been at Timbuctoo. Amongst these individuals was a Shieck of Wed-Noon, a man of great consideration in that country, who had been several times at Timbuctoo in company with trading parties; and who, after questioning Adams very closely respecting that city and its neighbourhood, assured me that he had no doubt that he had been there. Another Moorish trader who was in the habit of frequenting Timbuctoo gave me the same account. In short, it was their universal opinion that he must have been at the places he described, and that his account could not be a fabrication. D.

Note 58, p. 66: I did, about the time stated by Adams, send him to Fez to the Emperor, under the protection of one soldier and a muleteer. D.

Note 59, p. 67: Having visited Tangier myself a few months afterwards, I there learnt from Mr. Simpson, that he had sent Adams to Cadiz a few days after his arrival. D.

Note 60, p. 67: Upon a minute examination of Adams's Narrative, a considerable difference will be found to exist between his collective estimates of the time he remained in Africa, and the actual interval between the dates of his shipwreck and return; the aggregate of the former amounting to about four years and three months, whilst the real time does not appear to have exceeded *three years and seven months*. It is not difficult to conceive that the tedium of so long a period of slavery and wretchedness would easily betray Adams into an error of this nature; especially in a situation where he possessed no means of keeping a minute account of the lapse of time; and it is reasonable to presume,

---

* For a more detailed description of the *Shilluh*, see the Appendix, No. II.

that when he speaks of having resided six months at one place, eight at another, and ten at a third, he has, in each of these estimates, somewhat over-rated the real duration of these tedious and wretched portions of his existence.

When this discrepancy in his statements was pointed out to him, and he was led to reconsider in what part of his Narrative the error lay, it did not appear to change his persuasion of the accuracy of any detached portion of his estimates. He did however express his *peculiar* conviction that he was at least accurate in the number of days occupied in his journeys from place to place. On this occasion, as on many others in the course of his numerous examinations, it was impossible not to derive from the indisposition which he evinced to conform to the opinion of others, upon points on which he had once given an opposite deliberate opinion of his own, a strong impression of his general veracity and sincerity.

It was at Wed-Noon that the first opportunity occurred to him after his shipwreck, of correcting his reckoning of time; his arrival at which place, (as he was informed by the French renegade whom he found there) having occurred about the middle of August, 1812, or about eight months earlier than his own computation would have made it. Assuming therefore the Frenchman's account to have been correct, and deducting Adams's excess of time in relative proportions from his stationary periods at Tombuctoo, Woled D'leim, and other places, the following will be the probable dates of the several stages of his travels.

1810, October 11. – Shipwrecked at El Gazie.
December 13. – Set out on the expedition to Soudenny.
1811, February 5. – Arrived at Tombuctoo.
June 9. – Departed from Ditto.*
August 11. – Arrived at Woled D'leim.
1812, March 7. – Departed from Ditto.
June 20. – Departed from El Kabla.
August 23. – Arrived at Wed-Noon.

* He says they had a few drops of *rain* before his departure, which in some degrees confirms the accuracy of this date; since the tropical rains in the latitude of Tombuctoo, may be supposed to commence in early June.

1813, September 23. – Departed from Ditto.
       October 6. – Arrived at Mogadore
1814, April 22. – Departed from Ditto.
       May 17. – Arrived at Cadiz.

To this statement with respect to *time*, we may add the following summary of the *distances* of his respective journeys, collected from the Narrative at his highest estimates;

Journies	Days	Course	Rate in Miles	Distance
From *El Gazie* to the Douar				
in the Desert –	30	E. ½ S.	15	450
On the Journey to *Soudenny* –	13	S. S. E.	20	260
Ditto – Ditto	4	S. S. E. ½ S.	20	80
To the Village where the				
Moors were put to death –	10	E.	20	200
To *Tombuctoo* –	15	E. by N.	20	300
Distance in British Miles from				
the Coast to *Tombuctoo* –	–	–	–	1290
To the point of departure from				
La Mar Zarah –	10	E. N. E.	18	180
– *Taudeny* –	13	N.	20	234
– the border of the Sandy Desert	1	N. W.	20	20
In the Sandy Desert	14	–	18	252
Ditto	15	–	12	180
From the edge of the Sandy				
Desert to *Woled D'leim* –	1	–	12	12
To *El Kabla* –	2	N. by W.	–	30
Woled Aboussebàh –	9	N. E.	18	162
Woled Adrialla –	6	N. N. W.	25	150
Aiata Mouessa Ali –	3	N. W.	18	54
Wed-Noon –	5	–	16	80
Akkadia –	1	N.	30	30
Bled Cidi Heshem –	2	N. E.	30	60
Agadeer or *Santa Cruz* –	4	N. by W.	–	90
Suerra or *Mogadore* –	{4	N.	20	80
	{1	–	10	10
Distance in British Miles from				
Tombuctoo to *Mogadore* –	–	–	–	1624

These distances, as well as the course of his journies, will be found accurately represented by the ruled line in the Map: and it is impossible to observe how nearly they approach to what may be presumed to be the truth, without being astonished at Adams's memory, and at the precision with which he estimated his course with no other compass than the rising and setting of a vertical sun.

CONCLUDING REMARKS

We shall close our remarks on Adams's Narrative with a brief review, of the extent to which it has hitherto been confirmed, and of the credibility of those parts of it which still rest on his own unsupported testimony. The first part of this examination may be disposed of in a very few words.

The preceding notes will be found to contain an uninterrupted chain of evidence by which his course may be traced backwards from London, through Cadiz, Tangier, Mequinez, Fez, Mogadore, and Wed-Noon, to the Douar of El Kabla in the depths of the Desert. His adventure with Aisha at El Kabla – the fame of which preceded him to Mogadore, and adhered to him during his residence at Wed-Noon – sufficiently establishes the identity of the individual whom Mr. Dupuis received from the Desert. From Mogadore, he is delivered into the hands of the American Consul at Tangier, who, in his turn, transmits him to Cadiz, where he is traced into the service of Mr. Hall. The Cadiz gentleman who first discovered him in the streets of London, supplies the last link to this chain of identity; and completes the proof (strengthened by other circumstances) that the gallant of Aisha at El Kabla, and the *Tombuctoo-traveller* in London, whether known by the name of *Adams*, or *Rose*, is one and the same individual.

Passing now to the earlier part of his adventures, we find the time and circumstances of his shipwreck, and his conveyance eastward into the Desert, confirmed by three of the Charles's crew who were first ransomed; whilst, on the other hand, the fact of the individual in question being actually one of the seamen of the Charles, is fully established by the testimony of *Davison* and *Williams*, his comrades at Wed-Noon, who may be said to have delivered him, as such, into the hands of

Mr. Dupuis' agent, – and who confirmed the fact upon their subsequent arrival at Mogadore.*

Thus far Adams's story is supported and confirmed by direct external evidence. We have seen it accompany him far into the Desert; and there find him again, at a greater distance from the coast than any other Christian, we believe, has ever been traced in these inhospitable regions. But between these two points of his advance and return, a wide interval occurs, during which we entirely lose sight of him: and we must therefore be content to receive this part of his story on his own credit alone, illustrated by such indirect corroborations as we may be enabled to glean from other sources. This unsupported part of Adams's story extends, it will be seen, from the Douar to which he was first conveyed from the coast, until his arrival at El Kabla; occupying a period of fifteen or sixteen months; – a period which the Narrative fills up with the expedition to Soudenny, – the journey to, and residence at, Tombuctoo, – and the return through Taudenny across the Desert to Woled D'leim and El Kabla. We do not deem it necessary to extend our examination to the whole of these journeys, because if we shall be fortunate enough to satisfy the Reader that Adams is entitled to credit as far as Tombuctoo,

---

* It ought to be mentioned in this place, because it affords an additional proof of Adams's accuracy on such points as he ought to be well acquainted with, that *ten* of the eleven individuals composing the crew of the Charles at the time of her wreck, were either ransomed by Mr. Dupuis, or accounted for to him through other channels than Adams, by the *same names*, (his own excepted), which the latter has given in the first page of this Narrative. The following is Mr. Dupuis' memorandum on the subject.

Harrison, Capt. died immediately after the wreck.
Nicholas, Seaman.
Newsham, ditto, Ransomed three months after the wreck.
Nelson, ditto, Ransomed three months after the wreck.
Dolbie, Mate, died at Wed-Noon in 1813.
Rose, (alias Adams), ransomed ditto.
Clark, black seaman, ditto, 1814.
Davison, seaman, Renegade at Wed-Noon, but liberated in 1814.
Williams, boy, Renegade at Wed-Noon, but liberated in 1814.
Matthews, an old man, reported to have died in the Desert.

Recapitulation,	7	liberated,
	3	Dead,
	1	unaccounted for,
	11	Total number stated by Adams;

of whom Stephens alone, (whom he says he left at Woled D'leim), was never heard of by Mr. Dupuis. [This note confuses the names of the captains of the *Charles* (Horton) and the *Montezuma* (Harrison).]

we conceive that no doubt can be raised respecting his journey from thence to El Kabla.

We have already entered so fully into the question of the probability of the expedition to Soudenny, in Note 7 p. 70, that the reader would hardly excuse us for repeating in this place the arguments which were there adduced in support of it. We shall therefore confine our remarks to the journey from thence to Tombuctoo.

But before we enter upon this examination, we are anxious to caution our readers against suspecting us of setting up any pretensions to *minute* accuracy, either in the situation which we have assigned to Soudenny in the Note in question, or in any positions of places in the map adjusted from data necessarily so vague as those afforded by Adams: neither must it be forgotten on the other hand, that the precise situations of the places which we have used as the standards of his accuracy, are rather assumed than proved. There may be errors in both cases: and in the latter, it is at least as probable that such errors may contribute to increase the apparent inaccuracy of Adams's positions, as that they lend to those positions any undue degree of probability. Without, therefore, pretending to determine whether the Negro dominion does actually reach to the 16th degree of north latitude under the assumed meridian of Soudenny, (that the Negro *population* extends so far we presume no one will doubt), or whether Adams's real course lay further to the south than his Narrative warrants us in placing it, we must at least contend that the approximation of Adams's evidence on this part of his journey, to the best standards by which it can be tried, is astonishingly near; – so near indeed, that if we had not been assured, upon the undoubted authority of Mr. Dupuis, that the first account of his courses and distances which he gave when fresh from the Desert, afforded, with respect to Tombuctoo, *the same results as those which we are now remarking*, we should have been rather tempted to suspect that this degree of coincidence was the result of contrivance, than to have derived from the degree of his discordance with other authorities any doubts of the reality of his journies. Those who are most conversant with questions of this nature will best appreciate the extreme difficulty which an unscientific individual must find in even approaching to the truth in his computations of the direction and extent of a long succession of journies: even the evidence of so practised an observer as Park was not sufficiently precise to secure the eminent compiler of the Map of his first Journey from very considerable inaccuracies, which Park on his second mission, by the aid of his instruments of observation, was enabled to correct.

On the whole, since the circumstances stated by Mr. Dupuis entirely preclude all suspicion of contrivance in Adams's account of his route in Africa, (a contrivance which he was too ignorant to invent himself, and in which, when he arrived from the Desert, he had had no opportunity of being instructed by others) we do not conceive how it is possible to resist the circumstantial corroboration of his story which the application of his route to the Map affords; unless, indeed, by resorting to the preposterous supposition that so uniform an approach to the truth, throughout a journey of nearly three thousand miles, could be purely accidental. But to return to the particular question before us.

In addition to the grounds already adduced for placing Soudenny within the Bambarran territories, Adams may fairly claim the advantage of another circumstance mentioned by Park; we mean *the fluctuating state of the line of boundary itself.* Considerable changes in that respect had occurred within a few months of the period when Park crossed the frontier in question: – the seeds of further changes were perceptible, both in the restless and marauding disposition of the Moors, and in the preponderating strength of the King of Bambarra: and it would by no means follow (if the question were really of importance to Adams's story) that the northern frontiers of the state must, in 1811, be the same as they were supposed to be in 1796.*

Placing Soudenny, therefore, within the frontiers of Bambarra, in the sixteenth or possibly the fifteenth degree of North latitude, and about the fifth or sixth of West longitude, we shall find Adams's account of his course and distance from thence to Tombuctoo, approach with extraordinary accuracy to the *line* of journey required. We possess too little knowledge of the countries through which this route would lie, to pronounce with any confidence upon the probability of the *circumstances* of his journey. What we can at present know upon the subject must be learnt from Park; – who informs us, that to the eastward of

---

* In one direction at least, (to the West) the King of Bambarra's frontiers appear to have been much extended in 1810; for according to Isaaco's Journal, 4to. p. 194, they cannot be placed more than three or four short days journey from *Giocha (Joko)*; although according to Park's first map, the distance from *Joko* to the nearest frontiers of Bambarra is at least ten day's journey. There had been a war in 1801, in these parts; being the second war in six years.

Bambarra, between that kingdom and Tombuctoo, lies the Foulah kingdom of Masina. It is not known to what latitude the northern frontiers
of the latter kingdom extend; but we are told that it is bounded on
that side by the Moorish kingdom of Beeroo; and there is great reason
to suppose, with Major Rennell,* that the Moorish population which
to the westward touches the Senegal, does from that point incline in a
oblique line to the northward of east, as it advances from the west along
the limits of Soudan. Admitting this retrocession of the Moors towards
the Desert, the Negroes of Soudenny would find a secure route, through
Negro countries, along the extreme frontiers† of Bambarra and Masina
to the borders of Tombuctoo, generally in the direction described by
Adams.

Why the Negroes, if they were actually Bambarrans, should convey
their prisoners to Tombuctoo rather than to Sego, may not perhaps be
quite so apparent as some of Adams's readers may require: but it would
be pushing the caution of incredulity to an unreasonable extreme to
disbelieve the asserted fact on that account alone. Desirous as we may
be supposed to be, to obviate the doubts of the most sceptical, we can
hardly venture to suggest any motives for this journey which are not supplied by the Narrative itself, or by some collateral testimony. Yet, we will
hazard this brief remark, that if it were the object of the Negroes to place
their prisoners in a situation where they would be at once secure from
rescue, yet accessible to the interference of their fellows for the purpose
of ransom, (for it must be remembered that the imprisoned Arabs did
not belong to a neighbouring state, but were a troop of marauders from
a distant tribe of the Desert) we can hardly conceive a more probable
course than that of conveying them to Tombuctoo.

We are aware that it may be objected to these remarks that they take
for granted, that Tombuctoo is a *Negro* state, and at least in amity with,
if not a dependency of, the King of Bambarra: and we shall probably
be told that Tombuctoo is under the dominion of the Moors, and that
Adams's account of it must consequently be untrue.

---

* See Park's First Mission, Appendix, 4to. p. lxxxix.
† Adams states his route to have lain through barren and uninhabited districts; and Park
speaking of Soudan generally, says, first Mission, 4to. p. 261, "the *borders* of the different
kingdoms were either very thinly peopled, or entirely deserted." See also his Account of
the country, east of Benowm, near the frontiers of Bambarra, p. 116, – "a sandy country." –
p. 121, "a hot sandy country covered with small stunted shrubs."

In reply to such an objection we would by no means deny that Adams's *entire* liberation of Tombuctoo from the tyranny of the Moors or Arabs, does present a difficulty, – especially with reference to Park's information on the same subject. But let us fairly examine how the question stands with respect to Adams's testimony on the one hand, and the evidence to which it is opposed on the other.

In Adams we find an individual relating travels and adventures, which are indeed singular and extraordinary, but are told with the utmost simplicity and bear strong internal marks of truth. Placed in a wide and untravelled region, where a mere narrator of fables might easily persuade himself that no one would trace or detect him, we find Adams resisting the temptation (no slight one for an ignorant sailor) of exciting the wonder of the credulous, or the sympathy of the compassionate, by filling his story with miraculous adventures, or overcharged pictures of suffering. In speaking of himself he assumes no undue degree of importance. He is rather subordinate to the circumstances of the story, than himself the prominent feature of it; and almost every part of his Narrative is strictly in nature, and unpretending.

Unexpectedly to this individual, and in his absence, an opportunity occurs of putting his veracity and his memory to the test, on many of the important points of his story: and the result of the experiment is, that all the facts to which the test will reach are, in substance, confirmed, that none are disproved. Again, we are enabled by the same opportunity to try his consistency with himself at different periods: and we find him, after an interval of more than *two* years, adhering in every material point to the story which he told on arriving from the Desert.

But a difficulty arises in the course of his Narrative: he states a fact which his hearers did not expect, and respecting which they had previously received evidence of a contrary tendency. Nevertheless this unexpected fact contains nothing marvellous in itself, nothing even extraordinary; nothing which can be conceived to afford the slightest temptation to such an individual to invent it: but it occurs simply, and in some measure even indirectly, in the chain of his evidence.

If this is admitted to be a fair statement of the circumstances under which Adams informs us that Tombuctoo is a *Negro* state: and if there is nothing suspicious in the internal character of this part of his evidence, we are not at liberty lightly to disbelieve it, because we think it improbable, or because it happens to want those collateral proofs by which other parts of his story have accidentally been confirmed: but, a manifest preponderance of unexceptionable evidence to the contrary, can alone justify us in rejecting it.

For this evidence we must again have recourse to Park's first Travels (for the Journal of his Second Mission contains only one incidental notice on the subject) and we shall therein find a general description of Tombuctoo as a *Moorish* state, which he prefaces in these words (p. 213).

Having thus brought my mind, after much doubt and perplexity, to a determination to return westward, I thought it incumbent on me, *before I left Silla*, to collect from the Moorish and Negro traders, all the information I could, concerning the further course of the Niger eastward, and the situation and extent of the kingdoms in its vicinage;" – and the following account of Tombuctoo is part of the information which he says he thus collected at Silla (p. 215).

To the north-east of Masina is situated the kingdom of Tombuctoo, the great object of European research; the capital of this kingdom being one of the principal marts for that extensive commerce which the Moors carry on with the Negroes. The hopes of acquiring wealth in this pursuit, and zeal for propagating their religion, have filled this extensive city with Moors and Mahomedan converts; and they are said to be more severe and intolerant in their principles than any other of the Moorish tribes in this part of Africa. I was informed by a venerable old Negro, that when he first visited Tombuctoo he took up his lodging at a sort of public inn, the landlord of which, when he conducted him into his hut, spread a mat upon the floor, and laid a rope upon it, saying, 'if you are a Mussulman you are my friend, – sit down; but if you are a Kafir you are my slave; and with this rope I will lead you to market.' The present King of Tombuctoo is named Abu Abrahima; he is reported to possess immense riches. His wives and concubines are said to be clothed in silk, and the chief officers of state live in considerable splendour. The whole expence of his government is defrayed, as I was told, by a tax upon merchandize, which is collected at the gates of the city.

To this account Major Rennell adds (doubtless on the verbal authority of Park), that the *greatest proportion* of the inhabitants were, nevertheless, *Negroes*. (Appendix, p. xc.)

We are now to examine under what circumstances the information contained in this description was procured. Of his arrival and residence at Silla, Park gives us very minute details. His journey thither from Sego had been hurried, and his situation extremely distressing during its whole course; until, on the 29th July, at four o'clock in the afternoon, he arrived at Moorzan, a fishing town on the northern bank of the Niger, "from whence," he says, "I was conveyed across the river to Silla, a large town, where I remained until it was quite dark under a tree surrounded by hundreds of people. Their language was very different from [that of] the other parts of Bambarra. With a great deal of entreaty the Dooty allowed me to come into his balloon to avoid the rain; but the place was very damp, and I had a smart paroxysm of fever during the night. Worn down by sickness and exhausted with hunger and fatigue, I was convinced by painful experience that the obstacles to my further progress were insurmountable." Happily for himself, and for that science whose limits his return was so widely to extend, – this determination was no sooner adopted than executed; and at *eight o'clock the next morning* he stepped into a canoe, and commenced his painful return to the westward; having only spent at Silla one wretched night in sickness and despondency.

It is impossible for any of our readers to view the unquenchable zeal and intrepidity of Park with higher admiration than we do; and merely to express our belief that before he thus resolved to return he "had made," as he states, "every effort to proceed which prudence could justify," would be to render, in our opinion, very imperfect justice to his unparalleled ardour of enterprise and enduring perseverance. Joining to these higher qualifications, admirable prudence in his intercourse with the natives, and a temper not to be ruffled by the most trying provocations, he exhibited on his first journey an union of qualities often thought incompatible; an union which in our days we fear we cannot expect to see again, directed to the same pursuits. We will further add, that to our feelings scarcely an individual of the age can be named, who has sunk, under circumstances of deeper interest than this lamented traveller: whether we consider the loss which geographical science has suffered in his death, or whether we confine our views to the blasted hopes of the individual, snatched away from his hard-earned, but unfinished, triumph; and leaving to others that splendid consummation which he so ardently sought to achieve. True it is, that the future discoverer of the termination of the Niger must erect the structure of his fame on the wide foundation with which his great predecessor has already occupied the ground: but though the edifice will owe its very existence to the labours of Park, yet another name than his will be recorded on the finished pile:

Hos ego – feci, tulit alter honores.*

Feeling, as we do, this unaffected interest in the fate and fame of Park, it is hardly necessary to preface our further remarks with the declaration, that there is not a tittle of the evidence given upon the authority of his own observation, which we should not feel it a species of sacrilege to dispute. But the case is different with respect to those details which he gives on *hear-say* evidence only, – which we may fairly, and which we ought, to try by the circumstances by which Park himself enables us to estimate their pretensions to accuracy.

Availing ourselves of this undeniable, and as we hope, not invidious, privilege, we shall find that a situation can hardly be imagined less favourable to the acquisition of authentic information, than that which Park describes during the single melancholy night which he passed at Silla. He had before told us (p. 339), that he was not well acquainted with the Foulah language spoken in Bambarra; and he informs us that he found the language of Silla "very different" even from that of the more western parts of the kingdom: but the extent of his difficulty in that respect may be gathered from what he relates of his arrival even at Sansanding, where he found the people "speaking a variety of different dialects all equally unintelligible" to him, and where he was obliged to have recourse to the interpretation of his Sego guide; who, however, did *not* accompany him in his further progress to Silla.

Obtaining therefore, his information from Negroes at more than two hundred miles distance from Tombuctoo, and probably through the medium of Negro interpreters, we cannot be surprised either that it should not be accurate in itself, or that, such as it was, it should not be very accurately understood. We believe there is no person, who can speak from his own experience on the subject, who will not bear testimony to the extreme uncertainty, not to say general inaccuracy, of the information to be obtained from the natives of Africa, whether

* ["The honors I earned, another carries off."]

Mohammedans or Pagans. Jealousy and suspicion of the objects of such inquiries on the one hand, and unobserving ignorance on the other, render both Negro and Moor alike unwilling, or unable, to disclose the secrets of the interior to any European. The whole of Park's communications leave not the smallest doubt respecting the temper of the trading *Moors* towards him. He also remarks, page 383, how little information is to be expected from a *Negro* trader of the countries through which he passes in search of gain, – of which he affords us the following striking instance in the commencement of his Journey. "I was referred," he says, p. 10, "to certain traders called Slatees. These were free black merchants of great consideration in those parts of Africa, who come down from the interior countries. But I soon discovered that very little dependence could be placed on the accounts which they gave: for *they contradicted each other in the most important particulars.*" To what degree the natives of Silla would have contradicted each other in their accounts of Tombuctoo, Park's short stay there could not have allowed him time to ascertain; even if his knowledge of their language had enabled him to understand their accounts as well as he did those of the Slatees on the Gambia.

This appears to be the state of the evidence which places the government of Tombuctoo in the hands of the Moors: and it really does appear to us, that it is at least neutralized by other evidence which may fairly be opposed to it; we mean, the uniform testimony of the natives of Barbary, who have traded to Tombuctoo. The reader will not have forgotten that all the accounts which Mr. Dupuis collected from such individuals, some of them men of high authority and credit amongst their countrymen, spoke of Tombuctoo as being now in all respects a Negro state. The hear-say evidence of Mr. Jackson goes decidedly to the same point; and although that gentleman may have given an injudicious importance to such testimony in his book, it ought not on that account alone to be entirely disregarded. The fact then being undeniable that the most creditable of the Barbary traders who cross the Desert do *not* assign the dominion of Tombuctoo to the Moors; and their testimony being apparently free from suspicion, because, in opposition to that which would most gratify their vanity, we cannot but think that it is at least as likely to be accurate as the reports of the Negroes whom Park consulted at Silla; taking, as we ought, into account, the disadvantages both of language and situation under which he consulted them, and not forgetting the reserve with which he himself teaches us to receive their testimony.*

Having, as we trust, said sufficient to satisfy the Reader, that there is nothing in the character of Adams's general evidence which can warrant the arbitrary rejection of his authority on points which are merely improbable; and having shewn that the evidence of others on the particular point at issue, is at least of doubtful preponderance, we will just say one word on the probability that the story of the "old Negro," at Silla, may be strictly true, with reference to the early period of which he may be supposed to speak, and yet that Adams's account may be equally true, of a very different state of things *now*.

It is well known that the vernacular histories, both traditionary and written, of the wars of the Moorish empire, agree in stating, that from the middle of the seventeenth century, Tombuctoo was occupied by the troops of the Emperors of Morocco; in whose name a considerable annual tribute was levied upon the inhabitants: but that the Negroes, in the early part of the last century, taking advantage of one of those periods of civil dissension and bloodshed which generally follow the demise of any of the Rulers of Barbary, did at length shake off the yoke of their northern masters, – to which the latter were never afterwards able again to reduce them.† Nevertheless, although the Emperors of Morocco (whose power even to the north of the Desert has been long on the decline) might be unable, at the immense distance which separates them from Soudan, to resume an authority which had once escaped from their hands; it is reasonable to suppose that the nearer tribes of Arabs would not neglect the opportunity thus afforded to them, of returning to their old habits of spoliation, and of exercising their arrogated superiority over their

---

* Several instances of the contradictory testimony of the Negroes occur in Park's Travels. *Jinnie*, for instance, is stated in his first Mission to be situated on the Niger; but on his second Journey he renounces that opinion on the apparently good authority of an old *Somonie* (canoe-man) "who had been seven times at Tombuctoo." This informant places it on the Ba Nimma in the sketch which is copied into Park's Journal; and the latter accordingly says, p. 166, "we shall not see Jinnie in going to Tombuctoo." But *Amadi Fatouma* confirms the first account which Park received, and says, in describing their voyage down the Niger from Silla, "we went in two days to Jinnie."

† [A Moroccan army actually conquered Timbuctoo in 1591; the civil unrest referred to involved factions of the Ruma (the nominal ruling class descended from the Moroccan invaders, though intermarried with the black population) who employed Bambaran mercenaries (see Saad 203).]

Negro neighbours;* and that this frontier state would thus become the theatre of continual contests, terminating alternately in the temporary occupation of Tombuctoo by the Arabs, and in their re-expulsion by the Negroes.†

We have seen this state of things existing in Ludamar to the west of Tombuctoo, where a Negro population is subjected to the tyranny of the Arab chieftain *Ali*; between whom and his southern neighbours of Bambarra and Kaarta we find a continual struggle of aggression and self-defence: and the well-known character of the Arabs would lead us to expect a similar state of things along the whole frontier of the Negro population. In the pauses of such a warfare we should expect to find no intermission of the animosity or precautions of the antagonist parties. The Arab, victorious, would be ferocious and intolerant even beyond his usual violence; and the *Koran* or the *halter*, as described by the old Negro of Silla, would probably be the alternatives which he would offer to his Negro guest: whilst the milder nature of the Negro would be content with such measures of precaution and self-defence as might appear suffi-cient to secure him from the return of the enemy whom he had expelled, – without excluding the peaceful trader; and under the re-established power of the latter, we might expect to find at Tombuctoo, precisely the same state of things as Adams describes to have existed in 1811.‡

The reserve with which we have seen grounds for receiving the testimony of the natives of Africa, may reasonably accompany us in

---

* Mr. Jackson was informed, (See his "Account of Marocco," 4to. p. 250) that previous to the Moorish occupation of Timbuctoo (noticed in the text) the inhabitants had been subject to continual depredations from the Arabs of the adjacent countries.

† To elucidate the state of things which we have here supposed, we need not go further than to the history of Europe in our own days. How often, during the successful ravages of the great *Arab chieftain* of Christendom, might we not have drawn from the experience of Madrid, or Berlin, or Vienna, or Moscow, the aptest illustration of these conjectures respecting Tombuctoo? And an African traveller (if so improbable a personage may be imagined) who should have visited Europe in these conjunctures, might very naturally have reported to his countrymen at home, that Russia, Germany, and Spain were but provinces of France; and that the common sovereign of all these countries resided sometimes in the *Escurial* and sometimes in the *Kremlin*!

‡ In the second volume of the Proceedings of the African Association, it is stated on the authority of *l'Hagi Mohammed Sheriffe*, that the King of Bambarra, at the head of a nu-merous army actually did take the government of Tombuctoo out of the hands of "the Moors," in the year 1800. There is, however, a disagreement between this Sheriffe and Park, respecting the name of the said King of Bambarra, whom the former calls *Woollo*. See Note 8, p. 72, respecting *Woollo* and *Mansong*.

our further comparative examination of their accounts, and those of Adams, respecting the population and external appearance of the city of Tombuctoo. Notwithstanding, therefore, the alleged splendour of its court, polish of its inhabitants, and other symptoms of refinement which some modern accounts (or speculations), founded on native reports, have taught us to look for, we are disposed to receive the humbler descriptions of Adams as approaching with much greater probability to the truth. Let us not, however, be understood, as rating too highly the value of a Sailor's reports. They must of necessity be defective in a variety of ways. Many of the subjects upon which Adams was questioned are evidently beyond the competency of such an individual fully to comprehend or satisfactorily to describe; and we must be content to reserve our final estimates of the morals, religion, civil polity, and learning (if they now have any) of the Negroes of Tombuctoo, until we obtain more conclusive information than we can possibly derive from our present informant. Sufficient, however, may be gathered from his story, to prepare us for a disappointment of many of the extravagant expectations which have been indulged respecting this boasted city.

And here, we may remark, that the relative rank of Tombuctoo amongst the cities of central Africa, and its present importance with reference to European objects, appear to us, to be considerably overrated. The descriptions of Leo in the *sixteenth* century, may indeed lend a colour to the brilliant anticipations in which some sanguine minds have indulged on the same subjects in the *nineteenth*; but with reference to the commercial pursuits of Europeans, it seems to have been forgotten, that the very circumstance which has been the foundation of the importance of Tombuctoo to the traders of Barbary, and consequently, of much of its fame amongst us, – its frontier situation on the verge of the Desert, at the extreme northern limits of the Negro population, – will of necessity have a contrary operation now; since a shorter and securer channel for European enterprise into the central regions of Africa, has been opened by the intrepidity and perseverance of Park, from the south-western shores of the Atlantic.

Independently of this consideration, there is great reason to believe that Tombuctoo has in reality declined of late, from the wealth and consequence which it appears formerly to have enjoyed. The existence of such a state of things as we have described in the preceding pages, the oppressions of the Moors, the resistance of the Negroes, the frequent change of masters, and the insecurity of property consequent upon these intestine struggles, would all lead directly and inevitably to this result. That they *have* led to it, may be collected from other sources than Adams. Even Park, to whom so brilliant a description of the city was given by some of his informants, was told by others, that it was surpassed in opulence and size, by *Haoussa, Walet,* and probably by *Jinnie.* Several instances also occur in both his Missions, which prove that a considerable trade from Barbary is carried on direct from the Desert, to Sego and the neighbouring countries, without ever touching at Tombuctoo; and this most powerful of the states of Africa in the sixteenth century, according to Leo, is now, in the nineteenth, to all appearance, a mere tributary dependency of a kingdom which does not appear to have been known to Leo, even by name.

Such a decline of the power and commercial importance of Tombuctoo, would naturally be accompanied by a corresponding decay of the city itself: and we cannot suppose that Adams's description of its external appearance will be rejected on account of its improbability, by those who recollect that Leo describes the habitations of the natives *in his time,* almost in the very words of the Narrative *now;* * and that the

---

* One of the numerous discordances between the different translations of Leo occurs in the passage here alluded to. The meaning of the *Italian* version is simply this, – that "the dwellings of the people of Tombuctoo are cabins or huts constructed with stakes covered with chalk (or clay) and thatched with straw." – "le cui case sono capanne fatte di pali coperte di creta co i cortivi di paglia." But the expression in the *Latin* translation, (which is closely followed by the old English translator, Pory), implies a state of previous splendour and decay, – "cujus domus omnes in tuguriola cretacea, stramineis tectis, *sunt mutatæ.*"

As we shall have occasion hereafter to point out another disagreement between the different versions of Leo, it may be expedient to inform some of our readers that the Italian translation here quoted, is described to have been made by Leo himself, from the original Arabic in which he composed his work; and he appears, by the following extract from the Preface of his Italian Editor, to have learnt that language, late in life, for this especial purpose. See the first volume of Ramusio's *Raccolto delle Navigatione e Viaggi.* Venetia, 1588.

"Così habitò poi in Roma il rimanente della vita sua, dove imparò la lingua Italiana e leggere e scrivere, e tradusse questo suo libro meglio ch' egli seppe di Arabo: il qual libro scritto da lui medesimo, dopo molti accidente pervenne nelle nostre mani; e noi con quella maggior diligenza che habbiamo potuto, ci siamo ingegnati con ogni fedeltà di farlo venir in luce nel modo che hora si legge." "Thus he dwelt in Rome the remainder of his life, where he learnt to read and write the Italian language, and translated his Book from the Arabic in the best manner that he was able," &c. &c. Supposing the Latin version to be a translation direct from the Arabic, that circumstance, and the preceding explanation, may afford a clue to the discordances to which we have alluded; but a reference to the Arabic original (which we believe is not to be found in any of

flourishing cities of Sego and Sansanding appear, from Park's accounts, to be built of mud, precisely in the same manner as Adams describes the houses of Tombuctoo.

But whatever may be the degree of Adams's coincidence with other authorities, in his descriptions of the population and local circumstances of Tombuctoo, there is at least one asserted fact in this part of his Narrative, which appears to be peculiarly his own; the existence, we mean, of a *considerable navigable river close to the city*. To the truth of this fact Adams's credit is completely pledged. On many other subjects, it is *possible* that his Narrative might be considerably at variance with the truth, by a mere defect of memory or observation, and without justifying any imputations on his veracity; but it is evident that no such latitude can be allowed to him on the present occasion; and that his statement respecting the *La Mar Zarah*, if not in substance true, must be knowingly and wilfully false.

Those of our readers who have attended to the progress of African discovery, will recollect that Tombuctoo, although it is placed by the concurring testimony of several authorities, in the immediate vicinity of the Niger, is nevertheless represented to lie at a certain distance from the river, not greater than a day's journey according to the highest statement, nor less according to the lowest, than twelve miles. To these statements, which may be presumed to approach very nearly to the truth, may be added, on pretty much the same authorities, that the town of *Kabra* on the Niger is the shipping port of Tombuctoo, lying at the aforesaid distance of twelve miles, or of a day's journey, from the city. And neither Park, nor any other written authority (including the *English* translation of Leo, of which we shall say more hereafter) make any express mention of a communication by water with the city of Tombuctoo itself. Adams, however, as has been already observed, cannot have been mistaken in so important a fact as that which he has here stated. He never discovered the least hesitation in his repeated assertions of the proximity of the

our public libraries) could alone enable us to ascertain, whether the fault lay solely in the Latin translator's ignorance of Arabic, or in Leo's probable imperfect acquaintance with the Italian. We will only add, that in the passages which we have compared, the Italian and French, and the Latin and English translations, respectively agree with each other.

[The narrative of "Giovanni Leone" first appeared as "Della Descrittione dell'Africa et delle cose notabile che ivi sono," in volume one of Giovanni Battista Ramusio's *Navigatione et Viaggi* (Venice, 1550). It was published in Latin and French in 1556.]

river to the town, or of his subsequent journey, for ten days, along its banks; and we cannot entertain the smallest doubt that the river exists precisely as he has described it. We shall presently shew to what extent the probability of this fact is countenanced by other considerations: and in the mean time, the two following alternatives present themselves, respecting the probable course of the river beyond the south-western point, to which Adams's observation of it extended; – either, that it turns immediately, at a considerable angle, to the southward, and falls into the Niger in the neighbourhood of *Kabra*: or, that continuing its south-westerly course from Tombuctoo, it empties itself into the lake *Dibbie*, possibly at the northern inlet which Park's informants described to him as one of the two channels* by which that lake discharges the waters of the Joliba. Neither of these suppositions are inconsistent with the existence, or the importance to Tombuctoo, of the port of *Kabra*: for if, on the one hand, the communication of Adams's river with the Niger, lies through the lake *Dibbie*, it will be seen by a glance at the Map, what a circuitous water-conveyance would be cut off by transporting from Tombuctoo across to Kabra, and shipping *there* such merchandize as should be destined for the *eastward;* and even if Kabra should be situated at the confluence of the *La Mar Zarah* and the Niger, its importance as the rendezvous, or point of contact with Tombuctoo, for all the canoes coming either up or down the stream, – from the west or from the east, – needs no explanation.

We will now endeavour to shew what degree of countenance or corroboration other authorities afford to the general fact, that there *is* a water communication between the Niger, at some point of its course, and the city of Tombuctoo.

In the first place, notwithstanding the distinct notice of *Kabra* both by Leo and Park, as the great resort of the trade of the Niger, and as the port of Tombuctoo, both these writers, especially Park in his last journey, speak indirectly on several occasions of sailing to and from Tombuctoo, in such a manner as fairly to imply that they or their informants, meant,

---

* The fact of a large lake like the *Dibbie* discharging its waters by *two streams flowing from distant parts of the lake*, and re-uniting after a separate course of a hundred miles in length, has always appeared to us extremely apocryphal: at least we believe, that the geography of the world does not afford a parallel case. The separation of rivers into various branches, in alluvial tracts on the sea coast, is a well known geological fact; but the case is essentially different with reference to a lake at so great a distance inland.

not the distant port of Kabra, but the city of Tombuctoo itself. The Barbary traders, also, whose reports are quoted by Mr. Dupuis, mention a river (which they, however, consider to be the Niger) as running close past the city; and we are inclined to pay the greater attention to these reports, because we have always considered it extremely improbable, that the greatest trading depot in the interior of Africa (and such undoubtedly *has been* the city of Tombuctoo) lying so near to all the advantages of an extensive water communication like the Niger, should yet have no point of immediate contact with the river itself, or with any of its tributary branches.

But there is, in the second place, strong reason to believe that Leo Africanus, the only writer who professes to describe Tombuctoo from personal observation, will really be found to have noticed such a river as Adams has made us acquainted with. A comparison of the original Arabic in which Leo wrote, with the translations, could alone enable us to speak with perfect confidence on this subject; but we trust that we shall be able, by a brief examination of the latter, to shew that our opinion is not a gratuitous speculation.

There are two passages in which Leo speaks of the relative situations of Tombuctoo and the Niger; the one in his chapter on Tombuctoo, and the other in that on Kabra; and our opinion of his meaning, on a joint consideration of both these passages, and of the ambiguity or contradiction of his translators, is this; *that Tombuctoo is situated upon a branch or arm of the Niger twelve miles distant from the principal stream.* We are aware that this construction is not warranted by the English translation,* which (following the Latin) states, that "it is situate within twelve miles of a certain branch of Niger;" but there is a peculiarity in the expression of the Latin translation, an ambiguity in that of the Italian version, and an inconsistency in both, between the passage in question and the context, which are open to much observation. The Italian translation (subject, always, to the explanation given in the Preface†) must be considered as the best authority; its words are these: "vicina a un ramo del Niger circa a dodici miglia;" the ambiguity of which has been faithfully preserved by the French translator, who with a total disregard

---

* "A Geographical Historie of Africa, written in Arabicke and Italian by John Leo, a More. Translated and collected by John Pory, lately of Gonville and Caius College." London 1600.

† See Note, pp. 119–20.

of idiom, and apparently little solicitude about meaning, thus copies it, word for word:* "prochain d'un bras du Niger environ douze mile." The Latin Editor, however, takes more pains to explain his conception of the passage, which he conveys in the following words: "in duodecimo miliario *a quodam fluviolo* situm fuit quod è Nigro flumine effluebat."

Conjointly with this passage, thus translated, we must take into our consideration the other passage in the Chapter on Kabra, to which we before alluded; wherein Leo states (without any variation between his translators) that Tombuctoo is distant *twelve miles from the Niger*.

Now, supposing, on the one hand, that the literal meaning of the translations of the former passage implies, that Tombuctoo is situated twelve miles from a smaller river communicating with the Niger; and being certain, on the other, that the latter passage really means that Tombuctoo lies exactly the same distance from the Niger itself; admitting, we say that there may be two distinct streams, each precisely twelve miles distant from the city; is it probable that Leo, wishing to designate to his readers, in the former passage, the exact position of Tombuctoo, by its distance from some given point, should select for that purpose, not the far-famed Niger itself, but an equally remote, a smaller, and a nameless stream? Surely not. There can hardly be a doubt, that it is to the Niger, and to the same point of the Niger, that he refers in both passages; that the translators, by a very trifling mistake in the Arabic idiom, or by a want of precision in their own, have given a different colour to his meaning; and that the smaller stream, the "ramo del Niger," and the "fluviolum," is really the *La Mar Zarah* seen by Adams.

We have been led into a more detailed examination of this part of the Narrative than we had at first anticipated; but the question is of considerable interest, not merely with reference to the verification of Adams's story, but as containing in itself a probable solution of the mistakes and doubts by which the real course of the Niger (from west to east) was for so many ages obscured. If the *La Mar Zarah* really communicates with the Niger, either at Kabra, or through the Lake Dibbie, by a south-westerly course from Tombuctoo, we have at once a probable explanation of the origin of Leo's mistake, (so ably exposed and corrected by Major Rennell), in placing Ginea (Gana) to the westward of Tombuctoo. That Leo was never on the Niger itself is sufficiently

* Lyons Ed. folio 1556. [*Historiale Description de l'Afrique*, translated by Jean Temporal.]

evident, for he states it to flow from east to west; but knowing that the traders who embarked at Tombuctoo for Ginea* proceeded, in the beginning of their course, to the west or south-west with the stream, (which would be the case on Adams's river) he was probably thus misled into a belief that the whole of the course, as well as the general stream of the Niger, lay in that direction.

We shall here close these imperfect Remarks; in which we have endeavoured to bring before the Reader such illustrations as are to be collected from collateral sources, of the most original, or most objectionable, of those points of Adams's story which are unsupported by direct external evidence. We might have greatly multiplied our examples of the indirect coincidences between Adams's statements, and other authorities, respecting the habits, customs, and circumstances of the inhabitants of central Africa; which would have added to the other incontestible evidences of the genuineness and accuracy of his relations. But the detail will have been already anticipated by most of Adams's readers, and would, we hope, be superfluous to all. We shall therefore conclude, by noticing only two important circumstances, respectively propitious and adverse to the progress of discovery and civilization, which the present Narrative decidedly confirms; viz. *the mild and tractable natures of the Pagan Negroes of Soudan, and their friendly deportment towards strangers,* on the one hand, – and, on the other, *the extended and baneful range of that great original feature of African society – Slavery.*

---

* Leo says, that the merchants of Tombuctoo sailed to Ginea during the inundations of the Niger in the months of July, August, and September; which seems to imply, that at other seasons there was *not* a continuous passage by water. He also says in another place, that when the Niger rises, the waters flow through certain canals to the city (Tombuctoo). As these passages when considered together, seem to infer that the navigation of the river of Tombuctoo (the *La Mar Zarah*) is obstructed by shallows during the dry season, they afford grounds for believing that Adams, when he saw that river (which was in the dry season) may have had good reasons for doubting which way the stream really ran.

APPENDIX NO. I

At a time when the civilization and improvement of Africa, and the extension of our intercourse with the natives of that long-neglected country, seem to be among the leading objects of the British government and nation, – and when, with these views, great exertions are making to procure information respecting the interior of that vast and unknown continent; the following account of Tombuctoo, and the trade and navigation of the Niger, may perhaps prove not altogether uninteresting. It was procured on a journey to *Galam* in about the year 1764, for a gentleman who was then Governor of *Senegal*, by a person who acted as his Arabic interpreter.

*Après bien des difficultés, j'ai enfin trouvé un homme qui est revenu de *Tombuctoo* depuis peu, qui m'a mieux instruit du pays que personne. J'ai

---

* It may seem superfluous in the present enlightened age, to give a translation of a *French* paper; but there may still be some of our readers to whom the following, if not necessary, may be convenient.

After many difficulties, I have at length found a man lately returned from *Tombuctoo*, from whom I have obtained better information of the country than from any other person. I have spoken to several merchants, who have reported some things to me, but I confide most in this last, who is lately returned, who has assured me that the vessels which navigate in the river of Tombuctoo do not come from the sea; that they are vessels constructed at Tombuctoo, which are sewed either with cordage or with the bark of the cocoa tree, he does not exactly know which; that these vessels only go by tracking and by oars (or paddles).

He says, that the inhabitants of the city of Tombuctoo are Arabs, that it is a large city, and that the houses have three or four stories. He says, that the caravans which come to Tombuctoo, come from the side of Medina, and bring stuffs, white linens, and all sorts of merchandise. That these caravans are composed only of camels, that they stop at the distance of half a league from Tombuctoo, and that the people of Tombuctoo go there to buy the goods, and take them into the city; afterwards, that they equip their vessels to

parlé à plusieurs marchands, qui m'en ont compté quelque chose, mais je m'en rapporte mieux au dernier, qui en vient depuis peu; qui m'a assuré que les bâtimens, qui naviguent dans la rivière de Tombuctoo, ne viennent point de la grande mer; que ce sont des bâtimens construits à Tombuctoo, qui sont cousûs soit avec du cordage, soit avec de l'écorce de coco, il ne le sait pas au juste; que ces bâtimens ne vont qu'au traite et à l'aviron.

Il dit que ce sont des Arabes qui habitent la ville de Tombuotoo, que c'est une grande ville, que les maisons ont trois ou quatre étages. Il dit, que les caravanes qui viennent à Tombuctoo, viennent du côté de Medine,* et apportent toutes sortes de marchandises, des étoffes, et des toiles blanches; que ces caravanes ne sont composées que de chameaux; qu'elles s'arrêtent à une demi lieue de Tombuctoo, et que de là, les gens de Tombuctoo vont acheter les marchandises, et les apportent dans la ville; ensuite, qu'ils arment leurs bâtimens pour les envoyer à *Genné*, qui est une autre ville sous la domination de Tombuctoo, et que les habitans de Tombuctoo y ont des correspondans. Ceux de Genné arment à leur tour leurs bâtimens, et y mettent les marchandises qu'ils ont reçus des bâtimens de Tombuctoo, et font monter leurs bâtimens à leur tour, et leur font monter la rivière. Il est à remarquer, que la séparation des deux rivières est à une demi lieue de Genné, et Genné se trouve entre les deux rivières, comme une isle. Une de ces rivières court dans la *Bambarra*, et l'autre va a *Setoo*, qui est un pays habité par un peuple rougeâtre, qui fait sans cesse la guerre aux Bambarras. Lorsqu'ils vont a la guerre contre les Bambarras, ils sont toujours cinq mois dehors. Après que les barques de Genné ont monté la rivière bien avant, ils trouvent la chûte de *Sootasoo*; où ils s'arretent, et

---

send them to *Genné*, which is another city under the dominion of Tombuctoo, and that the inhabitants of Tombuctoo have correspondents there. The people of Genné in their turn equip their vessels, and put into them the merchandise which they have received from the people of Tombuctoo, with which they ascend the river. It is to be remarked that the separation of the two rivers is at half a league from Genné, and Genné is situated between the two rivers like an island. One of these rivers runs into *Bambarra* and the other goes to *Betoo*, which is a country inhabited by a people of a reddish colour, who are always at war with the Bambarras. When they go out to war against the Bambarras, they are always five months absent. After the barks of Genné have gone a great distance up the river, they arrive at the fall of *Sootasoo*, where they stop and can proceed no further. There they unload their salt and other merchandise, and carry them upon the backs of asses, and upon their heads to the other side of the fall, where they find the large boats of the Negroes, which they freight; and ascend the river to the country of the *Mandingoes*, who are called *Malins*, and who are near to the rock *Gouvina*.

* It appears from Mr. Ledyard's and Mr. Lucas's communications to the African Association, that the caravans from Mecca, Medina, and all Egypt, arrive at Tombuctoo, by the same route as those from Mesurata, going round by Mourzouk. Proceedings of the African Association, 4to. [London: C. Macrae,] 1790, pp. 38, 87 [Hallett, *Records* 60 and 67–8].

ne peuvent plus passer. Là ils déchargent leur sel et leurs marchandises, et les portent à l'autre côté de la chûte à dos d'ânes, et sur leurs têtes. Là ils trouvent les grandes pirogues des Negres, qu'ils fraitent, et montent la rivière avec ces pirogues jusqu'à chez les *Mandings*, qui s'appellent *Malins*, qui sont proche du roche *Gouvina*.

The gentleman, for whom these particulars were collected, states, that he has always had the greatest confidence in their correctness; not only on account of the character and talents of the person employed, but also from the means which he had, during a residence of three or four years at Senegal, to verify all the most material points in them, upon the information of others; which he lost no opportunity of obtaining. In his account of the position of Genné, the junction of the two rivers near to it, the course of one of these rivers from Betoo or Badoo, and *the course of the Niger itself, at that time* (1764) *generally supposed to be from east to west*; the Arabic interpreter has been proved, by the information obtained through Mr. Park, to be correct; and his representation of the trade upon the Niger is accurately confirmed by Mr. Park, in his conversation with the ambassadors of the King of Bambarra;* except that he carries it beyond Mr. Park's report.

If the interpreter's report be correct, it would seem that the Niger is navigable to a much greater distance westward, than it is represented to be in any of the existing maps of that part of Africa; nor does there appear to be any authority to oppose to this theory, except the information which Major Rennell states Mr. Park to have received, when at Kamalia, on his return from his first journey; that the source of the Niger was at a bearing of south, a very little west, seven journies distant, for which Mr. Park calculated one hundred and eight geographical miles.†
The name of the place was said to be *Sankari*, which the Major supposes to correspond with the *Song* of D'Anville. But this account is too vague to be implicitly relied upon, in a country, where men travel, as Mr. Park observes,‡ only for the acquirement of wealth; and pay but little

---

* "We sell them (the articles brought by the Moors) to the Moors; the Moors bring them to Tombuctoo, where they sell them at a higher rate. The people of Tombuctoo sell them to the people of Jinnie at a still higher price; and the people of Jinnie sell them to you." Park's Last Mission, 4to. p. 268. [This passage appears on page 152 of the first edition of *Park's Journal of a Mission to Africa in the Year 1805* (1815).]
† Appendix, First Journey, page xliv.
‡ Idem, page 214.

attention to the course of rivers, or the geography of countries. In other respects, the idea that the Niger is navigable to a considerable distance above Bammakoo, instead of being contradicted, is much supported by all the information which is to be collected from Mr. Park's Journeys, and particularly his Last Mission; though to a person looking only at the Map attached to his Notes, the fact would appear to be otherwise.

The Arabic interpreter speaks of a trade and extensive navigation above the falls of *Sootasoo*, which must be to the westward; as he states it to extend into the country of a Mandingo nation called *Malins*,* whose territories approach near to the rock Gouvina. His account is supported by the fact, that Bammakoo is at the commencement of the Mandingo Nations; but the representation of the river above it, according to our maps, gives no idea of the further voyage which he speaks of. Mr. Park does not notice the existence of the falls of Sootasoo, but from his description of the rapids at Bammakoo, there is every reason to believe that they are the same.† He tells us, that at that‡ season (21st August) the river was navigable over the rapids. We are consequently to understand, that at other seasons it is not navigable over them even downwards; and that, although he avoided the principal falls, where, as he says, the water breaks with considerable noise in the middle of the river, and paddled down one of the branches near the shore; still the velocity was such, as to make him sigh.§

Major Rennell, who appears to have obtained from Mr. Park information upon geographical matters, far beyond that which is to be collected by the mere perusal of his first Journey, states, that¶ the Niger first becomes navigable at Bammakoo, or perhaps, that it is only navigable upwards to that point in a continuous course from Tombuctoo. His

---

* We have no account of the people here spoken of under the name of *Malins*, and have ascertained by Mr. Park's discoveries, that the river does not actually approach the rock *Gouvina*; but it should be observed that the rock was the only point in that part of Africa to which the interpreter could refer as known to the person to whom his communication was addressed. The Mandingo nations commence to the eastward at about Bammakoo, and extend some distance to the north-west, and to the west almost to the sea coast. From this circumstance therefore, as well as from the mention of the rock Gouvina, it is evident that the country spoken of must be to the west of Bammakoo.

† The country in which Bammakoo is situated, and a very extensive tract to the westward, is stated by D'Anville to be inhabited by a people called *Soosos*.

‡ Last Mission, page 257 [page 144 in the first edition].

§ Idem, page 238 [p. 142].

¶ First Journey, Appendix, xliv.

latter supposition is most probably correct, as it does not militate against the existence of a navigation, not continuous, beyond, Bammakoo, nor against the fact proved by Mr. Park in his second mission, that at particular seasons the rapids may be passed downwards. It is also clear from Park, that there is, at least to a certain distance, above Bammakoo, a populous and trading country; as it was at Kancaba (called in the maps Kaniaba)* that Karfa Taura bought his slaves before proceeding to the coast. It is called a large town on the banks of the Niger, and a great slave market; and is placed by Major Rennell (doubtless on the authority of Park) above Bammakoo.† Most of the slaves, Mr. Park says, who are sold at Kancaba, come from Bambarra: for Mansong, to avoid the expense and danger of keeping all his prisoners at Sego, commonly sends them in small parties to be sold at the different trading towns; and as Kancaba is much resorted to by merchants, it is always well supplied with slaves, which are sent thither up the Niger in canoes. It cannot be supposed that this resort of merchants, is from places down the river; that they leave the great markets of Sego and Sansanding, to labour over the rapids to Kancaba; or that the slaves would be sent there to be bought by merchants who could receive them at places so much nearer. It must be for a trade down the river from populous countries situated *above* Kancaba, that they are sent there. Nor is it easy to believe, that a river, which Mr. Park states to be at Bammakoo, a mile across, and to be interrupted in its navigation only by a local cause, should not be navigable above that cause: or that a stream, which he states to be larger even there (at Bammakoo) than either the Gambia or the Senegal, should be distant from its source only 108 geographical miles, and draw its supplies from a country, which, by the map attached to Park's last mission, appears to be only 40 or 50 G. miles in breadth; when the Senegal has a course of not less than 600 G. miles, measured by the same map, across to the rock Gouvina, and from that to its mouth, without making any further allowance for its windings; and drains for its support, a country extending, according to the same authority, in breadth, not less than 300 G. miles. It will of course occur to any person, looking at the maps attached to Park's Journeys, that the places marked out as the sources of the Senegal and Gambia, preclude the possibility of the Niger's

---

* Idem. p. 275. [This actually appears on p. 257 in Park's *Travels*.]
† Idem, Major Rennell's Maps.

extending farther to the westward than is there represented; but upon a careful perusal of Park's Last Mission, there seems strong ground to believe, that the framers of his map, proceeding upon the old idea that the Senegal and Gambia take their rise in the Kong mountains, have here fallen into an error. It would appear that there are two distinct ranges of mountains, commencing at the *Foota Jalla* hills. The *Kong* mountains running to the east, but in a line curved considerably to the south, and supposed to be the greatest mountains in Africa; the other proceeding in a more direct line and increasing in its elevation, as it extends towards the east, seems to approach nearly to its full height at the Konkodoo mountains, and bending or returning to the North and N. W. beyond Toniba, where Mr. Park crossed it, to give birth to all the streams, which, united, form the Senegal.

Of the sources of the Gambia, we have no particular account, but it seems probable that these two ranges of mountains are united at their western extremity, and that the Gambia does not extend beyond this union; an idea in which there is ground to believe that Mr. Park would have concurred from expressions in two of his letters to Sir Joseph Banks, the first dated from Kayee, River Gambia, 26 April, 1805.* "The course of the Gambia is certainly not so long as is laid down in the charts." The second letter is dated Badoo, near Tambacunda, May 28th, 1805.† "The course of the Gambia is laid down on my chart too much to the south; I have ascertained nearly its whole course." The removal of the river more to the north by leaving a larger space for its course from the mountains, renders it more probable that it should be terminated at the point herein supposed; and if its sources were as distant as they are represented to be in our maps, it is difficult to imagine that Mr. Park could, as he states, have ascertained nearly its whole course.

The position of the northern range of hills is described by Mr. Park with considerable accuracy at Dindikoo,‡ where he speaks of the inhabitants looking from their tremendous precipices over that wild and woody plain, which extends from the Falemé to the Black River. This plain, he says, is, in extent from north to south, about forty miles; the range of hills to the south seems to run in the same direction as

---

* The Last Mission, p. 62 [p. lxii in the first edition].
† Idem, page 69 [p. lxix].
‡ Last Mission, page 176 [p. 60].

those of Konkodoo, viz. from east to west. The framers of his map have made them run north and south, because they could not otherwise carry the sources of the rivers beyond them. Dindikoo was on the northern range of hills, and supposing the southern range to be, as he states, distant about forty miles, it will be found sufficient to account for the size assigned to all the rivers passed by Mr. Park in his route from the Gambia.

The first of these is the *Falemé* river, which he had already crossed at Madina.* No particular account is given of the size of this river, or of the manner of passing it; but in his former journey, when he crossed it about the same place, he says,† that it was easily forded, being only about two feet deep. In his last mission,‡ he says, its course is from the south-east, the distance to its source six ordinary days' travel. Assigning to it this course, its source will not be beyond the hills, but the compilers of the map attached to his Journal have given it a course much more nearly south, and have placed its source, even in this direction, far beyond six days' journey by their own scale; and without making any allowance for the time, and the distance in an horizontal line, lost in travelling over a mountainous country. The next river is the *Ba Lee*, too insignificant to be noticed. The next the *Ba Fing*, the greatest of the rivers which form the Senegal. This was passed at Konkromo by canoes. He gives us no account of the course of this river or the distance to its sources, but merely says,§ "it is here a large river quite navigable; it is swelled at this time about two feet, and flows at the rate of three knots per hour." When fully flooded, its course must be much more rapid, as in his first journey,¶ he crossed it by a bridge, formed of two trees, tied together by the tops; and adds, that this bridge is carried away every year by the swelling of the river. Running, as we collect, from both Mr. Park's journies, but particularly the first, as this river does, at the foot of a high ridge of mountains,ǀ and through a country, which he calls every where "hilly, and rugged, and grand beyond any thing he had seen;"** and allowing for its

---

* Idem, page 167 [pp. 51–2].
† First Journey, page 346.
‡ Last Mission, page 167 [p. 51].
§ Last Mission, pages 193, 194, 195 [p. 79].
¶ First Journey, page 338.
ǀ First Journey, page 340.
** Second Mission, page 192 [p. 76], and First Journey, page 337, et passim.

necessary sinuosity in such a country, and its receipt of numerous smaller streams in passing through it, there can be no difficulty in accounting for it, such as described by Mr. Park at Konkromo, by placing its sources in the hills already described; for neither his descriptions of a river, which being flooded two feet is quite navigable, nor of one, which could be crossed by so simple a bridge, impress us with the idea of a mighty stream, or of one far distant from its source. It is also fair to presume, that this and the other rivers, forming the Senegal, have a part of their course at, or parallel with, the foot of these hills, collecting the waters which descend from them. The next river is crossed near to Madina, and is represented in the map as formed by the confluence of the *Furkomah* and *Boki* rivers, and not very greatly inferior either in magnitude or in the length of its course even to the Ba Fing. All that Mr. Park says of this great river, is, "at eleven o'clock, crossed a stream, like a mill-stream, running north"!* The last river we come to, is the *Ba Woolima* which its various streams, the Wonda, Ba Lee, Kokoro, &c.; which, after what has been said of the Ba Fing, scarcely require to be noticed; except, that by their windings and the numerous streams crossed in each day's journey, they serve to shew the small distance, in which a considerable river may be formed in such a country. They are all clearly bounded by the chain of mountains herein described, which, a little further eastward, bends or returns (as already observed) to the north and north-west to the kingdom of Kasson,† and forms the eastern angle of the triangle, described by Major Rennell, in his Appendix to Park's first Journey; a description corresponding very accurately with that here supposed; though the Major, in his Map, still carries the sources of the Senegal (the Ba Fing, &c.) across to the Kong mountains, and represents the mountains in that part of the country as running north and south, and extending southward to the same chain of mountains; and it is in this point only, that there appears to be reason for doubting his correctness. In Konkodoo, we have this northern range clearly described as running east and west at a distance of about forty miles. By the necessity for avoiding the difficulties of the Jalonka wilderness, we there lose sight of them for a time; but when we find them again at Toniba, they are there also running east and west, for Mr. Park crossed them in a course nearly from north to

---

* Second Mission, page 197 [p. 81].
† First Journey, Appendix, page xix.

south,* and we have endeavoured to shew, that the magnitude of the rivers passed in the intermediate space, is not such as necessarily to induce a belief, that the mountains do not there preserve the same direction; especially as the course of the greatest of these rivers is not given, whether from the south, or rather from the eastward of south, which seems the most probable; as the Major represents (and we believe with correctness), that the eastern level of the country is here the highest.

It is in the plain left between the Kong mountains and this ridge, which, according to Park, separates the Niger from the remote branches of the Senegal;† that the Niger has its course, "rolling its immense stream along the plain,"‡ and washing the southern base of these mountains.§ The extent of this plain to the west, and the distance to which the Niger is navigable through it, are points not yet known, and which, although of the very utmost importance to the prosecution of our discoveries or the extension of our trade in the interior, it does not appear that any attempt has yet been made to ascertain. From its situation between two such ranges of mountains, it may be presumed, that the plain is of great elevation; and from the report of the Arabic interpreter, supported by Mr. Park's account of Kaniaba or Kancaba, there is reason to believe, that the Niger is navigable through it, to a considerable distance westward. The information received by Mr. Park at Kamalia may still have been correct: one of the principal streams, forming the Niger, may have its source at the place described to him; another may flow down this plain from the westward, collecting in its course all the streams that run from the south side of the mountains which give birth to the Senegal, and from the northern declivity of the Kong mountains. In this way we have no difficulty in accounting for the magnitude of the Niger at Bammakoo; which we have already observed that it is impossible to do, by the course hitherto assigned to it; especially when it is considered that that course is nearly at a right angle with the Kong mountains, and consequently a great part of it through the plain, where it is not likely to receive much additional supply.

If these conjectures be well founded, it would seem that our pursuit should be, instead of endeavouring to perform the difficult, dangerous,

* Second Mission, pages 253, 254, 255 [p. 139].
† Idem, p. 256 [p. 140].
‡ Idem, page 256 [p. 140].
§ Idem, page 231 [p. 115].

and expensive operation of transporting a caravan to the remote station of Bammakoo; to search for the nearest point to the westward, at which the Niger is navigable; that we may commence our discoveries and trade by navigation as near as possible to the Western Ocean. With this view, the Gambia should be immediately occupied by this country; and indeed this, under any circumstances, would seem to be a wise measure, that we may not, at the moment that our discoveries begin to lead to results of value, find, that the right of navigating that river is disputed with us by the prior establishment of some rival and more active European nation.

An establishment should then be formed as high up that river as its navigation, and the state of the country will permit; and from this point, there could be no great difficulty or expense in sending a mission into the interior, to the south-east, to seek for the sources of the Niger, and the extent of its navigation to the westward. Nor can there be any question upon the possibility of establishing a settlement high up in the Gambia, from whence to commence our discoveries, after the example of the French Fort of St. Joseph at Galam on the Senegal. Galam is 150 leagues in a direct line from the mouth of the Senegal, or by the course of the river 350 leagues.* The fort was many years in the possession of the French; and at the time its garrison was removed after the capture of Senegal by this country in the year 1763, the officer in charge of it had been stationed there twenty-four years, the next in command sixteen, and others very long periods: the natives were so far from shewing any hostile disposition to the French trade upon the river, that they gave to it every possible protection and encouragement; as they were fully sensible that it was for their interest to support it: the navigation of the river was secure, and the officers at the fort upon the most friendly footing with the inland powers.

By commencing our operations from the Gambia in the manner proposed, we should have the important advantage of experiencing the least possible opposition from our rivals and inveterate enemies, the Moors; whose influence naturally diminishes in proportion as we recede from

---

* These distances are given according to a most beautiful and correct Chart of the River Senegal, drawn from an actual survey, which was in the possession of the gentleman here alluded to as having been in the government of Senegal, and was taken from him by the French, by whom he was captured on a voyage to England.

the Desert: and if we were once established on the Niger, our superior advantages in trade, would render nugatory any attempts which they might make to resist our further progress.

P.S. The writer of this Memoir thinks it right to disclaim all pretensions to any superior or exclusive knowledge of African geography. There appeared to him to be something inconsistent in the magnitude of the Niger as represented by Mr. Park at Bammakoo, and its sources according to our maps; and being in possession of a paper which seemed to throw some little light upon the subject, he has ventured to give it to the public, accompanied with a few remarks; and will feel highly gratified, if they should have the effect of engaging the attention of some person capable of doing justice to an inquiry which is certainly interesting and important.

APPENDIX NO. II[*]

The whole of the population of Western Barbary may be divided into three great classes (exclusive of the Jews) viz. Berrebbers, Arabs, and Moors. The two former of these are in every respect distinct races of people, and are each again subdivided into various tribes or communities; the third are chiefly composed of the other two classes, or of their descendants, occasionally mixed with the European or Negro races.

In the class of Beerebbers, of which I shall first treat, I include all those who appear to be descendants of the original inhabitants of the country before the Arabian conquest; and who speak several languages, or dialects of the same language, totally different from the Arabic. The subdivisions of this class are – 1st. the *Errifi*, who inhabit the extensive mountainous province of that name on the shores of the Mediterranean; 2dly. the *Berrebbers of the Interior*, who commence on the southern confines of Errif, and extend to the vicinity of Fez and Mequinez, occupying all the mountains and high lands in the neighbourhood of those cities; 3dly. the *Berrebbers of Middle Atlas*; and, 4thly. the *Shilluh* of Suse and Hàhà, who extend from Mogadore southward to the extreme boundaries of the dominions of the Cid Heshem, and from the sea coast to the eastern limits of the mountains of Atlas.

---

[*] This original and interesting Sketch of the *Population of Western Barbary* grew out of some observations made by the Editor to Mr. Dupuis, upon the frequent indiscriminate use of the names of *Arab* and *Moor*, in speaking apparently of the same people: and the explanation of these terms (as well as of the term *Shilluh*, see p. 101, Note 56) having led Mr. Dupuis into a longer detail than could be conveniently comprised in a Note on the Narrative, he kindly consented, at the Editor's request, to extend his Remarks to *all* the classes of the inhabitants of the Empire of Morocco; and the Editor is happy to have permission to present these Remarks, in their present entire form, to the reader.

The *Errifi* are a strong and athletic race of people, hardy and enterprising; their features are generally good, and might in many cases be considered handsome, were it not for the malignant and ferocious expression which marks them in common with the Berrebber tribes in general, but which is peculiarly striking in the *eye* of an Errif. They also possess that marked feature of the Berrebber tribes, a scantiness of beard; many of the race, particularly in the south, having only a few straggling hairs on the upper lip, and a small tuft on the chin. They are incessantly bent on robbing and plundering; in which they employ either open violence or cunning and treachery, as the occasion requires; and they are restrained by no checks either of religion, morals, or humanity. However, to impute *to them in particular*, as distinct from other inhabitants of Barbary, the crimes of theft, treachery, and murder, would certainly be doing them great injustice; but I believe I may truly describe them as more ferocious and faithless than any other tribe of Berrebbers.

The *Berrebbers of the districts* of Fez, Mequinez, and the mountains of Middle Atlas, strongly resemble the Errifi in person, but are said to be not quite so savage in disposition. They are a warlike people, extremely tenacious of the independence which their mountainous country gives them opportunities of asserting, omit no occasion of shaking off the controul of government, and are frequently engaged in open hostilities with their neighbours the Arabs, or the Emperor's black troops. They are, as I am informed, the only tribes in Barbary who use the bayonet. The districts which they inhabit are peculiarly interesting and romantic; being a succession of hills and vallies well watered and wooded, and producing abundance of grain and pasturage.

The *Shilluh*, or Berrebbers of the south of Barbary, differ in several respects from their brethren in the north. They are rather diminutive in person; and besides the want of beard already noticed, have in general an effeminate tone of voice. They are, however, active and enterprising. They possess rather more of the social qualities than the other tribes, appear to be susceptible of strong attachments and friendships, and are given to hospitality. They are remarkable for their attachment to their petty chieftains; and the engagements or friendships of the latter are held so sacred that I never heard of an instance of depredation being committed on travellers furnished with their protection, (which it is usual to purchase with a present) or on any of the valuable caravans which are continually passing to and fro through their territory, between Barbary and Soudan. However, the predominant feature of their character is self-interest; and although in their dealings amongst strangers, or in the towns, they assume a great appearance of fairness and sincerity, yet they are not scrupulous when they have the power in their own hands: and like the other Berrebbers, they are occasionally guilty of the most atrocious acts of treachery and murder, not merely against Christians (for that is almost a matter of course with all the people of their nation) but even against Mohammedan travellers, who have the imprudence to pass through their country without having previously secured the protection of one of their chiefs.

As the Shilluh have been said to be sincere and faithful in their friendships, so are they on the other hand, perfectly implacable in their enmities and insatiable in their revenge.* Their country produces grain in abundance, cattle, wax, almonds, and various valuable articles of trade.

I have already said, that the languages of all the *Berrebber* tribes are totally different from the Arabic; but whether they are corrupted dialects

---

* The following anecdote, to the catastrophe of which I was an eye-witness, will exemplify in some degree these traits of their character. A Shilluh having murdered one of his countrymen in a quarrel, fled to the Arabs from the vengeance of the relations of his antagonist; but not thinking himself secure even there, he joined a party of pilgrims and went to Mecca. From this expiatory journey he returned at the end of eight or nine years to Barbary; and proceeding to his native district, he there sought (under the sanctified name of *El Haje*, the *Pilgrim*, – a title of reverence amongst the Mohammedans) to effect a reconciliation with the friends of the deceased. They, however, upon hearing of his return, attempted to seize him; but owing to the fleetness of his horse he escaped and fled to Mogadore, having been severely wounded by a musket ball in his flight. His pursuers followed him thither; but the Governor of Mogadore hearing the circumstances of the case, strongly interested himself in behalf of the fugitive, and endeavoured, but in vain, to effect a reconciliation. The man was imprisoned; and his persecutors then hastened to Morocco to seek justice of the Emperor. That prince, it is said, endeavoured to save the prisoner; and to add weight to his recommendation, offered a pecuniary compensation in lieu of the offender's life; which the parties, although persons of mean condition, rejected. They returned triumphant to Mogadore, with the Emperor's order for the delivery of the prisoner into their hands: and having taken him out of prison, they immediately conveyed him without the walls of the town, where one of the party, loading his musket before the face of their victim, placed the muzzle to his breast and shot him through the body; but as the man did not immediately fall, he drew his dagger and by repeated stabbing put an end to his existence. The calm intrepidity with which this unfortunate Shilluh stood to meet his fate, could not be witnessed without the highest admiration; and, however much we must detest the blood-thirstiness of his executioners, we must still acknowledge that there is something closely allied to nobleness of sentiment in the inflexible perseverance with which they pursued the murderer of their friend to punishment, without being diverted from their purpose by the strong inducements of self-interest.

of the ancient Punic, Numidian, or Mauritanian, I must leave to others to determine. That of the Errifi, I am told, is peculiar to themselves. It has also been asserted that the language of the Berrebbers of the interior, and of the Shilluh, are totally distinct from each other; but I have been assured by those who are conversant with them, that although differing in many respects, they are really dialects of the same tongue.

Like the Arabs, the *Berrebbers* are divided into numerous petty tribes or clans, each tribe or family distinguishing itself by the name of its patriarch or founder. The authority of the chiefs is usually founded upon their descent from some sanctified ancestor, or upon a peculiar eminence of the individual himself in Mohammedan zeal or some other religious qualification.

With the exception already noticed, (that the *Berrebbers of the North* are of a more robust and stouter make than the *Shilhuh*) a strong family likeness runs through all their tribes. Their customs, dispositions, and national character are nearly the same; they are all equally tenacious of the independence which their local positions enable them to assume; and all are animated with the same inveterate and hereditary hatred against their common enemy, the Arab. They invariably reside in houses, or hovels, built of stone and timber, which are generally situated on some commanding eminence, and are fortified and loop-holed for self-defence. Their usual mode of warfare is to surprise their enemy, rather than overcome him by an open attack; they are reckoned the best marksmen, and possess the best firearms in Barbary, which renders them a very destructive enemy wherever the country affords shelter and concealment; but although they are always an over-match for the Arabs when attacked in their own rugged territory, they are obliged, on the other hand, to relinquish the plains to the Arab cavalry, against which the Berrebbers are unable to stand on open ground.

The Arabs of Barbary, are the direct descendants of the invaders of the country, who about the year 400 of the Hegira, according to their own histories, completed the conquest of the whole of the North of Africa, dispersing or exterminating the nations which either attempted to oppose their progress, or refused the Mohammedan creed. During the dreadful ravages of this invasion, the surviving inhabitants, unable to resist their ferocious enemy (whose cavalry doubtless contributed to give them their decided superiority) fled to the mountains; where they have since continued to live under the names of Berrebber, Shilluh,

&c. a distinct people, retaining their hereditary animosity against their invaders.

The Arabs, who now form so considerable a portion of the population of Barbary, and whose race (in the Sheriffe line) has given Emperors to Morocco ever since the conquest, occupy all the level country of the Empire; and many of the tribes penetrating into the Desert have extended themselves even to the confines of Soudan. In person they are generally tall and robust, with fine features and intelligent countenances. Their hair is black and strait, their eyes large, black and piercing, their noses gently arched, their beards full and bushy, and they have invariably good teeth. The colour of those who reside in Barbary is a deep but bright brunette, essentially unlike the sallow tinge of the Mulatto. The Arabs of the Desert are more or less swarthy according to their proximity to the Negro states; until, in some tribes, they are found entirely black, but without the woolly hair, wide nostril, and thick lip which peculiarly belong to the African Negro.

The Arabs are universally cultivators of the earth or breeders of cattle, depending on agricultural pursuits alone for subsistence. To use a common proverb of their own, "the earth is the Arab's portion." They are divided into small tribes or families, as I have already stated with respect to the Berrebbers; – each seperate tribe having a particular Patriarch or Head by whose name they distinguish themselves, and each occupying its own separate portion of territory. They are scarcely ever engaged in external commerce; dislike the restraints and despise the security of residence in towns; and dwell invariably in tents made of a stuff woven from goats' hair and the fibrous root of the *palmeta*. In some of the provinces their residences form large circular encampments, consisting of from twenty to a hundred tents, where they are governed by a *shieck* or magistrate of their own body. This officer is again subordinate to a *bashaw* or governor appointed by the Emperor, who resides in some neighbouring town. In these encampments there is always a tent set apart for religious worship, and appropriated to the use of the weary or benighted traveller, who is supplied with food and refreshment at the expense of the community.

Something has already been said in the preceding Notes of the character of the Arab. In a general view, it is decidedly more noble and magnanimous than that of the Berrebber. His vices are of a more daring, and (if I may use the expression) of a more generous cast. He accomplishes his designs rather by open violence than by treachery; he has less duplicity and concealment than the Berrebber; and to the people of his own nation or religion he is much more hospitable and benevolent. Beyond this, I fear it is impossible to say anything in his favour. But it is in those periods of civil discord which have been so frequent in Barbary, that the Arab character completely developes itself. On these occasions they will be seen linked together in small tribes, the firm friends of each other but the sworn enemies of all the world besides. Their ravages are not confined merely to the Berrebber and Bukharie tribes to whom they are at all times hostile, and whom they take all opportunities of attacking, but every individual is their enemy who is richer than themselves. Whilst these dreadful tempests last, the Arabs carry devastation and destruction wherever they go, sparing neither age nor sex, and even ripping open the dead bodies of their victims, to discover whether they have not swallowed their riches for the purposes of concealment.

Their barbarity towards Christians ought not to be tried by the same rules as the rest of their conduct; for although it has no bounds but those which self-interest may prescribe, it must almost be considered as a part of their religion; so deep is the detestation which they are taught to feel for the "unclean and idolatrous infidel." A Christian, therefore, who falls into the hands of the Arabs, has no reason to expect any mercy. If it is his lot to be possessed by the Arabs of the Desert, his value as a slave will probably save his life; but if he happens to be wrecked on the coast of the Emperor's dominions, where Europeans are not allowed to be retained in slavery, his fate would in most cases be immediate death, before the Government could have time to interfere for his protection.

The next great division of the people of Western Barbary are the inhabitants of the cities and towns, who may be collectively classed under the general denomination of Moors; although this name is only known to them through the language of Europeans. They depend chiefly on trade and manufactures for subsistence, and confine their pursuits in general to occupations in the towns. Occasionally, however, but very rarely, they may be found to join agricultural operations with the Arabs.

The *Moors* may be subdivided into the four following classes – 1st. the tribes descended from *Arab* families; 2d. those of *Berrebber* descent; 3d. the *Bukharie*; 4th. the *Andalusie*.

The *Arab* families are the brethren of the conquerors of the country; and they form the largest portion of the population of the southern towns, especially of those which border on Arab districts.

The *Berrebber* families are in like manner more or less numerous in the towns, according the proximity of the latter to the Berrebber districts.

The *Bukharie*, or black tribe, are the descendants of the Negroes brought by the Emperor Mulai Ismael from Soudan. They have been endowed with gifts of land, and otherwise encouraged by the subsequent Emperors; and the tribe, although inconsiderable in point of numbers, has been raised to importance in the state, by the circumstance of its forming the standing army of the Emperor, and of its being employed invariably as the instruments of government. Their chief residence is in the city of Mequinez, about the Emperor's person. They are also found, but in smaller numbers, in the different towns of the Empire.

The *Andalusie*, who form the fourth class of Moors, are the reputed descendants of the Arab conquerors of Spain; the remnant of whom, on being expelled from that kingdom, appear to have retained the name of its nearest province. These people form a large class of the population of the towns in the north of Barbary, particularly of Tetuan, Mequinez, Fez, and Rhabatt or Sallee. They are scarcely, if at all, found residing to the south of the river Azamoor; being confined chiefly to that province of Barbary known by the name of El Gharb.

The two last named classes of *Bukharie*, and *Andalusie*, are entire in themselves, and are not divisible into smaller communities like the Moors descended from the Arab and Berrebber tribes, the latter imitating in that respect their brethren in the country, and retaining the names of the petty tribes from which their ancestors originally sprung; for instance, the *Antrie, Rehamni*, &c. which are Arab tribes, and the *Edoutanan*, the *Ait Amoor*, &c. amongst the Berrebbers. All these smaller tribes are very solicitous to maintain a close family alliance with their brethren, who still pursue their agricultural employment in the country, which they find of great advantage in the event of intestine commotions.

The length of time since the settlement of these tribes in the towns cannot be accurately ascertained; but the manner in which they were first separated from their kindred in the country, may probably be exemplified by the following modern occurrence. When the father of the present Emperor had built the town of Mogadore, he caused a certain number of individuals to be selected, or drafted, from Arab and Berrebber (or Shilluh) tribes, and also from some of the towns; whom he compelled to settle in the new town. The young colony was afterwards encouraged and enriched by the removal of the foreign trade of the empire from Santa Cruz to Mogadore, which led to the settlement of other adventurers there. The probability that other towns were peopled by a similar compulsory proceeding, is confirmed by the known repugnance of the Arabs to quit their tents for houses, and by the aversion and even contempt which they feel for the restraints of a fixed residence in towns.

These are the component parts of that mixed population which now inhabits the towns of Barbary, and which is known to Europeans by the name of *Moors*. In feature and appearance the greater part of them may be traced to the Arab or Berrebber tribes from which they are respectively derived; for marriages between individuals of different tribes are generally considered discreditable. Such marriages however do occasionally take place, either in consequence of domestic troubles, or irregularity of conduct in the parties; and they are of course attended with a corresponding mixture of feature. Intermarriages of the other tribes with the *Bukharie* are almost universally reprobated, and are attributed, when they occur, to interested motives on the part of the tribe which sanctions them, or to the overbearing influence and power possessed by the *Bukharie*. These matches entail on their offspring the Negro feature and a mulatto-like complexion, but darker. In all cases of intermarriage between different tribes or classes, the woman is considered to pass over to the tribe of her husband.

Besides the Moors, the population of the towns is considerably increased by the Negro slaves, who are in general prolific, and whose numbers are continually increasing by fresh arrivals from the countries of Soudan.

In conclusion, the following may be stated as a brief leading distinction between the habits and circumstances of the three great classes of the inhabitants of Western Barbary.

The Berrebbers, (including the Shilluh) are cultivators of the soil and breeders of cattle; they occupy the mountainous districts, and reside in houses or hovels built of stone and timber.

The Arabs, occupying the plains, follow the same pursuits as the Berrebbers, and live in tents.

The Moors are traders, and reside in the towns.

It will, perhaps, be observed, that this distinction will not apply to the tribe described by Mr. Park on the southern confines of the Desert, whom he calls *Moors*, and distinguishes by that name from the *Arabs* of the Desert. It is evidently quite impracticable to assign precise denominations to the many possible mixtures of races which in process of time naturally occur: but a roving people, living in tents, as these are described to be, certainly cannot be entitled to the appellation of *Moors*. Neither can the people in question, whom Park describes to have short bushy hair, be a pure *Arab* tribe; though their leader, Ali, appears to have been an Arab. But by whatever name they ought to be distinguished, it seems very probable that they are descended from the ancient invaders of Soudan, who having been left to garrison the conquered places, remained on the southern borders of the Desert after the authority which originally brought them there, became extinct; and who by occasional intermarriages with the Negroes have gradually lost many of the distinguishing features of their Arab ancestors.

Viewing the term *Moor* as a translation or corruption of the Latin word *Mauri*, by which the Romans designated a particular nation, it is evident, that it cannot with strict propriety be used even in the limited sense to which I have here confined it; for, the people who now occupy the towns of Western Barbary, (with the exception, perhaps, of that small portion of them allied to the Berrebber tribes) are certainly not descendants of the ancient Mauritanians. The name, as I have said before, is not used amongst the people themselves, as the names of *Arab, Berrebber*, &c. are: but the *class* is quite distinguished from the other inhabitants of Barbary by the modes of life and pursuits of those who compose it. And as Europeans in their loose acceptation of the name *Moor*, have successively designated by it all the different races who have from time to time, occupied this part of Africa; applying it even to the Arab invaders of Spain, who proceeded from hence; they may very naturally appropriate it to those *stationary* residents of the Empire of Morocco with whom, almost exclusively, they carry on any intercourse. The only distinguishing term which the Arabs occasionally give to the Moors is that of *Medainien*, towns-people; which is a depreciating appellation in the estimation of an Arab. If you ask a Moor; what he calls himself? he will naturally answer you that he is a *Mooslim*, or believer; – his country? *Bled Mooselmin*, the land of believers. If you press him for further particulars, he will then perhaps tell you the tribe to which he belongs, or the district or city in which he was born. Neither have they a general name for their country; in other Mohammedan states it is distinguished by the name of *El Ghârb*, the West; but the natives themselves only apply this name to a province in the northern part of the Empire beyond the River Azamoor.

The term *Moor*, therefore, seems to stand, with respect to the people to whom we apply it, exactly in the same predicament as their term *Romi* with respect to us; which having survived the times when the extended power of the *Romans* rendered it not an improper appellation for all the inhabitants of Europe known to the Mauritanians, continues, in the dialects of Barbary, to be the general name for *Europeans of every nation* at this day.   D.

CONTEMPORARY ESSAYS

INTERIOUR OF AFRICA
(*NORTH AMERICAN REVIEW*, MAY 1817)

Much interest has been lately excited in England by the narrative of an American sailor, who goes by the name of Robert Adams. He was accidentally found strolling in the streets of London in a state of wretchedness and want, a little more than a year and a half ago; and the singularity of his appearance, together with the account he gave of his travels and sufferings, excited the curiosity of several gentlemen of eminence. As he could neither read nor write, he was examined by a gentleman belonging to the African Trading Company, and his narrative was written according to his relation. It was read before Sir Joseph Banks, and several other gentlemen, approved by them, and printed in a splendid quarto form. Our readers will doubtless recollect the notice taken of it in a late number of the Edinburgh, and of the Quarterly Review, and also in several other English publications.

The following narrative is the substance of what was collected from Adams on the subject, while he was in Cadiz, more than a year before he went to London, by a gentleman of Boston, and has never before been published. It was withheld from the publick, because the writer upon further inquiry, found reasons for suspecting the veracity of Adams, particularly in regard to what he says about Tombuctoo, and of his travels among the negroes. The subject is important in itself, and has become more especially so from the general excitement it has produced, on the other side of the Atlantick. We propose hereafter to inquire what degree of credit is to be attached to Adams' story, particularly to that part relating to the city of Tombuctoo, about which so much has been said and conjectured, and so little is known. We are glad to learn, that the London narrative will soon be republished in this country.

On the seventh day of May, in the year 1810, I sailed from New York for Gibraltar as a common sailor, on board the ship Charles, John Norton, master. Our complement of men, including the captain, mate, and supercargo, was eleven, We arrived at Gibraltar on the twelfth day of June, and remained there till the middle of September, when we sailed for the Cape de Verd islands, with the same men on board, except the supercargo. Our voyage was sufficiently favourable till the eleventh of October, when, being on the coast of Africa, as I think, near Cape Noon, in latitude about twenty eight, the vessel stranded on a reef of rocks, projecting out from the continent. This disaster happened at about six o'clock in the morning, but the darkness of the previous night, and the haziness of the weather at that time, prevented us from knowing our nearness to the shore. The boats were immediately hoisted out, but were dashed in pieces by the violence of the waves. Being apprehensive that the ship herself might share the same fate, we threw ourselves into the water in order to swim to the land.

We had no sooner reached the shore, than we were seized and made prisoners by a party of wandering Arabs, who had discovered us at a distance, and waited our approach. They rushed upon us, while we were yet in the water, and each one claimed as his own property the person, whom he had taken. We made some struggle, but without avail.

On the succeeding day, the wind and sea abated, so that the vessel was left dry on the rocks. The Arabs went on board, plundered her of every thing worth taking away, and afterwards set her on fire. Having done this, they made a distribution of us by lots. Dalby, the mate, and myself, fell to the share of the same person. They had previously stripped us of our clothes, and we were compelled to follow them, wandering from place to place, entirely naked. They belonged to a wandering tribe in the interiour, and had now come to the seacoast in number thirty or forty for the purpose of procuring fish. They seemed to be miserably wretched, and to have no other object than that of mere existence. We continued this kind of life for the term of a month, suffering excessively from hunger and exhaustion, from the heat of the day and dews of the night. The captain, unable to endure these sufferings, soon died. This event took place while we were in our accustomed motion, and gave the Arabs not the least trouble or uneasiness. They threw the body aside, and there would have left it, had we not begged permission to bury it in the sand.

After a month had elapsed, the party separated in order to return to their several places of rendezvous in the interiour, taking with them their slaves. Dalby and myself followed our master to a place in the district of Woled Doleim, where was the encampment of the rest of the tribe. After travelling about eighty miles over a sandy country in a southeast, easterly direction, we arrived at our place of destination. It consisted of a small cluster of tents, and was inhabited by about two hundred people, and was chosen as a place of encampment by reason of its affording a little shrubbery and one or two wells of brackish water. Every thing wore the aspect of poverty, filth, and wretchedness. They had a few camels and asses, which it was my duty to attend. Our food consisted of a scanty allowance of barley flour and water; theirs was the same, with the occasional addition of camels' milk.

We remained in this place about two months, when a party was formed to go to a place called Soudeny, for the purpose of stealing negroes. This party consisted of about thirty, myself included. We were mounted on camels, armed with short daggers, and supplied with barley flour and water, as our only food. From Woled Doleim we proceeded in a southeast, southerly direction over a barren sandy country, which afforded water but in a single instance, where there was a cluster of rocks; and this water was bitter and slimy. After having travelled eighteen days at an average rate of about fifteen miles a day, we arrived at the mountains in the vicinity of Soudeny. These mountains are of rock and sand, and among them we hid ourselves until an opportunity should offer of seizing such negroes as might pass that way.

We remained in this concealment thirteen days; but, on the fourteenth, the people in the neighbourhood, having discovered our hiding places, came out in a body, attacked us, and made prisoners of the whole party. The natives beat and abused the Arabs, whom they had taken, but they treated me with less rudeness. During the first night we were all put into the same prison; but in the morning I alone was released, and the rest remained in strict confinement during our short continuance in the place.

The soil of the country around Soudeny was very much better than of that we had passed over in our journey from Woled Doleim. The town itself appeared to consist of thirty or forty mud houses, or rather huts, containing perhaps, four or five hundred inhabitants, who hold themselves subject to the king or Wooloo of Tombuctoo. They had several springs of good water; their land was a little cultivated and produced some vegetation. I observed date trees, and a tree bearing a large fruit, the name of which I did not learn; likewise Guinea corn, beans, barley, a species of artichoke and a small, black grain, called in their language *moutre*. The place and its inhabitants were dirty and miserable, but not so much so as the Arabs. The children were commonly naked. People of full age had a sort of clothing in the form of a shirt, made of wool and goats' hair, dyed blue. Their weapons of warfare were bows and arrows. I observed that every person was marked with three scores on each cheek. They had horses, cows, goats, sheep, dogs, dromedaries, and camels, all of which, excepting the two last, were weak and miserable.

We remained here but a single day, at the end of which our whole party was ordered to Tombuctoo, under a guard of forty negroes, armed with bows and arrows. We pursued a southeast direction, which we continued for ten days at the rate of about twenty miles a day. We rested only a short time during the day, and at night for sleep. Our food consisted of moutre, formed into a kind of pudding, and occasionally a few ostrich's eggs. We sometimes saw this bird during our march. We passed over an uneven country, varying in the quality of its soil; sometimes affording shrubbery, and sometimes nothing but sand. We saw no water, or marks of cultivation, or even of human existence. During the whole of this journey, my former masters were pinioned and closely guarded. I was left at liberty and walked with the negroes, or occasionally rested myself by riding on the camels.

At the end of the tenth day, we arrived at a miserable village of about fifteen mud huts, as many tents, and perhaps two or three hundred inhabitants, who were the first human beings we had seen since leaving Soudeny. They were naked, and of a much more wretched appearance than the people of Soudeny. They were distinguished by the loss of the cartilage of the nose. They were not, as the Arabs told me, subject to the Wooloo of Tombuctoo.

We tarried in this place but one day, after which we continued our march in the same direction as before, and in two days came into a much better country than any we had yet passed. We began to see villages and evidences of cultivation, and found frequent springs of good water. After the fourth day, the change became still more perceptible. We passed several villages, the inhabitants of which seemed to enjoy many of the comforts of life, and appeared in every respect in a much better condition than any I had before seen in Africa. At the end of the sixth day, we arrived at our point of destination, the city of Tombuctoo. My companions and myself were immediately thrown into prison. I was released, however, after one night, although the others were confined till they left the city.

Tombuctoo is built at the distance of about two hundred yards from a river, which the natives call *La Parsire*, and consists probably of not less than twelve thousand inhabitants. The houses are scattered irregularly over a large space of ground, and not badly built. They are from thirty to seventy feet square, single storied, and flat roofed. The sides are composed of mud and straw cemented together, and raised and supported without wood. The partitions within are of the same materials. The rafters supporting the roof, which is of the same composition as the walls, are made of the date tree. In the whole fabrick no use is made of iron. Each house has its apertures, serving for windows, without shutters. There is nothing in the external appearance of these houses, which would indicate a difference of rank in their inhabitants, except that of the Wooloo, which is distinguished from the others by its size only.

The inhabitants in shape and general appearance are very much like the Africans commonly seen in Europe and America. The peculiar features of the face, and shape of the legs, are the same. They are generally inclined to corpulency, especially the females. Their dress is the same among all ranks, with this slight difference, that the shirt, the only garment worn, is among the poorer class blue; among the higher, white. This article is sometimes manufactured among themselves of wool and goats' hair, and sometimes bought of traders visiting the city from distant parts. A few of the inhabitants wear a sort of slipper made of goats' skin, and the skins of other animals. The dress of the women consists of a garment called a hayk, being a long piece of cloth, not attached to the body, but worn loosely about it like a cloak. In addition to this a small turban, or bandage, bound round the head, forms the whole of their dress. They never labour in the fields, but are employed in cooking, attending their children, weaving the cloth above mentioned, or other domestick concerns.

The women appear to be under no undue restriction from the men, nor are two or more of them ever obliged to bind themselves in marriage to the same person. They are considered marriageable at the age of twelve or thirteen. When a marriage is to take place, an agreement is previously made between the parents of the parties, who give their mutual consent. After this, the bridegroom leads the bride before the Wooloo, and there publickly promises fidelity and protection; they then proceed to the house of the bridegroom, and celebrate the marriage by three days of dancing and festivity. The women are generally prolifick and frequently bear twins, in which case, for some motives of superstition, one of them is suffered to die. The men are addicted to jealousy, and in the indulgence of this passion, they are often led to extreme cruelty in beating and maltreating their wives. Instances have occurred in which the husband in a fit of jealousy has poisoned his wife, and the whole of her offspring, and escaped to avoid punishment. Divorces may be obtained by the consent of the Wooloo, and in the following manner. The husband, if he be the complainant, appears at the door of the Wooloo, with a present, such as a goat, calf, or sheep, which, after he has killed it, is received by a servant of the Wooloo, who makes known his wish to gain admittance. When this is done, he states his accusation, and the wife is called, and witnesses are produced on both sides. The Wooloo decides as he thinks proper, and should the wife be adjudged criminal, she returns to her father's house with her children, the burthen of whose support is afterwards to rest on her. Should she be pronounced innocent, her husband is obliged to receive her again, and protect her according to the original contract.

Indolence prevails to an excess. A large portion of their time is taken up in sleep and drowsiness. They eat three times a day, but sparingly. Their food consists of fish and flesh boiled, roasted or baked; corn and moutre boiled; and bread made of pounded Indian corn, and baked in the ashes. They use salt and red pepper to season their food. This is prepared in a large, rough shapen, wooden dish, around which the master of a family and his children sit, serving themselves with their fingers. The women generally eat by themselves afterwards.

The wants of these people are very limited, and their employments are light, though various. Some are engaged in their rude manufactures, some in fishing, others in cultivating the fields and gardens; but in no case does any one appear to devote himself exclusively to any particular object, or to follow any pursuit as a trade; and, in fact, were they ever so enterprizing, they could do little under their present form of government. They are in the most abject slavery to the Wooloo, and the greater portion of those, who fish, do so by his order; and for a certain compensation they deliver the proceeds of their labour to him. The fields adjacent to the town are entirely under the direction of the Wooloo, who divides them into parcels, and allots certain portions to individuals. The whole amount of the produce goes into his store houses, and all, which the labourers receive, is barely sufficient for a temporary subsistence. The mode of living, and every external appearance of wealth, are the same in all classes, yet there is an evident distinction of rank, of respectability of standing, and exemption from labour.

The absolute authority of the Wooloo extends to the trade, as well as to every other concern of the people, whom he governs. In him is vested the sole privilege of selling, purchasing or holding any commodity whatever. His whole trade is with the Caravans, which arrive from Woled Abusbak, and various other Moorish settlements. They bring with them the articles of their own growth and manufacture, as well as of the manufacture of Europe, and receive in return the raw materials of the country, and slaves. On entering Tombuctoo these itinerant merchants are received by the Wooloo, and lodged by him at their own expense in a kind of caravansary. All negotiations pass between him and them, and as he has no such thing as money or any thing like coin in his dominions, articles of one commodity are exchanged for those of another. The articles brought to Tombuctoo are cotton cloth, fire arms, gun powder, leaden balls, weapons of every sort, tobacco and dates; for which are given in return ivory, gums, gold dust, ostrich feathers and slaves. A pound of gold dust has often been given for a quantity of gun powder of equal weight. The commodities thus received are deposited in the store houses of the Wooloo, and such as he does not otherwise dispose of are distributed, as his own pleasure or policy may dictate, among his subjects. Although they have no coin, yet they use small shells as a circulating medium, to which they have attached a certain value; and this is the only currency with which they are acquainted. They seem ignorant of the true value of gold, and use it only in manufacturing a few rude ornaments. I have been often asked why Christians sought gold so eagerly, and to what use they applied it.

The Wooloo is absolute. All law and government centre in him. He is the sole dispenser of justice. He alone frames and executes the laws. I could never ascertain whether this rank and its privileges were elective or hereditary, though I was led to believe the former. He has power over the liberties and lives of his subjects, and directs their occupations as he pleases. The people seem formed, in fact, but for his purposes; to amuse, benefit, and aggrandize him. The greater part of his subjects are in his immediate service; some as soldiers of his army, some are engaged in fishing, some in agriculture, some in tending his herds, some in procuring gold dust. They are sometimes rewarded according to a previous stipulation, but more commonly according to his own pleasure and caprice. Being sole merchant, as well as sole governour, he receives all the commodities which are in any way procured by his vessels, and deposits them in his store houses. These he considers his own, and uses them as he thinks proper, either for his own purposes, or as articles of exchange with foreign merchants. The person, also, of every individual in his dominions is at his disposal, whenever he chooses to deprive any one of liberty.

In return for this surrender of every privilege, the people look to him for relief, support, and protection. As he possesses all the conveniences and most of the necessaries of life, they look to him for relief from their wants. As he is the supreme judge, they apply to him to settle their differences and redress their wrongs; and as he has the whole control of their occupation, they expect solace and support from him when they are no longer able to labour. In discharge of these several duties he dispenses employment, adjusts disputes, and supports the aged and decrepid. This last office is supposed to devolve on children, when they have ability to bear the burthen; and when they have not, the Wooloo takes the charge on himself. A large house is set apart for this purpose, which I observed was always full.

The revenue of the Wooloo arises not merely from the exclusive privilege of trade, but from an excessive tribute exacted from his subjects, over and above the labour just mentioned. With funds thus acquired, he supports an army of five or six hundred men under continual exercise, armed with muskets and swords, and not entirely without skill in the use of them. These troops occasionally attend him in his walks, at which time the people bow to him, and kiss his hands. Beyond this little show of exterior distinction, his life, manners, and habits are the same with those of his people. There appear to be a few in the community, to whom the Wooloo delegates more power than to others, and who, as a kind of inferiour officers, take cognizance of certain petty transactions. These officers, however, appear to be wholly employed in relieving the chief of a portion of his burden, by attending to some minor concerns, and not in giving him their advice and counsel.

The Wooloo's punishments rarely go beyond the chastisement of those, who have failed in their duty and personal respect to him. Theft is common, and if the thief be taken in the act, the punishment is in the hands of the party aggrieved. Lying is incessant, and passes unnoticed and apparently without disgrace. Murders occur occasionally, and are always punished by the Wooloo, who inflicts death in return, generally by decapitation. Imprisonment, privation, and hard labour are used as punishments for minor offences.

I never discovered any thing among these people, that indicated the least notion of any kind of religion, or of a divine agency. No houses, no particular rank of people, no allotment of time, nor any particular portion of ground, were set apart for any devotional exercises or super-stitious rites. They seem to have no idea of any existing relation between man and his Creator. They perform some ceremonies, which seem orig-inally to have had some reference to a sort of religious belief; but no ideas of this kind are now attached to them. Circumcision is universal, and performed between the age of one and two years. The ceremony is attended with considerable pomp, and as the operator is one, who in other cases acts as a surgeon, the notion seems to prevail, that it is rather a surgical operation, than a religious rite. Just before death, and afterwards, I have seen some unintelligible gesticulations and actions of those standing round the body of the sick or deceased person. I had no particular evidence, that they were the result of any religious impres-sions. I had no reason for supposing, that they regulated their conduct by any moral or religious precepts.

The soil around Tombuctoo, though sandy, is generally good. A suf-ficient proof of this is, its producing any thing with the very little labour, which the natives bestow upon it. They cultivate Guinea corn, moutre, barley, a kind of black grain, the name of which I have forgotten, turnips, carrots, watermelons, and some other vegetable productions known in Europe and America. The climate is unvarying, and the heat uniformly extreme. It is rarely cloudy, and never rains, except during the rainy sea-son, which continues for a single month only of the winter. Nor is the ground at all refreshed by the nightly dews; so that during a large por-tion of the year, the suffering from drought is excessive. The proximity to the river alone affords the inhabitants and their cattle the means of continuing life. The winds are light and scarcely apparent, but variable. The most troublesome wind, which I experienced, and that fortunately but seldom, was from the south. It was so hot and oppressive, that my life seemed almost to sink under it. The brute creation were much more sensibly affected by it, than the human, and during its continuance, although it was generally short, they would be seen panting and languishing, apparently in great agony, and to seek a temporary relief, would often plunge into the river.

Among the animals, which I saw, were dogs, cats, horses, asses, cows, goats, sheep, dromedaries, camels; the most of them, except the two last, of an inferiour race and character. The cats and dogs were exceedingly miserable; the horses poor, small, and weak. They were accoutred for riding, with a rude sort of pack saddle, and a bridle made of grass rope. The cows were large and tolerably good. The goats and sheep were small and lean. The sheep are hairy, and are sheared once a year, or rather shaved, as the operation is done with a knife. The grazing animals are driven to the fields adjacent to the city, where they remain during the day, attended by herdsmen to protect them from wild beasts. At night they are driven again into the city. On my way to Tombuctoo, and in its vicinity, I saw wolves, foxes, rabbits, antelopes, wild hogs, porcupines and elephants. In the river are muskrats, and in the vicinity are many serpents, some of which are venomous. Lizards are found, and likewise smaller vermin of various kinds. Among the birds are the cuckoo, crow, sparrow hawk, kingfisher, a species of black robin, many river birds, peacocks, and Guinea hens. The two last are domesticated.

The river, which runs in front of the town, is called by the natives *La Parsire*, and its direction is from east to west. Before the town it is about three quarters of a mile wide. But here the water is shallow, and the channel is narrower both above and below. At a short distance below, it is very much compressed, by passing between two mountains. At a day's journey above the town, to the eastward, it is diminished to a furlong in width, not by reason of passing through any defile, as below, but from the diminution of water. Its appearance before the town is rather that of a lake than a river, and has very little current; below, it flows more rapidly, and at a day's journey toward the east it moves at the rate of a mile and a half an hour. This river affords clear water of a good taste, and furnishes the natives with a large portion of their food in such kinds of fish as are generally found in fresh water streams. Perch, mullet, suckers, and several other kinds are found in great abundance. They are caught in a small net of grass cords, made and used in the manner of a seine. The natives use, for the navigation of this river, a small canoe of a rude shape and inept construction. It is made of two pieces of the date tree, each hollowed and joined together with pegs. The seams are partially filled with grass and mud, but so imperfectly, that it is always necessary for those who manage them, to be constantly bailing. These canoes are used merely for crossing the river, or occasionally for fishing. During my residence at Tombuctoo, and subsequent march to the eastward, I never saw any of them ascending or descending the river, or used in any way for the conveyance of baggage or merchandize. The quantity of water in this stream appeared always the same. I was in the city nine months, and neither during the rainy season nor the excessive drought was the river sensibly increased or diminished. The natives seemed to have no knowledge of this river, except that it passed the city in a direction from east to west. I could learn nothing from them respecting its source or termination, or any tribes of inhabitants living on its banks.

After I had acquired some knowledge of their language, I made them acquainted with my misfortunes, my shipwreck, and the manner in which I had been made a slave. They expressed some degree of commiseration, but manifested no desire of knowing any thing further of me or my country, than what I voluntarily told them; yet I could not understand that there was any tradition or remembrance that a white man had ever been seen among them before. During my residence among them I was lodged in the house of a person connected with the Wooloo, and at his expense. They told me that they knew there was a difference between me and the Moors, and that the abhorrence in which they held them afforded no reason why they should treat me with severity.

At the end of nine months, a party of Moorish traders purchased of the Wooloo the whole party, which had been taken prisoners at Soudeny. They paid sixteen pounds of tobacco for each man. The Moors, their countrymen, were bought to be restored to liberty, and I to my former condition as a slave.

In the early part of the month of December, 1811, our caravan left Tombuctoo, consisting in all of about fifteen camels and fifty persons, including the merchants, those who had been purchased, myself, and a few negro slaves. Our destination was Taudeny. For the first eight days we followed the course of the river, which was due east, leading us over a country partially cultivated and interspersed with occasional settlements. We had travelled at the rate of about sixteen miles a day, and had ascended the river to the extent of one hundred and thirty miles. The width and depth of the river was such as to induce a belief, that we had not advanced, more than one fourth part of the way to its source. We halted at a small village of huts about two miles distant from the river, where we remained four days to refresh our camels by grazing and to prepare for crossing the great desert.

Our next direction was north, northwest, leaving the river directly behind us. We had no sooner quitted the borders of the river, than every trace of vegetable life disappeared. We immediately entered on an immense waste of sand. We met with a little burnt shrubbery, on which the camels sometimes browsed, but saw no water from the river to Taudeny. I subsisted entirely on a scanty portion of barley and water taken once a day, and the rest of the party fared little better. The excessive heat of the sun and sand, and exhaustion for want of food, soon rendered me unable to walk; and occasionally, when I became absolutely unable to move, I was suffered to relieve myself for a short time by riding on one of the camels.

At the end of the fourth day a negro child died of hunger, thirst, and fatigue, and the body was thrown carelessly upon the sand. Two days afterwards the mother of the child died, being overcome with fatigue and grief for the loss of her child. Her body was left in the same manner as that of the child, exposed on the sand. In the course of the journey one of the camels died, and his flesh served us for food. We arrived at Taudeny in ten days, having travelled about fourteen miles a day.

Taudeny has a miserable appearance, contains fifty or sixty huts, and apparently about six hundred inhabitants, including strangers, of whom many resort thither in caravans for purposes of trade. It is governed, as I understood, by a Shiek, who is appointed by the Wooloo of Tombuctoo, to whom the place is tributary. It contains one or two springs of good water, and likewise salt mines. In every respect, except the difference of size, Taudeny is like Tombuctoo. The Moors remained here four days, engaged in traffick, during which time I was employed in tending the camels. At the beginning of the fifth day we resumed our march with a destination for Heligobla. Our direction was northwest, and we soon entered a plain of burning sand, still more horrible than that we had passed. The allotted time for our journey was twelve days, and we had supplied ourselves with twelve goat skins of water, one for each day. On the second day two of them burst and left us an allowance scarcely sufficient for subsistence. Our sufferings were indescribable, from heat, thirst, hunger, and exhaustion. We daily began our march at the dawn, after the Moors had finished their morning devotions, and continued till sunset, when we received our scanty allowance of food. We stretched ourselves on the sand to sleep in the night, after having removed the upper surface, the heat of which was so great, that we could not endure it. In this dreary waste the Moors directed their course by the sun. During this journey two negro boys died of fatigue, and also a camel, whose flesh served us for food. On the tenth day we came to a small elevation of soil, where was a good spring of water and a little verdure, and on the twelfth we had the joyful sight of Heligobla.

We were now in the country of the wandering and savage Moors. We had left the territory of the negroes on quitting Taudeny. Heligobla is not a place of fixed residence; but merely a well of water surrounded by a little herbage, where tents are pitched during a certain season of the year. When the herbage is exhausted by the grazing animals, the tribe migrates to another place. The tribe consisted of about two hundred persons, men, women, and children, inhabiting thirty or forty tents. They are Mahometans, and as strict in their religious duties as at Tangier and elsewhere. Their faces are nearly black, their hair long and of the same colour, their persons squalid and dirty, and in their manners and customs they are brutal and cruel. They do not cultivate the ground, but live entirely on dates and the milk, and occasionally the flesh of camels and goats. They have many of the latter animals, and sometimes sell them to the passing caravans. They speak the Arabick language, and are governed by a Shiek from their own numbers. They are much more wretched and uncivilized than the negroes.

After we had been fourteen days in this dismal place, I found that my master had sold me to the Shiek for two camels and two bags of dates. The caravan left me, and I immediately commenced my labours under my new master, which consisted in attending the camels and goats. I continued in this employment six months, during which time my only food was goats' milk and water, given me twice a day in a scanty allowance. My labours were unremitted, and I was treated with great severity and often cruelty. To slaves of every description they are morose and severe, but Christians in particular are objects of inveterate hatred.

After having remained in this wretched condition for six months, I was at length sold by the Shiek to a Woled Abusbak trader passing in a caravan through Heligobla, to Lagassa, or Heligassa. After leaving Heligobla we pursued a northwest, westerly, direction, which we continued for fifteen days at the rate of about ten miles a day, passing over a country much better than the sandy desert between Taudeny and Heligobla. The ground was uneven, affording a little shrubbery, and water in one or two places. We met with two or three Moorish encampments, and arrived at Lagassa at the end of the fifteenth day. This place in every respect resembles Heligobla. The inhabitants are a few shades lighter in their complexion, and they differ from those of Heligobla by being an abandoned set of thieves and robbers. Their whole employment consists in plundering travellers and strangers of the adjacent tribes. This was the first place in which I found gold and silver known as a circulating medium.

We remained here two days, after which I was sold to a Shiek of Wadnoon for sixty dollars, and he returned with me soon to the district to which he belonged. Our course was northeast, northerly, which we continued fifteen days, stopping occasionally for the purposes of trade. The whole distance from Lagassa to Wadnoon is not more than eight full days' march. The country, which we passed over, was better than that between Heligobla and Lagassa. It was sometimes mountainous, of a good soil, was not badly watered, and in some places it was covered with shrubbery. We passed many encampments, and met many travellers. I likewise observed several herds of deer and antelopes. On the fifteenth day we arrived at Wadnoon. Nothing could exceed my surprise, when, on entering this place, I found four of the crew of the Charles prisoners like myself. The reason of our all having been brought to this place, was the importance and wealth of the city of Wadnoon, which made it a great market for slaves.

Wadnoon is the name of an extensive district; the capital of which bears the same name, and consists of forty or fifty houses and gardens, built and arranged in the Moorish style, and differing in no respect, excepting size, from Tangier and similar cities. It is independent of the emperour of Morocco, and governed by a Shiek from among themselves. The people are not so savage as those of Heligobla and Lagassa, but more so than those nearer the seacoast. I continued in this place with my fellow slaves for twelve months, subject throughout to the same master. My employment was to labour in the fields and gardens, and my food was barley, water, and dates, once, and sometimes twice a day; but these were given me so sparingly, that to support life I was obliged to steal every thing like food, which I could find.

Four months after my arrival, Dalby, the former mate of the Charles, finding himself exhausted by labour and privation, declared himself unable to perform some duty which was assigned him, at which his master was so enraged that he stabbed him with a dagger, and killed him on the spot. To protect his remains from the dogs, I and my fellow slaves obtained permission to bury him. A few months after my three surviving fellow prisoners, suffering incessantly from beating, privation, and insults, declared their intention of escaping these calamities by turning Mahometans. This determination they put into effect, and were consequently circumcised and allowed all the privileges of the people of the country. After this my life became doubly wretched. My master wished me to follow the example of the others and change my religion, and endeavoured to prevail on me to do so, by alternate persuasion and the most abusive treatment. But I was soon relieved from my sufferings and from slavery, for within a month or two afterwards a person came to Wadnoon, empowered by the consuls of the United States and of Great Britain at Mogadore, to purchase such Christian slaves as might be found in this district. To my unspeakable joy I found myself ransomed for one hundred and five dollars, with liberty to go with my purchaser to Mogadore. The sad resolution of my fellow prisoners prevented them from sharing with me this happiness. In five days after leaving Wadnoon, having travelled in a west, northwest direction, about one hundred and fifty miles, we reached Santa Cruz. From thence I walked on the seashore three days, at the end of which, in the latter part of August 1812, I arrived at Mogadore.

"ARTICLE IX. *THE NARRATIVE OF ROBERT ADAMS.*" A REVIEW ESSAY BY JARED SPARKS. (*NORTH AMERICAN REVIEW*, JULY 1817).

"Article IX. *The Narrative of Robert Adams, a sailor, who was wrecked on the western coast of Africa, in the year 1810, was detained three years in slavery by the Arabs of the great Desert, and resided several months in the city of Tombuctoo. With a map, notes, and an appendix.* pp. 200. Boston, Wells and Lilly. 1817."*

In our last number we published a notice of this book, together with a similar narrative, which was taken at Cadiz several months previously to this, expressing at the same time our suspicion, that the whole of that part, which related to the interiour, and particularly to the city of Tombuctoo, was a fabrication. We propose now to examine the subject more at large, and to bring forward such reasons as have induced us from the beginning to regard the story as a fiction, and a gross attempt to impose on the credulity of the publick. To us, indeed, this has appeared so obvious, that we should not think it worthy of any serious examination, had it not excited so much interest, and gained universal belief in England.

* [This review of the first American publication of Adams's narrative was written by Jared Sparks (1789–1866), American historian and educator, who served as the editor of the *North American Review* in 1817–18. He bought the journal in 1824 and served as its editor until 1830. He became McLean Professor of History at Harvard in 1838 and served as president of the university from 1849 until 1853.]

The narrative first appeared there in a splendid quarto form; or rather it occupied a small corner in a book of this description; by much the greater part being composed of introductory details, copious explanatory notes by various hands and on various subjects, elaborate concluding remarks in defence of the story and the notes, together with two learned and well written appendices, which have no connexion with any other part of the book. It was sent into the world, also, under the sanction of some of the most distinguished men in England, as will be seen from the following notice, taken from the editor's Introductory Details.

The story having come to the knowledge of Earl Bathurst, the Right Honourable the Chancellor of the Exchequer, Major General Sir Willoughby Gordon, the Right Honourable Sir Joseph Banks, John Barrow, Esq. George Harrison, Esq. Henry Goulburn, Esq. M. P. and other members of the government, who interest themselves in African affairs, and they having expressed a desire to see Adams, he waited upon them in person, and the Narrative was at the same time transmitted to them for perusal. It is unnecessary to give stronger evidence of the general impression derived from this investigation, than is afforded by the fact, that the Lords of the Treasury were pleased to order the poor man a handsome gratuity for his equipment and passage home; – and Sir Willoughby Gordon in a letter, which the editor had subsequently the honour to receive from him, expressed his opinion in the following words; – 'The perusal of his statement, and the personal examination of Adams, have entirely satisfied me of the truth of his deposition. If he should be proved an impostor, he will be second only to Psalmanazar.'

Thus supported, the narrative gained credit every where, and made an article in almost every periodical publication in the British dominions. It was gravely and elaborately reviewed in the Edinburgh and Quarterly Reviews, and the latter in particular entered into a manful defence of its most glaring absurdities. Considered in this light, it assumes an importance, and deserves a notice, to which it would not otherwise be entitled.

In other views, also, the subject is not without claims to our attention. During these twenty years past an uncommon enthusiasm has prevailed on the other side of the Atlantick, particularly in England, on the subject of Africa. The peculiar condition of this ill fated country has called into action at the same time two of the most powerful principles of the human mind, sympathy and curiosity. The noble design of abolishing from the earth the detestable traffick in human blood, which was prompted by the philanthropy and prosecuted by the zeal of a few great men – the results of the investigations which took place in consequence of this design – the wrongs, oppressions, and cruelties, which were found to be practised on an inoffensive and unprotected race of beings – their intellectual degradation – their wretched state of existence, arising from an entire ignorance of the arts of civilized life, and of the first principles of moral and religious obligations; – all these have operated powerfully in touching the springs of benevolent feeling, and exciting a generous wish that these unhappy people might be relieved from this burden of wretchedness – made acquainted with the joys and comforts of social life, and the cheering hopes and influences of Christianity.

These causes have excited a desire of making more particular inquiries into the geography of the interiour, and the condition and character of the inhabitants. But such inquiries have only increased, without satisfying curiosity. All here is mysterious and uncertain. The Romans are said to have crossed the great desert, and penetrated as far as the Niger, but no European in modern times, if we except Leo Africanus, has advanced so far in this direction, or been able to bring, from the most interesting part of the interiour, any correct information. Several individuals, within a few years past, have fallen a sacrifice to the ardour of their zeal in attempting to prosecute discoveries into these unknown and inhospitable regions. Among them we have to lament our unfortunate countryman, Ledyard, who, in native love of adventure, and persevering energy of character, has probably never been surpassed. But the world has seldom united in stronger feelings of sympathy for the fate of any individual, than that of Park, "the flower of modern chivalry," and the most enthusiastick practical advocate for African emancipation. We are not more astonished at the irresistible curiosity and unabated ardour of this bold adventurer, than at his coolness and deliberation on the approach of danger, his patient endurance of suffering, and calm resignation to the most disastrous and appalling events that could await him. From him we have learned more concerning the interiour of Africa, than from every other traveller. The grand object of his first mission was to discover the direction and termination of the Niger, and to gain some definite knowledge of the great central mart of Africa. This object he accomplished but in part. After many perils and sufferings, he succeeded in discovering the Niger, and travelled several days along its banks, – but prudence prevented his proceeding as far as Tombuctoo, and all the knowledge he gained of that city was derived from the authority of others.

Nothing was known with certainty of the kingdom or city of Tombuctoo till the beginning of the sixteenth century, when Leo Africanus wrote his description of Africa. He was a native of Spain, and going over to Africa during the political disasters of his country, he travelled in various parts of the interiour, and resided for some time at Tombuctoo. He gives a full and apparently honest account of this city, and represents it as a place of great importance, and the capital of an extensive and powerful empire. It was the residence of the king, who possessed vast wealth, and was surrounded with splendour and magnificence. The king's palace and a stately mosque were built of stone and lime by an artist from Spain, and many of the other buildings were also of the same materials. He speaks of merchants of great wealth residing there, and of a trade being carried on by means of caravans from Barbary, and through the port Kabra, to almost every part of Africa.

This account of Leo has always been credited, though he has sometimes been found a fallible guide in geography. It was requisite from the nature of his work, that he should relate many things on the authority of others, and he was thus occasionally led into errours; – but when he speaks from personal observation, we have no reason to doubt his veracity or suspect his honesty. Succeeding researches have generally verified his statements. What he says of the power of the king of Tombuctoo, and the consequent importance of his dominions, was confirmed fifty years afterwards by Marmol, a Spanish writer,* who had been taken prisoner and carried into the interiour of Africa. "The cheriff, Mahomet," says he, "in the height of his prosperity, [1540] had thoughts of conquering this and other kingdoms of the blacks, as had been done in former ages by the Leptunes. He set forward with a thousand eight hundred horse, and an infinite number of camels, loaded with ammunition and provision; but being informed, that the king of Tombut was marching to meet him with *three hundred thousand men,* he made his way back to

---

* [From Mármol's *Descripción general del Áffrica* (3 vols., 1573–99)].

Tarudant." Marmol says he was himself in this expedition. The French at Galam, a settlement on the Senegal, received similar accounts relative to Tombuctoo from the Mandingo merchants, who went annually on a trading expedition to that city.* They spoke of the merchandize collected there from various parts as immense, and described the articles, which were commonly brought from the northern parts. This description agreed entirely with the truth, as was ascertained by M. Brue,[†] who several times saw the caravans set out from Tripoli to cross the desert.

What we have here related, we believe, is the substance of all that was known of Tombuctoo for nearly three hundred years, – from the beginning of the sixteenth to the close of the eighteenth century.

This was not a period very auspicious for African improvement. The want of enterprize in Europe, resulting from the decline of ten centuries, left men without motives either of interest or curiosity sufficient for prompting them to extend their researches into a country, which was known only for its deserts, and the piracies, barbarism, and stupidity of its inhabitants. And when the mind again recovered its energies in the more civilized parts of the world, it was long occupied with objects less remote and less doubtful. The revival of letters in Europe – the resuscitation of commerce – the formation of political establishments – the new relations, which were beginning to exist between different nations, – all these afforded sufficient scope for the noblest exertions of intellect, and the grandest schemes of enterprize. When the changes, arising from these, ceased to attract by their novelty, and to awaken attention by their importance, the new world, which had lately been discovered, was a theatre amply capacious for carrying into effect any adventurous project. The tide of discovery turned wholly in this direction. To ascend the rivers and penetrate the interiour of this unknown region – to traverse its forests – explore its lakes – and clamber to the summits of its mountains, were exploits of no ordinary hazard or trifling fame. New bays, and islands, and straits were daily added to the charts of the mariner – till finally the project of a northwest passage absorbed every other. This spirit of discovery gave rise to the grand expeditions under

---

* Nouvelle Rélation d'Afrique, par Labat, Tom. iii, p. 661, et suiv. [Jean Baptiste Labat (1663–1738) published his *Nouvelle Rélation d'Afrique Occidentale* in 1728.]
† [Adrien Hubert Brue (1786–1832) was a French cartographer and publisher.]

Cook, and the valuable acquisitions of Bougainville – the disastrous fate of La Perouse, and the ill success of D'Entrecasteaux.*

The commercial, scientifick and political world were equally engaged in these enterprizes, and the idle and curious gazed with admiration, because they saw nothing more wonderful to admire. But when these had lost their novelty and their motives, the active spirit, which had prompted to them, did not slumber. The accumulated ills of Africa, as well as the natural disadvantages and privations to which it is subjected, had already awakened the sympathy of the friends of humanity. It became now the object of general attention and interest. The travels of Bruce, Valiant, Barrow, Lucas, and Horneman were read with eagerness, although the knowledge they gave respecting the interiour, and the state of Africa in general, was exceedingly limited.†

The old account of the wealth and magnificence of Tombuctoo was revived – and various speculations were raised for the purpose of solving that great geographical problem, the course and termination of the Niger.

The first regular and well digested account of Tombuctoo, and its trade with the Barbary states, was published by Mr. Jackson in his description of Morocco.‡ He resided many years in that country, and obtained his information respecting the interiour, as he says, by a long

---

* [Captain James Cook (1728–1779), famed English explorer of the Pacific Ocean; Louis Antoine de Bougainville (1729–1811), first Frenchman to circumnavigate the globe; Jean-François de Galoup, Comte de La Pérouse (1741–1788), French explorer whose ship was lost in a storm near the Solomon Islands; Antoine Raymond Joseph de Bruni D'Entrecasteaux (1739–1793), explorer sent to find La Pérouse, failed in that mission, but collected important scientific information about the region (*Nouvelle Biographie Générale*).]

† [James Bruce (1730–1794) served as Consul General in Algiers before going on to become the most celebrated explorer of tropical Africa of his day and publishing his five-volume *Travels to Discover the Source of the Nile* (1790). The *Voyage dans l'intérieur de l'Afrique, par le cap de Bonne-espérance, dans les années 1783, 84 et 85* of François Le Vaillant (1753–1824) appeared in both French and English in 1790. Sir John Barrow, who was among those who questioned Adams in the offices of the African Company, had established his leading role in African affairs with the publication of *An Account of Travels into the Interiour of Africa in the years 1797 and 1798* (1801). William Lucas published an account of his effort to reach the Fezzan from Tripoli in the *Reports* of the African Association (1790), which had sponsored his journey (see Hallett, *Reports* 48–69). The African Association also sponsored the effort by Friedrich Hornemann (1772–1801); his journal from the first part of the journey, *The Journal of Frederick Hornemann's Travels from Cairo to Mourzouk, the Capital of the Kingdom of Fezzan, in Africa in the Years 1797–1798*, was published by the Association in 1802.]

‡ [James Grey Jackson's *An Account of the Empire of Marocco* (1809).]

series of inquiries, and from sources on which he could rely. He had himself received caravans of merchandize from Tombuctoo, and seems to have succeeded in drawing information from the traders, without awakening their apprehensions, or exciting their jealousy. These people have always looked with a jealous eye on those inquisitive Europeans, who have made inquiries, which in any way affected their commercial concerns, and have been often induced for these reasons to make false representations. No one had thought of questioning the general truth of Mr. Jackson's account, till the new story of Adams made its appearance, with such high pretensions and under so imposing a form, – but then, as a thing of course, it began to be believed erroneous.

We have conversed on this subject with Mr. Court, an English gentleman, who has resided in a mercantile capacity more than twenty years at Mogadore. He speaks in the most unqualified terms of the correctness of Jackson's statements in what relates to Morocco, and assures us, that what he has said of the interiour was derived from the very best authorities, and such as might, in most cases, be relied on with confidence. Mr. Court has been frequently engaged in an intercourse with merchants from Tombuctoo, and what he has been able to learn from them corresponds entirely with the account given by Jackson. He says there are regular trading establishments in Morocco connected with others in that city, and that caravans are passing more or less frequently every year.

From what Mr. Jackson could learn, as well as from the uniform testimony of the caravan merchants in other parts, this city is of great extent – the emporium of central Africa – the resort of traders from every part of the continent – inhabited by people from different countries, all of whom are tolerated in their religious belief and worship – the soil productive, and the climate favourable. This is a general outline, and as such it disagrees entirely with the story of Adams; – this story, in fact, has scarcely a single point of resemblance to any other description which has been given, either ancient or modern.

We come now to a more immediate examination of the narrative under consideration. From what has been said of the present state of knowledge on the subject, our readers will be able to judge with some accuracy of the degree of credit, which ought to be attached to any novel pretensions. We take it for granted, that, as far as internal evidence is concerned, the Cadiz and London narratives are to be considered of equal value, – or if any difference exist, it will be in favour of the former, as this was taken more than a year before the other, when the recollection of the narrator must have been more vivid than at so long a time afterwards. We propose to compare these narratives in some of their more important parts, and to point out discrepancies, which we believe are alone sufficient effectually to destroy the credibility of both.

At the very outset we are presented with a difficulty, which seems incapable of solution, and which goes very far towards overthrowing the whole story. When at Cadiz, Adams represented the shipwreck to have taken place near Cape Noon, in latitude twenty eight degrees north, but at London he makes it happen at Cape Blanco, five hundred miles farther south. The London editor has consequently begun at this latter point on the map to trace the route of Adams according to his representation of courses and distances, and finds that such a route must approach near the known position of Tombuctoo, and come out near Wednoon where it ought to terminate. But let us trace the same line from Cape Noon, and we shall not approach within four hundred miles of the city, and shall come out, not to the place where we started, as we ought, but into the Mediterranean near Algiers. If the wreck actually took place, therefore, at Cape Noon, it is obvious, that the formal detail of courses and distances, in making which Adams was so particular and so obstinate, is a mere fabrication. But, disconnected with his own statements, which are in this particular contradictory, and therefore of no weight, there is every reason for believing, that the ship was stranded at this place. It is a fact well established, that no wrecks have been known to happen on this coast much south of Cape Bajador, in latitude twenty six north. Mr. Court was very positive that during the twenty five years, in which he has resided at Mogadore, there has been no instance of a shipwreck south of this point, – wrecks had not been unfrequent, but they uniformly happened between Cape Bajador and Cape Noon. The same remark is made by Jackson, who adds, that the coast between these capes is subject to an almost perpetual haziness, which prevents mariners from seeing the land, till they are driven ashore by a strong current setting from the west. Adams mentions a haziness, and a violent surf at the place of his shipwreck. Captain Riley, whose narrative has lately interested the publick, was wrecked on this coast, and his description corresponds exactly with what is here related.

It is essential to remark, that in his first narrative at Cadiz, Adams was quite as particular in mentioning the directions, distances, and times of his different journeyings across the desert, as he was afterwards at London, but there is scarcely a single point of agreement between the two accounts. The whole distance, according to the first, would not take him but little more than half way from the sea coast to the city of Tombuctoo, if the line were traced from Cape Noon, – and if from Cape Blanco, it would extend south, instead of east, as it ought, quite across the Senegal, nearly as far as the Gambia. There is no mode of reconciling those differences, nor any way of accounting for them, except by supposing the whole of this part of the narratives to be a tissue of inventions, brought forward in this positive manner to give plausibility to the pretended intervening incidents. It seems very probable, that before he went to London, he had discovered the blunders of his first statements, and learnt to adapt his distances to his places;* – for Mr. Storrow, the gentleman who examined him at Cadiz, assures us that while there, Adams was not the stupid, unthinking, simple being, which we are led to suppose him from the remarks of the London editor. He saw it gave him consequence, and was disposed to take advantage of it.

From the sea coast to Tombuctoo there is a general resemblance in the outlines of the two narratives, but much is added to the last, which is not found in the first, by way of eking out and giving it an air of the marvellous. In the former he says the captain died of fatigue and exhaustion, – in the latter he gives a particular account of his having been murdered by the Arabs. A more romantick description is here found, also, of the adventurous expedition to Soudenny for the purpose of stealing negroes; – he talks of a "remarkably ugly negro chief – enlarges on the dress, manners, and amusements of the inhabitants, their weapons of warfare, the higher and lower orders of people, their houses and furniture, and may other things which appear to be rather the answers to detached questions, than a continuous voluntary relation.

---

* We shall here insert a table, which was made by the English editor, from the London narrative, – and one, which we have collected from the narrative at Cadiz. It will require but a single glance to discover that they are totally dissimilar – and few probably will desire stronger evidence of their both having been fabricated when the narratives were taken.

	Days	Course	Dist. in m.
Travelling to the Douar in the desert,	30	E. ½ S.	450
To *Soudenny*,	17	S. S. E.	340
To a village in the interiour,	10	E.	200
To Tombuctoo	15	E. by N.	300
Distance in miles to Tombuctoo			1290
Up the river La Mar Zarah	10	E. N. E.	180
From the river to Taudeny	13	N.	234
To Woled Doleim	31	N. W.	464
– El Kabla,	2	N. by W.	30
– Woled Abousebàh,	9	N. E.	162
– Woled Adrialla,	6	N. N. W.	150
– Aiata Mouessa Ali,	3	N. W.	54
– Wednoon,	5		80
– Akkadia,	1	N.	30
– Mogadore,	11		240
Distance from Tombuctoo to Mogadore in miles			1624
Staid on the sea coast	14		
At the town in the interiour	30		
In concealment near Soudenny	11		
At Soudenny	4		
At Taudeny	14		
At Tombuctoo, six months			

	Days.	Course.	Dist. in m.
From the sea coast to the town in the interiour,		S. E. by E.	80
To Soudenny,	18	S. E. by S.	270
– To Tombuctoo	16	S. E.	320
Distance to Tombuctoo			670
Up the river La Parsire	8	E.	100
From the river to Taudeny	10	N. by W.	140
– to Heligobla [El Kabla]	12	N. W.	168
– to Lagossa,	15	N. W. by W.	150
– Wednoon,	15	N. E. by N.	150
– Mogadore,	8		120
Distance from Tombuctoo to Mogadore			828
Staid on the sea coast	30		
At the town in the interiour,	60		
At Soudenny,	1		
At Tombuctoo, nine months			
At Taudeny,	4		

He tells a story of a certain tribe of negroes near Soudenny, who have large holes in the cartileges of their noses, in which they wear gold rings. He had probably seen people of this description in the south of Morocco, and learnt that they come from beyond the desert. Mr. Jackson mentions having seen in this part of Morocco, a number of negroes from Wargarra ornamented in this way.

Our limits will not allow us to enter into a minute examination of his description of Tombuctoo, – we can only mention some of the more important particulars, from which the merits of the whole may be easily estimated. Both narratives, in what relates to this city, have the appearance of having been extorted by a series of questions, which being necessarily on kindred topics, often received similar answers, because it would be impossible, without direct contradiction, to answer them otherwise. But there are many striking disagreements, and such as could not have arisen from forgetfulness or want of observation.

At London he describes the king and queen as old, greyheaded personages, – but Mr. Storrow, who questioned him very particularly on this point, is confident that he told him the king was a man in middle life, robust and active. In his answers concerning the king's family and court, upon which he was closely questioned, he never mentioned a queen or any female of distinction. Had he really seen the extraordinary Fatima, dressed in the manner he describes, it is not likely he would have passed her over at that time without notice. It will be in place here to remark, that in all his answers relating to his residence at Tombuctoo, Mr. Storrow found him exceedingly vague and unsatisfactory, and was often obliged to put his questions in a variety of forms before he could collect from him any thing definite on the subject of inquiry.

There is nothing more extraordinary or improbable, perhaps, in the whole story, than what he says of the character and occupations of the king. All the mercantile concerns of the city are represented as being transacted by him individually. He is the only acting merchant, and his palace the only warehouse in his dominions. Now all this is exceedingly absurd, – and if we reflect on the immense trade which is known to be carried on here by caravans from every part of Africa – from the borders of the Red Sea – from Egypt, Barbary, and the western coast – and probably by an extensive inland navigation on the Niger, we shall not hesitate to say it is absolutely impossible. With Barbary alone the trade is sufficient to employ constantly a large number of acting merchants – and to pretend that the whole comes under the personal inspection of an individual, and he a king, who is at the same time sole governour, law-maker, and judge, is a tax on our credulity, which we cannot conceive any one in his right mind will consent to pay. Besides, Mr. Dupuis himself, who is a very strong advocate for Adams, says he has always understood from the merchants, that there are shops in this city, in which are exposed to sale foreign and domestick commodities. At Sansanding, which we must suppose, from its vicinity to Tombuctoo, bears a strong resemblance in its general character to that city, Mr. Park saw vast numbers of shops and traders' stalls, in which various kinds of merchandise were sold or exchanged. There was, also, "a large space appropriated for the great market every Tuesday, when astonishing crowds of people came from the country to purchase articles in wholesale, which they retailed in the different villages." Finally, we believe there is no instance of a city or village of much size in any part of the world, in which there are not resident merchants engaged in purchasing and vending goods, with such privileges and under such municipal restrictions, as are deemed proper by the government under which they live.

This is a point on which it was not possible for Adams to be mistaken, – he could not be daily in the streets of a large city for nine, or even six months, without learning the occupations of its inhabitants, and being able to describe them minutely, – and if, in attempting to do this, he is inconsistent and absurd, we have the best grounds for supposing him to practise an equal imposition in such particulars as are less obvious, and of which our knowledge is too limited to detect false representation.

The people are said to give no indication of any religious belief or impressions, – they have no forms of worship or religious rites. But this is not to be credited. Great numbers of Mohammedans are constantly visiting the city, and it would be folly to suppose, that many do not live there, especially when we recollect that the place has been, till very lately, if it is not at present, under the government of Moors, or people of Moorish descent. Mr. Dupuis is convinced that Mohammedans reside there, and adds, "it is also generally believed in Barbary, that there are mosques at Tombuctoo." Mr. Park saw Mohammedan negroes on the borders of Bambarra, who read the Koran, and possessed Arabick manuscripts.

In one account, Adams speaks of circumcision as being universal, and describes the ceremony as being performed with a good deal of pomp; – in the other he intimates, that it was not practised at all among the negroes, for he saw only a few who had been circumcised, and he supposed them to have been in possession of the Moors. These are things in which it would not be possible for him to mistake or forget. The ceremonies of marriage and divorce are also very differently described.

In regard to the occupations of the inhabitant, there are few special disagreements, – and yet there is not much similarity in the representations. The assertion, that no particular classes of people were devoted to mechanical employments of any kind, or to manufactures, wants at least the support of probability. When at London he seems to have been in more of a story telling mood, than when examined the year before – and he has accordingly embellished this last narrative with more curious relations and striking incidents, than the former. But the same want of particularity and definite statement is apparent in both.

The animals, which he describes, are such as are common in Barbary, and such as he might have seen within the confines of Morocco. We will pass over the wonderful stories of the elephant twenty feet high, with *four* enormous tusks, all growing out of the under jaw, – of the curious animal, which had "a hollow in its back like a pocket," as well as some others equally wonderful, and which came near shaking the faith of Sir Joseph Banks, as we believe they were all invented after Adams left Cadiz. Neither can we stop to examine the editor's speculations on the probability of his having mistaken a *calabash* for a *cocoa nut*.

At Cadiz, among other animals, he spoke of horses, and described them as small and weak, and as being "accoutred for riding with a rude sort of packsaddle, and a bridle made of grass rope." In the other narrative he says expressly, *there are no horses*, – and we hardly know how to understand the assertion in the Quarterly Review, in defence of this statement of Adams, that it is conformable to the account given by Leo Africanus. The fact is directly the contrary. It is certain he speaks of a large company of body guards of the king, who were mounted on horses – and also of the courtiers riding on these animals. He says the best horses were brought from Barbary, but the smaller ones were raised at Tombuctoo.* Horses are common in this part of Africa; – Park found them abundant in Kaarta and Bambarra, and rode on horseback several days in those countries.

No part of the story has excited more speculation, than that in which a river is described as passing westerly within two hundred yards of the city. This part of the narrative, as his editor observes, is peculiarly his own, – no hint has been given any where else, of a river passing in this direction near the city. The Niger has always been mentioned, from the time of Leo Africanus himself, as not approaching within twelve miles of the town, – and it is known also to flow easterly. The editor acknowledges, "that on this fact respecting the river, the credit of Adams is completely pledged." But in our estimation, the contradictions and vagueness, which appear in his several relations at Mogadore, Cadiz, and London, are sufficient to destroy all claims to belief in this instance, even without any farther direct evidence. In his story to Mr. Dupuis at Mogadore, he did not speak of this river as flowing westerly, "but discovered some uncertainty on the subject, observing that he had not taken very particular notice" – nor did he give it any name. Mr. Dupuis had often heard the traders mention a river near Tombuctoo – but they uniformly described it as running easterly, and he had always understood it to be the Niger. Adams told Mr. Dupuis, also, that "he had seen the natives navigate the river in fleets of from ten to twenty canoes together, that he had been informed they were absent occasionally a month or more, and frequently returned to Tombuctoo laden with slaves and merchandize." At Cadiz, he called the river *La Parsire*, and said, "its waters were clear and of good taste;" – and in speaking of the canoes, he represents them as "used merely for crossing the river, or occasionally for fishing. During my residence at Tombuctoo," he observes, "and subsequent march to the eastward, I never saw any of them ascending or descending the river, or used in any way for the conveyance of baggage or merchandize." At London, the name is transformed into *La Mar Zarah* – the water becomes brackish, and the river is made to assume a decided westerly direction.

There is no authentick account or even tradition of a river running nearer the city than the Niger. In Labat's Collection (vol. ii, p. 163)

---

* Description d'Afrique, Liv. 7, p. 324 ["Lyons" edition (1556), tr. Jean Temporal].

mention is made of a river, by the name of Guien, which is said to run in the vicinity of Tombuctoo, – but no information is given about its source or direction; – and we need only be told, that Labat adopts the opinion of Edrisi and Abulfedain* supposing the Niger to run west, and that in fact he considers it the same as the Senegal, to be convinced of the little credit, which is to be attached to his authority on this subject.

The editor, in his concluding remarks, has levied no ordinary tax on his invention, to prove that Leo Africanus has been misunderstood in what he says of the relative position of the city and the Niger. He labours this point with great parade of learning and philological criticism. He collates the various readings of the Italian, Latin, French, and English translations, and would make it appear that some of them are ambiguous, some unintelligible, and some contradictory; but in our apprehension there is not a clearer passage in the whole Description of Africa, than the one in question. We select the Italian, because this version is allowed to have been made by Leo himself from his original Arabick. Speaking of the city, he says, "Vicina a un ramo del Niger circa a dodici miglia," which in our conception has but one meaning, and that a very obvious one – the city is *about twelve miles from a branch of the Niger*. This is also confirmed afterwards where he describes the port Kabra, as situated on the Niger, *twelve miles from the city*. The editor would have it all mean, "that Tombuctoo is situated on a branch of the Niger, twelve miles from the principal stream," and on this false construction of Leo he rests the credit of Adams, relative to this important part of his narrative, and on which he considers it "completely pledged."

All accounts agree in making Kabra the grand port of trade for all merchandize brought from different countries up or down the river, – but if a navigable river pass by the city, as Adams represents, is it probable that all the commercial business would be transacted at so great a distance? Is it probable, that he would have remained several months

---

* [A native of Ceuta, Edrisi, or Al-Idrisi (1100–1166) described the known world in a work written for his patron, Roger II, Norman King of Sicily, entitled *Al-Kitab al-Rudjari* ("The Book of Roger," 1154). A Latin translation was published in 1619. Abulfedain, or Abulfeda (Abu'l Fida), historian and geographer, was born in Damascus in 1273 and died in 1331. Parts of his great compilation of geographical knowledge (*Takwim al-Buldan*, 721) appeared in Europe as early as 1650, though a full translation (into French) did not appear until 1840.]

so near this great depository of merchandize without hearing of it? Leo says the city was watered by sluices or canals running from the Niger; – would this have been necessary, if a stream of water passed within its precincts?

Park had no hints of such a river, although he was within two hundred miles of Tombuctoo, and received his information from an intelligent trader, who had been there seven times, and on whom he seems to place reliance; – but the editor, as well as the writer in the Quarterly Review, affects to treat Park's authority in this particular with very little deference, and assigns as a principal reason, that he did not understand the language of the natives, with whom he conversed. We presume these writers had forgotten, that Park made a long speech in the Bambarra language to Modibinnie, the king's minister, explaining his motives for coming into his master's dominions. This was, to be sure, during his second mission; but it was immediately after his arrival in the country, before he could have had time to learn any thing of the language, had he been ignorant of it when he came there. He must, therefore, have acquired the language during the first mission, and there is no reason for supposing him to have been ignorant of it, when he made his inquiries about Tombuctoo at Silla. Besides, he assures us, "that he received his information from such various quarters, as induced him to believe it authentick."*

The state of government at Tombuctoo is another point in which Adams' story differs from every other account. It has always been represented to be in the hands of the Moors. Park was told at Silla, "that the king [or chief] himself, and the principal officers of state were Moors," and that the Mohammedans there were very zealous in propagating their religion. It is a well known fact in Moorish history, that Tombuctoo was for a long time subject to the emperour of Morocco previous to the death of *Muley Ishmael* in 1727. After this event the tribute began to be irregularly transmitted, and was finally discontinued. The Moors, stationed in garrison there, had intermarried with the natives, and lost in some degree their attachment for the country of their ancestors, – but still they preserved their influence, their manners, and religion. Jackson observes, and he seems to speak with a knowledge of the fact, "that the

---

* Last Mission, p. 244. [This appears actually to be a reference to a passage from Park's first mission, p. 217. The passage in the next paragraph is found on p. 215 in the *Travels*.]

Cadi, or chief magistrate of Tombuctoo in 1800, had been a principal trader in Mogadore, and was son in law to the governour – who being unsuccessful in his commercial affairs, crossed the desert, and soon obtained the appointment of Cadi. He was a shrewd man, about thirty five years old."* Mr. Jackson had resided long at Mogadore, and it is very unlikely he would have made such a statement without knowing it to be true. It is not understood from Jackson, nor necessarily from Park, that Tombuctoo is at present an independent kingdom of itself, but rather a province in the dominions of the king of Bambarra; – and this Cadi, it would seem, held his office under him.

We have not time to pursue Adams through all the improbabilities, inconsistencies, and contradictions of his story. We have mentioned some of the more important only, and such as could not possibly arise from defect of memory or observation, – we will notice only two or three more. In the last narrative he talks a good deal about a Portuguese boy, by the name of Stevens, who accompanied him throughout his whole tour, – in the other he does not once hint at this circumstance, but gives the impression constantly that he was alone. He saw no canoes more than *ten feet* long, and according to one account, these were made of the *date tree*, and to the other, *of the fig tree*. Park bought canoes at San-sanding *forty feet* long, out of which he constructed the schooner Joliba. At Cadiz he said the natives regarded him with indifference, "and manifested no desire of knowing any thing more of him or of his country, than what he voluntarily told them," – at London he tells of the "people coming in crowds to stare at him and his companion," and of having "afterwards understood that many persons came several days' journey on purpose." At one place he makes his residence in Tombuctoo *nine months*, – at the other, *six months*.

With regard to the size of Tombuctoo, we have no disposition to magnify it vastly beyond the dimensions, which it would be made to have from the description of Adams. Mr. Court told us it had generally been represented to him as less, than the city of Morocco. We have no doubt it has been on the decline for many years, and that Haousa, being in a more central position, may have become a place of more importance; – but still it is certain, that Tombuctoo is yet the theatre of a very extensive commercial intercourse, and the only resort of the large caravans from

* [Jackson, p. 300.]

the north and the west, – and as such, it would be idle to consider it any other than a place of wealth, activity, and large population. Such it would appear to be from every other account except the one before us, whose pretensions we have sufficiently examined. It may be remarked, that Sansanding contains eleven thousand inhabitants, although it has never been known as a place of trade or importance. We put no confidence, however, in any part of Sidi Hamet's stories about his journeyings into the interiour, which occupy so large a portion of Captain Riley's book, and which make Tombuctoo contain two hundred and sixteen thousand inhabitants.*

We will only observe further, that were the narratives we have been considering pursued from Tombuctoo to Mogadore, they would be scarcely recognized as describing the same events. The times and distances, which, let us repeat, were in both cases pertinaciously insisted on by the narrator, entirely disagree throughout, as may be seen by a slight inspection of them in the preceding note. The London narrative in this part is duly set off with appropriate adventures and incidents, which probably had not been thought of at Cadiz, but which serve to give effect and interest, and what was of equal importance to the editor and booksellers, to swell the book into a comely size.

We shall add here such external evidence, as we have been able to collect from different sources, in confirmation of the opinion we have advanced. The following is a letter from Mr. Storrow.

Boston, June 2, 1817.

– I first saw Robert Adams during the summer of the year 1814 in Cadiz. Mr. Simpson, the American Consul at Tangier, stated to Mr. Charles H. Hall of Cadiz, that an American sailor was with him, who had been redeemed from slavery among the Moors, and who was said, during the period of his captivity, to have been carried to a greater distance into the interiour of Africa, than any white person had before advanced. The man was represented to be in extreme wretchedness, and Mr. Hall, as well from benevolence as from the desire to learn his history, requested that he might be sent to him in Cadiz. I saw him immediately after his arrival at that place. My first impressions were not in his favour; he seemed ignorant and stupid, but on farther acquaintance I found him crafty and observing. As his general conversation was incoherent, I requested him to give me a special detail of the occurrences of his captivity

* [Captain James Riley's *Narrative of the Loss of the American Brig Commerce . . .* (1817).]

in such shape as might be committed to paper. The only method of arriving at this was by a series of inquiries, embracing the whole period. In that part of his narration relating to his residence in Morocco, I had no reason to doubt him, but as soon as he represented himself to have been carried beyond the confines of that kingdom, I perceived an evident difference of manner. His answers were more vague; there seemed a greater dependence on invention than memory; a willingness to be assisted and readiness, as I thought, to assent to any thing I suggested.

He was irritated by the expression of any doubt of his veracity, although when it was called in question he adduced no other proof of it than a more positive assertion. When the story was completed, my doubts had so far prevailed that I affixed to it no value whatever; – partly from the meagreness of the narrative itself, and partly from the mode in which it was communicated. I assented to the leading facts of the shipwreck and captivity, and to his having been carried from place to place within the limits of Morocco, and imagined that by imputing what he saw in that kingdom to other parts of Africa, he found it easy to impose on those who had never been in either. His inducement to frame a story was apparent, as by means of it he had acquired a currency and temporary livelihood, which he had sufficient shrewdness to anticipate at the commencement. Shortly after examining Adams, I met an intelligent man by the name of Jewet, who had been in the interiour of Africa, as far as Bambarra; he rejected the story as improbable and unlike his own experience. Shortly afterwards intelligence arrived through Mr. Simpson, from one of Adams' shipwrecked comrades, stating that his story was false; that he had never been separated from his companions in captivity for a sufficient length of time to warrant his account.

The process of acquiring information from Adams was tedious. After a short trial I found it ineffectual to depend on what might be suggested by himself unassisted. I therefore divided the whole time into small portions, making special inquiries as to the employment of each part. When on a march, I endeavoured to refresh his memory by inquiring into the occurrences of each day in regular succession. When stationary in any village or encampment, I endeavoured to elicit every thing by a minute reference to whatever I imagined might belong to such place. At the end of the inquiry on each subject, I read to him the result, and requested him to communicate whatever else might suggest itself. In relation to several topicks, on which I was doubtful, he told me repeatedly, that he had nothing more to offer – among these were the king and royal family of Tombuctoo, and the birds and beasts of that region generally.

The times, directions, and distances of his several journies were calculated by him with care and apparent precision. In these he depended on memory solely. The courses were ascertained, as he said, by observing the sun and stars.

It may appear singular that I made no exertion to expose what I considered to be an imposture. In the early part of the narrative I entertained no doubts; in the subsequent part after doubts had arisen, I contented myself with my own conviction, without seeking for means of explaining it to others; – more especially as there appeared no reason for attaching any importance either to Adams or his journal.

Yours,

SAMUEL A. STORROW.

We insert here also an extract from a letter which we have lately received on the subject, from a gentleman of respectability at Gibraltar, dated March 27, 1817.

We have just returned from Tangier, where I saw Mr. Simpson, and conversed with him about Robert Adams. I wrote you sometime ago what Mr. Shaler told me of Mr Simpson's detecting the imposture. I have with me his copy of the narrative, containing his marginal notes. Adams is indeed' second only to Psalmanazar.' The testimony of several of the crew proves, that he was never more than two or three days journey distant from Wednoon, and some of his shipmates were always with him. Mr. Hall, brother to the merchant with whom he resided thirteen months at Cadiz, and who was there at the time, is now in this place. He has read the narrative with me, and says the story is different from the one he told at Cadiz, and in many parts contradictory, especially in what relates to Tombuctoo. Mr. Samuel A. Storrow, who was then at Cadiz, questioned him repeatedly, and carried to the United States in manuscript the result of his examinations. It was unfortunate that Mr. Dupuis left his papers at Mogadore, for his memory certainly failed him, and as it respects dates, his statements in London contradict his letters now in possession of Mr. Simpson. All agree, that Adams was shrewd, observing, and of a retentive memory.

Adams said in London, that he was a native of Hudson, in the state of New York, and that he sailed from New York, June 17th, or as he said at Cadiz, May 7th, 1810. We state with confidence, on the authority of a gentleman who has resided at Hudson ever since its first settlement, that no family of this name has been known there till within twelve years, and that no person of the character and pretensions of Adams has ever been heard of in that place. We have seen a letter from the collector of

New York, which certifies, that no vessel answering Adams' description of the Charles has cleared from that port.*

We leave our readers to draw such inferences from these facts, as they think proper. To us they appear conclusive, and connected with the fabulous character of the narrative, they impress a conviction of deception and bold imposition, on the part of Adams, which we think no one, who examines the subject with much interest or candour, can resist.

---

* [Unfortunately, there is a gap in the National Archives' record of "Foreign Clearances" from the Port of New York for the period from July 1809 through the end of 1817. However, a search of the crew lists for ships departing New York in May and June of 1810 reveals no trace of the *Charles*. Similarly, a search of the first federal census reveals no one named either Rose or Adams living in the town of Hudson in 1790, at a time when one should expect to find some record of Adams's "sail maker" father.]

INDEX

*Marked entries indicate a topic indexed in the original publication of *The Narrative of Robert Adams* (1816)

Abdà, 94
Abu Bakr, Pasha, xix
Abulfedain (Abulfeda), 176
Abyssinia, 77
Accra, xxiii
Adams, John, l
*Adams, Robert
    alternative version of narrative told by,
        147–161
    as Christian hero, xlvii–xlix, 98–100, 179
    credibility of, xii–xiv, xvi–xxiii, xxxvii–xl,
        22, 72–91, 102–105, 106–124,
        162–179, 182
    in sub-Saharan Africa, 31–34, 70–72,
        149–150
    in Timbuctoo, 35–48, 72–91, 149–157
    racial identity of, xliii, 89, 91
    ransom of by Dupuis, 64–66, 100
    relations with the African Company,
        ix–xi, xiv, xxxii, 9–14, 147
    shipwreck and first enslavement of, 22,
        26–31, 68, 69, 70, 148–149, 169–170
    transported as slave from Timbuctoo to
        Wed-Noon, 49, 63, 91–101, 157–161
    uncertainty regarding identity of, x–xi, 17,
        70, 147
    voyage of from Wed-Noon to England,
        67, 161
Admiralty, x, xi, xxiii, 13
Africa
    exploration of, xxiii, xxxii–xxxiii, liii, 8,
        163–167
    shipwrecks on coast of, 9, 15, 22, 69, 148
    slavery in, x, xxv, xxvi, xlii, lii, 8, 99

sub-Saharan, xx, 16, 32–34
western knowledge of, xiv, xv, xxi, xxiv,
    xxvii, xxviii–xxx, xxxii, xxxvii–xxxviii,
    xlii, 9–14, 23–25, 59, 76, 79, 82,
    106–109, 124, 125–135, 144
African Association, xi, xxii, xxiv, xxvii,
    xxviii, xxx, xxxii–xxxiii, xxxviii, 13,
    117, 126
*African Company (Company of Merchants
    Trading to Africa) xxii, li
    and publication of the *Narrative*, x, xi, xiv,
        xxviii–xxxi, xxxvii–xxxix, xlii, xliii,
        147
    Committee of the, x, xiii, xiv, xvi, xxii,
        xxiii, xxvii, xxix, xxx, xxxii, xxxvi,
        xxxvii, xxxviii, 9, 10, 18, 67
    Gold Coast possessions of, xxiii–xxiv, xxvi
    history of, xxiii–xxxi
    parliamentary investigation of, xxv–xxviii
    slave trading and, xxiii–xxiv,
        xxxviii–xxxix, xlii, liii
African Institution, xxv, xxvii, xxviii, xxx
Agadeer Bomba, 31. *See also* Ághadír Dóme
Agadir, 15, 65, 95, 104, 143, 161. *See also*
    Santa Cruz
*Agadir Doma (Ághadír Dóme), 70. *See also*
    Agadeer Bomba
Aiata Mouessa Ali, 57, 58, 59, 104, 171
Aisha, 56–57, 93, 106
Ait Amoor, 142
Akkadia, 64, 104, 171
al-Aqib, Muhammed, xix
al-Fasi. *See* Leo Africanus
Algiers, xlv, xlix, lii, 169

al-Idrisi. *See* Edrisi
al-Kunti, Sidi al-Mukhtar, xix
Allison, Robert, xlix
al-Zayani, xlvi
Amadi Foutouma, 72, 96, 97–98, 116
Anagoos, 24
*Andalusie, 142
Annamaboe, xxiii
Antrie, 142
Appolonia, xxiii
*Arabs
  Adams's resemblance to, 15, 91
  and slavery, xi, 15, 28, 69, 70, 83, 90, 92,
    93, 96, 98–100, 110, 116, 148–149,
    150, 170
  and trade, 68, 73, 76, 125
  as objects of European science, xlii, 136,
    139–141, 142
  culture and character of, 68, 74, 78, 88,
    89, 91, 93, 94, 117, 137, 138, 139, 142,
    143, 144
*arrows, poisoned, 41, 81
Ashanti, xxiv
Association for Promoting the Discovery of
  the Interior Parts of Africa. *See* African
  Association
Atlas Mountains, 136, 137
Azamoor, 142, 145

Badoo, 130
Baepler, Paul, xliii, liv
Bahar-Nile, 75. *See also* Niger River
*Ba Fing (Bafing) River, 131, 132
Bajedore, Cape, 96, 169
*Ba Lee River, 131
*Bamako, 128–130, 133, 135
Bambara, xx, xliii, 77, 86, 117, 126, 175,
  177, 180
  and Niger River, 47, 90, 127
  and Timbuctoo, 72, 85, 110, 112, 114,
    117, 173, 178
  extent of, 71, 109, 110
  slavery and, xxxix, 45–46
Ba Nimma River, 116
*Banks, Sir Joseph, xi, xii, xxii, xxiv, xxxii,
  xxxiii, xxxviii, 13, 97, 130, 147, 163,
  174
*Barbary, 38, 71, 74, 82, 174
  peoples of described, 18, 136–145
  representation in captivity narratives, xlvi
  shipwrecks on the coast of, 69, 96
  slavery in, 78, 85, 95

Timbuctoo's trade with, xxxv, 72, 73, 75,
  76, 79, 81, 87, 88, 89, 101, 115, 118,
  122, 165, 172
Barbary captivity narratives, xiv, xlv–lv
  abolitionists' use of, li–liii
  American cultural identity and, xlix–l
  Christian-Moslem conflict in, xv, xlvi–li
Barbary States, xlvi, xlix, li, 73, 167. *See also*
  states by name
Barbary War, l
Barros, João de, xxxv
*Barrow, Sir John, xi, xii, xxxiii, xxxviii, 13,
  82, 163, 167
*Barry, John, 69
Barth, Heinrich, xviii, xix
*Bathurst, Earl, 13, 163
*Ba Woolima River, 132
Beasley, Consul R. G., 10
Beeroo, 110
Bel-Cossim, xlviii–xlix, 60, 61, 95, 98
Beni Hassan, 55
Benin, Bight of, 24, 25, 77
Benowm, 71, 110
Berbers, xlii, 28, 136–139, 140, 142, 143. *See*
  also Errifi, Imraguen, Shilluh
*Berrebbers. *See* Berbers
*Betoo (Betou), 126, 127
Biafra, Bight of, xxxiii, 24
Black River, 130
Blanco, Cape (Cap Blanc), 15, 23, 169
Boerick, 57
Bojador, Cape. *See* Bajedore
Boki River, 132
Bondou, 47, 72, 74, 81
Boston, l, 147, 179
Bougainville, Louis Antoine de, 167
Bouré, xl
Brancker, P.W., 96
Bristol, xxiii, 67
Bruce, Consul James, 167
Brue, Adrien Hubert, 166
Buffon, 79
Bukharie, 141, 142, 143
Burckhardt, Johann Ludwig, xxxiii

Cabara, xviii, 120–124, 165, 176
Cadamosto, Alvise, xxxv
Cadiz, x, xii, xvi, xvii, 8, 9, 26, 66, 67,
  83, 102, 104, 106, 147, 162, 175,
  179–181
"Cadiz Narrative" of Robert Adams, xiii,
  168–171. *See also* "Interiour of Africa"

"Calculation Upon The Returns" (Simon Cock), xxvi–xxvii, xxxi
Caillié, Réné, xvii–xviii, xix, xx, xxxix–xl, xli, 37
Cairo, xxxii, xxxiii. *See also* Egypt
Calabar, xxxiii
Cambridge, xli
Canary Islands, 29, 69, 93
*cannibals, 85
*canoes, use of in Sub-Sahara, 76, 157, 178
Cape Coast Castle, xxiv
Cape Verde Islands, 27, 68, 148. *See also* May, Isle of
*caravans, desert trading of, 87–89, 153, 179
Carlyle, Thomas, liii
Castlereagh, Lord, xxvii, 10
Charles (ship), xlv, 9, 15, 17, 22, 23, 26, 29, 67, 68, 70, 93, 94, 98, 99, 106, 148, 160, 161, 182
*Christians, 107, 153
as slaves in North Africa, lii–liv, 15, 57, 59, 61, 62, 63, 69, 70, 89, 93, 95, 98–100, 138, 141, 159, 161
representations of in Barbary narratives, xv, xlvi, liv
Cidi Hamet, 179
*Cidi Hamet a Moussa, 65
great market of, 101
Cidi Heshem, 64, 87, 101, 136
*Cidi Mohammed Monsoul, 65
Clarke, Martin, 27, 101
Cock, Simon, xxii, xxiii
mediation of *Narrative* by, xiii, xx, xxi, xxix, xxx, xxxii, xxxvii, xxxviii, xlii, xliii, xliv, xlvi, xlvii, 19
relations of with Robert Adams, x–xi, xvi, xxxii, 8–14
relations of with the British government, xxv–xxviii, xxxvi
Colley, Linda, xlv, xlviii, li
Colonial Office, xxix, xxx, 8
colonialism, xiv, xv, xxx–xxxi, xxxii, li, 134–135
Columbia County (NY), xvi
Commenda, xxiii
Company of Merchants Trading to Africa. *See* African Company
Congo, Kingdom of, 25
Consulate in London, American, 9, 10
Cook, Captain James, 167
Cooper, James Fenimore, xlii

*courcoo, xxi, 40, 80, 174
Cresques, Abraham, xxxiv, xlii

Dahomey, 24
Dalby, 148, 161. *See also* Dolbie, Stephen
dancing, 44, 84–85
*D'Anville, Jean-Baptiste Bourgignon, 24, 76, 96, 127, 128
*Davison, James, xlvii, 27, 60, 63, 106
Decatur, Stephen, l
D'Entrecasteaux, Antoine Raymond Joseph de Bruni, 167
Desert, The, 12, 15, 16, 18, 51–52, 68, 69, 71, 74, 75, 78, 92, 93, 98, 106, 108, 135, 140, 144. *See also* Sahara Desert
trade across, 87, 89, 100, 101, 115, 118, 178
*Dibbie, Lake, 121, 123
Dindikoo, 130
Dixcove, xxiii
Djenné, xl, 126, 127. *See also* Jinnie
*Dolbie, Stephen, 26, 30, 31, 59, 63, 98
*Douar, 68, 90, 107
Douglass, Frederick, xlv
*Dupuis, Joseph
as ethnographer, xlii, 136–145
contributions to the *Narrative* of, xi, xiii, xiv, xv, xx, xxi, xxxii, 19, 68–102, 115, 122, 136, 173
Journal of a Residence in Ashanti (1824), xxxi
ransom of Adams by, xii, 63
relations of with Adams at Mogador, xvi, xliii, xlviii, 14–18, 28, 65, 106, 108, 175, 181

E' Dákhela. *See* Agadeer Bomba
Edinburgh Review, 147, 163
Edoutanan, 142
Edrisi, 176
Egypt, xvii, xxxiv, 126, 172
El Araische, 66
*elephants, xviii, 39–40, 48, 79–80, 174
El Gharb, 142, 145
*El Gazie, 28, 29, 52, 68, 103
*El Kabla, xxi, 15, 16, 54–57, 92, 93, 103, 106, 171
el-Wazzan-ez-Zayyati, El-Hasan ben Muhammed. *See* Leo Africanus
*Errifi (Berbers), 136, 137, 139
*Exchequer, Chancellor of the, xxiii, 13, 163

Fabian, Ann, xxii
*Falemé (Falémé) River, 130, 131
*Fatima, Queen, xx, 35–36, 39, 42, 72, 172
Fez, xxxv, xliii, 66, 89, 95, 102, 106, 136,
    137, 142
Fezzan, xxxii
Foota Jalla, 130
Foreign Office, xi
Formosa, xxi
Foulah, 71, 73, 77, 110, 112, 114. See also
    Fulani
France, xvii, xxi, xxxviii, xli, xlvii, 29, 37,
    60, 61, 69, 96, 103, 122, 125, 134, 166
Frederick's Place, x, xxvii
Fulani, xliii. See also Foulah
*Furkomah River, 132

Galam, 77, 125, 134, 166
*Gambia River, xxxi, xxxii, xxxvii, 23, 25,
    115, 129, 130, 131, 134–135, 170
Gardner, Brian, xx
Garrison, William Lloyd, xlv
*Genné. See Djenné
Ghana, xxiii, 96, 123
Ghent, Treaty of, x
Gibraltar, 16, 17, 26, 67, 96, 148, 181
Giovanni Leone. See Leo Africanus
gold, xxxiii–xxxvii, xxxix, 35, 42, 46, 81,
    101, 153
Gold Coast, xxiii–xxiv, xxv, xxviii, xxxi,
    xxxix, 27, 77
*Gollo, 85–86
Good Hope, Cape of, xxiii
*Gordon, Sir James Willoughby, xxi, 13, 19,
    163
Goree, xxx
*Goulburn, Henry, 13, 163
*Gouvina, Rock of, 126, 128, 129
Granada, ix, xxxv, 79
Gray, Major William, 8
Guien, 176
Guinea, xxxvii, 25
*gunpowder, 45, 60, 96
*guns (Arab and Sub-Saharan possession of),
    63, 64, 69, 74, 83, 93, 153

Hàhà, 136
Hall, Charles H., 67, 106, 179, 181
*Haoussa. See Hausa
Harrison, Captain, 23, 60. See also Horton,
    Captain John
*Harrison, Sir George, 13, 163

Hausa, 24–25, 60, 88, 96, 97, 119, 178
Hawata. See Imraugen
*heirie (mahri), 39, 78, 94
Heligassa. See Lagassa
Heligobla, 159, 160, 171. See also El Kabla
Hieta Mouessa Ali. See Aiata Mouessa Ali
*Hilla Gibla. See El Kabla
Holyhead, xii, xvi, 9, 67
Hornemann, Frederick, xxxiii, 167
*horses, 39, 78, 156, 174
*Horton, Captain John, 23, 26, 28, 29, 70
Hottentots, xliv
Houghton, Major Daniel, xxxii, xxxiii
Houssa, Abdullah, 57
Hudson (NY), xvi, 26, 181
Hudson River. See North River

Ibn Battuta, xxxiv–xxxv, xxxvii, xli
imperialism, xiv, xv, li. See also colonialism
impressment, l, 10, 17
Imraugen, 28
Indian captivity narrative
"Interiour of Africa" (North American
    Review), xiii, 162–182
Isaaco, 72, 85, 96
*Isha. See Aisha
*Issa, 76. See also Niger River

Jackson, James Grey, xxxvi, xxxvii, 72, 115,
    117, 167, 169, 172, 177
Jalonka, 132
Jama'a (of Timbuctoo)
Jefferson, Thomas, xxxii, l, liii
Jerba, xxxv
Jerusalem, xxxv
Jews, North African, xlii, 64, 136
Jibbel Kumri. See Mountains of the Moon
Jingereber (mosque), xix
*Jinnie, 47, 76, 88, 116, 119. See also
    Djenné
John Murray (publishers), x
Joko, 109
Joliba, 47, 90. See also Niger River
Jomard, Edme-François, xvii–xviii, xl, 48
*Joos. See Oyos

Kaarta, 117, 175
Kabra. See Cabara
*Kancaba, 129, 133
*Kanno (Kano), 60, 96
*Kashna, 97
Kasson, Kingdom of, 132

Kayee, 130
*Kong Mountains, 25, 130, 133
Konkodoo, 130, 131, 132
Konkromo, 131
Koran, 99, 117, 173
Koster & Co., 96
Kumasi, xxxi
Kunta, xx

Labat, Jean Baptiste, 166, 175
Lagassa, 160, 171
*Lagos, 24
*Lahamar River, 76
l'Hagi Mohammed Sherriffe, 117
Laing, Gordon, xli
*La Mar Zarah, xvii, 23, 37–38, 74–76, 104,
    120, 171, 175–177. See also La Parsire
Lander, Richard and John, 25
La Parsire, xvii, 151, 156, 171, 175. See also
    La Mar Zarah
La Pérouse, Comte de, 167
Laubed, Mahomet, 53, 55
Ledyard, John, xxiv, xxxii, xxxiii, 126, 164
Leo X, Pope, xxxv
*Leo Africanus, ix, xxviii, xxxv–xxxvi,
    xxxvii, xxxviii, xl, 78, 118, 119, 120,
    121, 122–124, 164, 165, 174, 175,
    176
Leptunes, 165
Lincoln, Abraham, lii
Lisbon, xviii, 26, 37
Liverpool, xxiii, xxvi, 26, 67, 96
Liverpool, Lord, 13
London, ix, x, xii, xiii, xiv, xvi, xx, xxi, xxiii,
    xxix, xxxvi, xxxvii, xliv, 8, 9, 10, 15,
    67, 106, 147, 168, 172, 174, 175, 179
Lucas, Simon, xxiv, xxxii, 126, 167
Ludamar, 71, 117

Madina, 131, 132
Madison, James, l
Maghreb, xxxiii, xxxvii, xxxix
Mahees, 24
mahri. See heirie
Mali (Empire of), xxxiii–xxxv, xli
*Malins, 126, 128
Mande, xxxiv
Mandingo, xliv, 47, 77, 86, 91, 126, 128,
    166
Mansa Musa, xxxiii, xxxvii, xlii
*maps, African, 22–25, 102–105, 108–109,
    125–135

Maqil, 52
*Mármol y Carvajal, Luis de, 76, 165
Marrakesh, xxxvi, 138
Marrakech, Treaty of, 16
Martin, Eveline, xxiii, xxv
Masina, 110, 112, 114
Matthews, John, 27
*Mauri, 144
Mauritania, xii, 139, 144, 145
May, Isle of, 27, 68. See also Cape Verde
    Islands
Mecca, xxxiii, 126, 138
*Medainien, 144
Medina, 125, 126
Meknes, xii, 66, 106, 136, 137, 142
Mequinez. See Meknes
Mesurata, 126
Middle Passage, xxvi
Milton, John, xlvii
*Mogador (Essaouira), 64, 94, 104, 106,
    136, 138, 142, 169, 171. See also
    Suerra
  and ransom trade in European captives,
    xlvii, 31, 57, 70, 94–101, 161
  as trading center, 69, 92, 168, 178
  Joseph Dupuis' interview of Adams at, xi,
    xiii, xvi, xxi, xliii, 14–18, 63, 65, 68,
    74, 75, 76, 78, 79, 81, 83, 93, 102,
    175
  Sub-Saharan slaves at, 83, 84, 85, 91
Moghtari, 62
Mohammedan. See Moslems
Monroe, James, l
*Montezuma (ship), 60, 96
*Moors, xliii, l, 48, 64, 65, 66, 85, 99, 100,
    134. See also Andalusie, Bukharie
  as objects of European science, xlii, 136,
    141
  at Timbuctoo, 44, 47, 72, 88, 110–120,
    173, 177
  enslavement of Adams by, xii, xliii, xlvii,
    28–33, 49, 59–64, 98, 148–149,
    157–161
  Europeans slaves held by, 69, 157
  slavery of Sub-Saharans and, 31–34, 71,
    78, 109, 110, 149–150
  trade of with Sub-Saharan Africa, xxxvii,
    xl, 36, 37, 39, 42, 44, 71, 73, 74, 76, 81,
    87, 127, 153
Moorzan, 113, 115
Morocco, xi, xii, xvii, xviii, xix, xl, xlii, 16,
    78, 87, 136, 167, 172, 174, 178, 180

Morocco, Emperor of, xlvi, 18, 64, 65, 78, 84, 87, 94, 95, 96, 101, 137, 138, 140, 142, 160, 177
  meeting with Adams of, xi, xii, 66, 102
  occupation of Timbuctoo by, 116, 177
Moslems, 144
  and sub-Saharan Africa, xx, 82, 84, 173, 177
  as Other, xv, xlvi, xlviii, 115
  as persecutors of Christians, 60, 63, 98–100, 112, 161
Moulay Suliman, Sultan, 16
Mountains of the Moon, 25
Mourzouk, 126
Muggs, Captain Jonathon Washington. See "Specimens of a Timbuctoo Anthology"
mulatto, xxix, xliii, xliv, 17, 140
Mulai Ismael, Emperor, 87, 142, 177
musical instruments, African, 44
muskets. See guns
Musselman. See Moslems
Mutnougo, 47

Napoleon, 29, 37, 117
Narrative of Robert Adams, The
  and African Company relations with Parliament, xxviii–xxxi
  and Moslem-Christian conflict, xv
  and race, xlii–liv, 15
  and western knowledge of Africa, xiv, xxviii–xxx, xxxii, xxxvii
  as performance, xxix
  credibility of, xi–xiv, xvi–xxiii, 102–105, 106–124, 162–182
  modern interest of, xiv–xv
  parody of, xliv
  publication of, x, xi, xiv, xxvi, xxviii, xxxi, l, liii
  relationship to popular literary forms, xiv, xliv–lv
*Negroes (Sub-Saharan Africans), 91, 147
  Adams's resemblance to, xliii, 15, 91
  as pagans, xxxi, xxxii, 81, 82, 115, 124
  as slaves, 31–33, 57, 60, 64, 71, 142, 143, 157, 170
  and the Soudan, 16, 24, 102, 108, 124, 140, 165
  and Timbuctoo, 35–48, 72–91, 110–120, 149–157
  customs of described, 32–34, 50–51, 61, 70–72, 126, 149–157

Nelson, Unis, 27, 70, 95
New Monthly Magazine and Literary Journal, xliv, xlv
New York, ix, x, 14, 15, 17, 26, 38, 148, 181
Newsham, Unis, 27, 30, 31, 70, 95
Nicholas (seaman), 27, 28, 70, 95, 99
*Niger River
  at Timbuctoo, ix, xviii, xxxv, 74–76
  names of the, 75, 76, 90
  Park's missions to, xxix–xxxi, xxxiii, 8, 112, 113, 114, 116, 164
  trade along the, xxxi, xl, 172
  western knowledge of, 18, 23–25, 47, 75, 96, 120–124, 125–135, 164, 167, 175–177
Nile-Abide, 76. See also Niger River
Nile River, 23, 75
Noon, Cape (Cap Noun), 96, 148, 169
North American Review, xiii, xvi, xvii
North River (Hudson), 26
Norton, Captain John, 148. See also Horton, Captain John
Numidian, 139
Nupe, xxxiii

Oil Rivers, 25
Old Jewry (London), x
orientalism, xv, xlvi, xlviii, liv
Ottomans, li
Oued Noun. See Wed-Noon
Oulad Adrialla. See Woled Adrialla
Oulad Bou Sbaa. See Woled Aboussebàh
Oulad Delim. See Woled D'Leim
Oulad El-Hadj Ben Demouiss. See Woled-el-Hadj
Oulad El Kabla. See El Kabla
Oxford, xxii, xxvii
Oyos, 24

Paddock, Judah, xlv
*Park, Mungo, xxviii, xxxiii, xliii, 24, 144
  Adams's account compared with that of, xxix–xxxi, xxxv, xxxviii, 71–72, 74, 76, 81, 82, 83–84, 86, 87, 88, 108, 109, 110, 111, 112–124, 173, 175, 177–178
  exploration of the Niger by, xxxii, 8, 23, 25, 96, 97–98, 118, 120, 127–135, 164
Parliament, xxiii, xxiv, xxv–xxviii
*Peddie, Major John, xxix, 8, 14, 24
Pennant, Thomas, 78
Phillips, Wendell, xlv

Pina, Ruy de, xxxiv
Pory, John, xxxv, 78, 113, 119, 122
Punic, 139
Psalmanazar, George, xxi, 13, 163, 181

Quaque, xxvii
Quarterly Review (London), xvii, xlv, 25, 147, 163, 174, 177
Quartermaster General. *See* Sir James Willoughby Gordon

Rabat. *See* Rhabatt
Ramusio, Giovanni Battista, 119
Ras Nouâdhibou. *See* Cape Blanco
Red Sea, 172
Reichard, Christian Gottlieb, 25
Regency, ix, xxv, li
Rehamni, 142
*Rennell, Major James, xxx, 23, 24, 90, 97, 110, 112, 114, 123, 127, 128, 132
Rhabatt, 142
Riley, Captain James, xlv, li, 169, 179
Robbins, Archibald, xlv, 55, 57
Romans, 144, 145, 164
*Romi, 145
*Rose, Benjamin, x, xi, xiii, xiv, xvi, xxxii, 17, 70, 106, 182. *See also* Robert Adams
Royal African Company, xxiii, xxiv
Royal Navy, x, xi, xlix, 10, 17
Royal Society, xi, 13
Ruma, 116

Saffy (Safi), 94
Sahara Desert, ix, xii, xiii, xiv, xxix, xxxiii, xxxiv, xl, xli, xliii, li, 30–32, 70, 158. *See also* Desert
Said, Edward, xv, xlviii
St. Joseph, Fort of, 134
Salem, Amedallah, 60
Sallee, xxiii, 142
Sankari, 127
Sankore (mosque), xix
Sansanding, xl, 87, 96, 112, 114, 120, 129, 173, 178, 179
Santa Cruz (Canary Islands), 29
Santa Cruz (Morocco), 64, 69, 95. *See also* Agadir
Secretary of State for War and the Colonies, xxiii, xxv, xxvii, 13, 19
Sego (Ségou), 85, 88, 110, 112, 114, 119, 120, 129

*Senegal River, xxxiv, 22, 28, 31, 70, 76, 110, 125, 127, 129, 131, 132, 133, 134, 166, 170, 176
September 11 attacks, xv
Seville, 26
Shiedma (province), 94
*Shilluh (Shluh), xliii, 15, 101, 136, 137–139, 143
Sidi Yaya (mosque), xix
Sierra Leone Company, xxiv, xxv
Silla, 23, 112, 114, 115, 117, 177
*Simpson, Consul James, 16, 66, 67, 70, 102, 179, 180, 181
Sinclair, Sir John, xxxvi
Slatees, 113, 115
slave narratives, xliv, li
slave trade
  abolition of, xiv, xxviii, xxxviii, li, liii, 164
  British, xiv, xxiii, xxv, xxvi, xxvii, xxxviii–xxxix, xlii
  North African, xiv, xxxix, 49, 63, 81, 85, 87, 93, 95, 96, 149, 157
slavery, xv, xxxi
  of Adams in North Africa, x, xiv, xlv, 8, 28–33, 49, 63, 148–149, 157–161, 179
  of Sub-Saharan Africans by North Africans, xiv, xxxix, 31–33, 49, 60, 81, 83, 84, 96, 124, 157, 170
  of Sub-Saharan Africans by Europeans, xxvi, li
  of Sub-Saharan Africans by Sub-Saharans, 43, 45–46, 124, 129
  of North Africans by Europeans, xxxv
  of westerners in North Africa, xiv, xlv, li, 76, 89, 93, 98–100, 179
Slavery No Oppression, xxiv. *See also* Company of Merchants Trading to Africa
slaves. *See* slavery
Sloan, Sir Hans, xxii
Société de Géographie de Paris, xvii
*Soosos, 128
*Sootasoo, 126, 128
Soudan
  people of, xxxi, 73, 82, 84, 86, 110, 124, 140, 142, 144, 149–157
  products and animals of, 73, 76, 79, 80, 92
  trade of with North Africa, xxxiii, xxxvi, 88, 91, 93, 101, 116, 138, 143
*Soudenny, xx, 31–34, 70–72, 81, 83, 89, 90, 103, 107, 108–110, 149–151, 170, 171

Sparks, Jared, xiii, xvi–xvii, xxviii
"Specimens of a Timbuctoo Anthology",
   xliv
Stephens (also Stevens), John, 27, 31, 35, 37,
   39, 47, 178
Sterne, Laurence, xxii
Stillwell, Charles, 26
Storrow, Samuel A., xiii, xvi, 170, 172,
   179–181
Succondee, xxiii
Sudan. See Soudan
*Suerra, 31, 53, 70, 89, 104. See also
   Mogador
Sultan, 70. See also Morocco, Emperor of
Sumner, Charles, lii
Suse (Suz), 64, 101, 136
Swanzey, James, 27

Takkeda, xxxiv
Tamashek, 48
Tangier, xii, xlv, xlix, 16, 17, 66, 70, 100,
   102, 106, 160, 179, 181
Tantumquerry, xxiii
*Taudeny. See Toudenny
Temporal, Jean, 123, 175
Teneriffe, 69
Tennyson, Alfred Lord, xli–xlii
Tensift, 94
Tetuan, 142
*Timbuctoo, xliii, 50, 54
   Adams's account of, ix, x, xi, xii–xiv, xv,
      xvi–xxi, xxii, 8, 9, 11, 13, 14, 15,
      16–17, 35–48, 51, 72–91, 102, 103, 106,
      108, 109, 147, 149–157, 158, 162, 170,
      171, 172–179, 180, 181
   and Islam, xv, xviii–xx, 82–83, 173–174
   relations of with sub-Saharan region, 33,
      45–46, 110, 149–151
   trade of, xxxvii, xl, 36, 37, 39, 42, 44, 46,
      49, 50, 73, 87, 88, 96, 172–173
   western knowledge of, xvi–xxii, xxviii,
      xxxi–xlii, l, 22–23, 72–91, 110–124,
      125, 128, 165–168
"Timbuctoo" (poem), xli
Toniba, 130
Toudenny, xl, 47, 50, 59, 90, 91, 92, 104,
   107, 157, 158, 171
Travels in the Interior Districts of Africa
   (1799). See Park, Mungo

*Treasury, Lords of the, xvi, 14, 163
Tripoli, xxxiii, xlv, xlix, 166
Tuaregs, 39, 47
Tuckey, Captain (R.N.), 24
Tudenny. See Toudenny
Tunis, xlv, xlix

Vaillant, François Le, 167
Vansittart, Nicholas, 13
Villa Adrialla. See Woled Adrialla
Villa de Bousbach. See Woled Aboussebàh
Vled Duleim. See Woled D'Leim

*Wadinoon. See Wed-Noon
Walet, 119
Wangara, xxxiv, xxxvi, 85, 96, 172
War of 1812, x, 10, 66, 70, 128
Wargee (the Astrakhani), xviii
Washington, George, l
Waterloo ix
Wed-Nile, 75, 86. See also Niger River
*Wed-Noon, xlvii, xlviii, 15, 16, 22, 54,
   57, 58, 59–64, 65, 67, 93, 94–101,
   102, 103, 106, 160–161, 169,
   171
Wells and Lily (publishers), l, 162
West Africa, xx, xxviii
Westminster, ix, x, xxviii, xxx, xxxviii
Whitehall, ix
*white men, 47, 49, 55, 60
Wilberforce, William, xxv
*Williams, Thomas, xlvii, 26, 60, 63, 100,
   106
witchcraft, 16, 82, 83–84
Windward Coast, xxix, 8
Winnebah, xxiii
*Woled Aboussebàh, 55, 57, 70, 78, 91, 92,
   93, 95, 104, 153, 160, 171
*Woled Adrialla, 57, 104, 171
*Woled D'Leim, 28, 52–54, 55, 90, 91, 92,
   103, 149, 171
Woled-el-Haje, 94
*Woolo, xx, 35, 36–37, 39, 42, 49, 72, 73,
   74, 82, 85, 88, 117, 149, 150, 151,
   152–155, 157

Yamina, xl

*Zaire River, 23